Longfellow's Miles Standish and Poems.
Longfellow's Tales of a Wayside Inn.
Lowell's Earlier Essays.
Lowell's The Vision of Sir Launfal.
Macaulay's Essay on Addison.
Macaulay's Essay on Hastings.
Macaulay's Essay on Lord Clive.
Macaulay's Essay on Milton.
Macaulay's Lays of Ancient Rome.
Macaulay's Life of Samuel Johnson.
Malory's Le Morte d'Arthur.
Milton's Minor Poems.
Milton's Paradise Lost, Books I and II.
Old English Ballads.
Old Testament Selections.
Palgrave's Golden Treasury.
Parkman's Oregon Trail.
Plutarch's Lives of Cæsar, Brutus, and Mark Antony.
Poe's Poems.
Poe's Prose Tales (Selections).
Poems, Narrative and Lyrical.
Poole's The Harbor.
Pope's Homer's Iliad.
Pope's Homer's Odyssey.
Pope's The Rape of the Lock.
Reade's The Cloister and the Hearth.
*Representative Short Stories.
Roosevelt's Writings.
*Rossetti's (Christina) Selected Poems.
Ruskin's Sesame and Lilies.
Ruskin's The Crown of Wild Olive, and Queen of the Air.
Scott's Guy Mannering.
Scott's Ivanhoe.
Scott's Kenilworth.
Scott's Lady of the Lake.
Scott's Lay of the Last Minstrel.
Scott's Marmion.
Scott's Quentin Durward.
Scott's Rob Roy.
Scott's The Talisman.
Select Orations.
Selected Poems, for Required Reading in Secondary Schools.
Selections from American Poetry.
*Selections for Oral Reading.

Shakespeare's Hamlet.
Shakespeare's Henry V.
Shakespeare's Julius Cæsar.
Shakespeare's King Lear.
Shakespeare's Macbeth.
Shakespeare's Merchant of Venice.
Shakespeare's Midsummer Night's Dream.
Shakespeare's Richard II.
Shakespeare's Richard III.
Shakespeare's Romeo and Juliet.
Shakespeare's The Tempest.
Shakespeare's Twelfth Night.
Shelley and Keats: Poems.
Sheridan's The Rivals and The School for Scandal.
*Short Stories.
*Short Stories and Selections.
Southern Orators: Selections.
Southern Poets: Selections.
Southey's Life of Nelson.
Spenser's Faerie Queene, Book I.
*Stevenson's Kidnapped.
*Stevenson's The Master of Ballantrae.
*Stevenson's Travels with a Donkey, and An Inland Voyage.
*Stevenson's Treasure Island.
Swift's Gulliver's Travels.
*Tennyson's Idylls of the King.
*Tennyson's In Memoriam.
*Tennyson's The Princess.
*Tennyson's Shorter Poems.
Thackeray's English Humorists.
Thackeray's Henry Esmond.
Thompson's The Hound of Heaven.
Thoreau's Walden.
*Trevelyan's Life of Macaulay. Abridged.
Virgil's Æneid.
Washington's Farewell Address, and Webster's First Bunker Hill Oration.
Whittier's Snow-Bound and Other Early Poems.
Wister's The Virginian.
Woodman's Journal.
Wordsworth's Shorter Poems.

* Cannot be sold in British Dominions.

THE MACMILLAN COMPANY
NEW YORK · BOSTON · CHICAGO
ATLANTA · SAN FRANCISCO

MACMILLAN & CO., Limited
LONDON · BOMBAY · CALCUTTA
MELBOURNE

THE MACMILLAN CO. OF CANADA, Ltd.
TORONTO

" By the rude bridge that arched the flood,
    Their flag to April's breeze unfurled,
Here once the embattled farmers stood,
    And fired the shot heard round the world."

SELECTIONS FROM
AMERICAN POETRY

WITH SPECIAL REFERENCE TO
POE, LONGFELLOW, LOWELL,
AND WHITTIER

EDITED BY
MARGARET SPRAGUE CARHART, A.M.
TEACHER OF ENGLISH IN PASADENA HIGH SCHOOL

New York
THE MACMILLAN COMPANY
1923

All rights reserved

Norwood Press
J. S. Cushing Co. — Berwick & Smith Co.
Norwood, Mass., U.S.A.

TABLE OF CONTENTS

INTRODUCTION

IF we define poetry as the heart of man expressed in beautiful language, we shall not say that we have no national poetry. True, America has produced no Shakespeare and no Milton, but we have an inheritance in all English literature; and many poets in America have followed in the footsteps of their literary British forefathers.

Puritan life was severe. It was warfare, and manual labor of a most exhausting type, and loneliness, and devotion to a strict sense of duty. It was a life in which pleasure was given the least place and duty the greatest. Our Puritan ancestors thought music and poetry dangerous, if not actually sinful, because they made men think of this world rather than of heaven. When Anne Bradstreet wrote our first known American poems, she was expressing English thought; "The tenth muse" was not animated by the life around her, but was living in a dream of the land she had left behind; her poems are faint echoes of the poetry of England. After time had identified her with life in the new world, she wrote "Contemplations," in which her English nightingales are changed to crickets and her English gilliflowers to American blackberry vines. The truly representative poetry of colonial times is Michael Wigglesworth's "Day of Doom." This is the real heart of the Puritan, his

conscience, in imperfect rhyme. It fulfills the first part of
our definition, but shows by its lack of beautiful style that
both elements are necessary to produce real poetry.

Philip Freneau was the first American who sought to express his life in poetry. The test of beauty of language
again excludes from real poetry some of his expressions and
leaves us a few beautiful lyrics, such as "The Wild Honey-
suckle," in which the poet sings his love of American nature.
With them American poetry may be said to begin.

The first historical event of national importance was the
American Revolution. Amid the bitter years of want, of
suffering, and of war, few men tried to write anything beautiful. Life was harsh and stirring and this note was echoed
in all the literature. As a result we have narrative and
political poetry, such as "The Battle of the Kegs" and "A
Fable," dealing almost entirely with events and aiming to
arouse military ardor. In "The Ballad of Nathan Hale,"
the musical expression of bravery, pride, and sympathy raises
the poem so far above the rhymes of the period that it will
long endure as the most memorable poetic expression of the
Revolutionary period.

Poetry was still a thing of the moment, an avocation, not
dignified by receiving the best of a man. With William
Cullen Bryant came a change. He told our nation that in
the new world as well as in the old some men should live for
the beautiful. Everything in nature spoke to him in terms
of human life. Other poets saw the relation between their
own lives and the life of the flowers and the birds, but Bryant
constantly expressed this relationship. The concluding
stanza of "To a Waterfowl" is the most perfect example of
this characteristic, but it underlies also the whole thought
of his youthful poem "Thanatopsis" (A View of Death).

If we could all read the lives of our gentians and bobolinks as he did, there would be more true poetry in America. Modern thinkers urge us to step outside of ourselves into the lives of others and by our imagination to share their emotions; this is no new ambition in America, since Bryant in "The Crowded Street" analyzes the life in the faces he sees.

Until the early part of the nineteenth century American poetry dealt mainly with the facts of history and the description of nature. A new element of fancy is prominent in Joseph Rodman Drake's "The Culprit Fay." It dances through a long narrative with the delicacy of the fay himself.

Edgar Allan Poe brought into our poetry somber sentiment and musical expression. Puritan poetry was somber, but it was almost devoid of sentiment. Poe loved sad beauty and meditated on the sad things in life. Many of his poems lament the loss of some fair one. "To Helen," "Annabel Lee," "Lenore," and "To One in Paradise" have this theme, while in "The Raven" the poet is seeking solace for the loss of Lenore. "Eulalie — A Song" rises, on the other hand, to intense happiness. With Poe the sound by which his idea was expressed was as important as the thought itself. He knew how to make the sound suit the thought, as in "The Raven" and "The Bells." One who understands no English can grasp the meaning of the different sections from the mere sound, so clearly distinguishable are the clashing of the brass and the tolling of the iron bells. If we return to our definition of poetry as an expression of the heart of a man, we shall find the explanation of these peculiarities: Poe was a man of moods and possessed the ability to express these moods in appropriate sounds.

The contrast between the emotion of Poe and the calm

spirit of the man who followed him is very great. In Henry
Wadsworth Longfellow American poetry reached high-water
mark. Lafcadio Hearn in his "Interpretations of Literature" says: "Really I believe that it is a very good test of
any Englishman's ability to feel poetry, simply to ask him,
'Did you like Longfellow when you were a boy?' If he says
'No,' then it is no use to talk to him on the subject of poetry
at all, however much he might be able to tell you about
quantities and metres." No American has in equal degree
won the name of "household poet." If this term is cor-
rectly understood, it sums up his merits more succinctly
than can any other title.

Longfellow dealt largely with men and women and the
emotions common to us all. Hiawatha conquering the deer
and bison, and hunting in despair for food where only snow
and ice abound; Evangeline faithful to her father and her
lover, and relieving suffering in the rude hospitals of a new
world; John Alden fighting the battle between love and
duty; Robert of Sicily learning the lesson of humility; Sir
Federigo offering his last possession to the woman he loved;
Paul Revere serving his country in time of need; the monk
proving that only a sense of duty done can bring happiness:
all these and more express the emotions which we know are
true in our own lives. In his longer narrative poems he
makes the legends of Puritan life real to us; he takes English folk-lore and makes us see Othere talking to Arthur,
and the Viking stealing his bride. His short poems are even
better known than his longer narratives. In them he expressed his gentle, sincere love of the young, the suffering,
and the sorrowful. In the Sonnets he showed that deep appreciation of European literature which made noteworthy
his teaching at Harvard and his translations.

He believed that he was assigned a definite task in the world which he described as follows in his last poem:

> "As comes the smile to the lips,
>   The foam to the surge;
>
> So come to the Poet his songs,
>   All hitherward blown
> From the misty realm, that belongs
>   To the vast unknown.
>
> His, and not his, are the lays
>   He sings; and their fame
> Is his, and not his; and the praise
>   And the pride of a name.
>
> For voices pursue him by day
>   And haunt him by night,
> And he listens and needs must obey,
>   When the Angel says: 'Write!'"

John Greenleaf Whittier seems to suffer by coming in such close proximity to Longfellow. Genuine he was, but his spirit was less buoyant than Longfellow's and he touches our hearts less. Most of his early poems were devoted to a current political issue. They aimed to win converts to the cause of anti-slavery. Such poems always suffer in time in comparison with the song of a man who sings because "the heart is so full that a drop overfills it." Whittier's later poems belong more to this class and some of them speak to-day to our emotions as well as to our intellects. "The Hero" moves us with a desire to serve mankind, and the stirring tone of "Barbara Frietchie" arouses our patriotism by its picture of the same type of bravery. In similar vein is "Barclay of Ury," which must have touched deeply the heart of the Quaker poet. "The Pipes of Lucknow" is dramatic in its intense grasp of a climactic hour and loses none

INTRODUCTION

of its force in the expression. We can actually hear the
skirl of the bagpipes. Whittier knew the artists of the
world and talked to us about Raphael and Burns with clear-
sighted, affectionate interest. His poems show varied characteristics; the love of the sterner aspects of nature, modified
by the appreciation of the humble flower; the conscience
of the Puritan, tinged with sympathy for the sorrowful; the
steadfastness of the Quaker, stirred by the fire of the patriot.

The poetry of Ralph Waldo Emerson is marked by seri-
ous contemplation rather than by warmth of emotional
expression. In Longfellow the appeal is constantly to a
heart which is not disassociated from a brain; in Emerson the
appeal is often to the intellect alone. We recognize the force
of the lesson in "The Titmouse," even if it leaves us less
devoted citizens than does "The Hero" and less capable
women than does "Evangeline." He reaches his highest
excellence when he makes us feel as well as understand a lesson, as in "The Concord Hymn" and "Forbearance." If we
could all write on the tablets of our hearts that single stanza,
forbearance would be a real factor in life. And it is to this
poet whom we call unemotional that we owe the inspiring
quatrain:

> "So nigh is grandeur to our dust,
> So near is God to man,
> When duty whispers low, *Thou must,*
> The youth replies, *I can!*"

James Russell Lowell was animated by a well-defined purpose which he described in the following lines:

> "It may be glorious to write
> Thoughts that make glad the two or three
> High souls like those far stars that come in sight
> Once in a century.

> But better far it is to speak
>   One simple word which, now and then
> Shall waken their free nature in the weak
>   And friendless sons of men.
>
> To write some earnest verse or line
>   Which, seeking not the praise of art,
> Shall make a clearer faith and manhood shine
>   In the untutored heart."

His very accomplishments made it difficult for him to
reach this aim, since his poetry does not move "the untutored
heart" so readily as does that of Longfellow or Whittier. It
is, on the whole, too deeply burdened with learning and too
individual in expression to fulfil his highest desire. Of his
early poems the most generally known is probably "The
Vision of Sir Launfal," in which a strong moral purpose is
combined with lines of beautiful nature description:

> "And what is so rare as a day in June?
>   Then, if ever, come perfect days."

Two works by which he will be permanently remembered show a deeper and more effective Lowell. "The Biglow
Papers" are the most successful of all the American poems
which attempt to improve conditions by means of humor.
Although they refer in the main to the situation at the time of
the Mexican War, they deal with such universal political traits
that they may be applied to almost any age. They are written
in a Yankee dialect which, it is asserted, was never spoken,
but which enhances the humor, as in "What Mr. Robinson
Thinks." Lowell's tribute to Lincoln occurs in the Ode
which he wrote to commemorate the Harvard students who
enlisted in the Civil War. After dwelling on the search for
truth which should be the aim of every college student, he

turns to the delineation of Lincoln's character in a eulogy of
great beauty. Clear in analysis, far-sighted in judgment,
and loving in sentiment, he expresses that opinion of Lincoln
which has become a part of the web of American thought.
His is no hurried judgment, but the calm statement of
opinion which is to-day accepted by the world:

> "They all are gone, and, standing like a tower,
>   Our children shall behold his fame,
> The kindly-earnest, brave, foreseeing man,
> Sagacious, patient, dreading praise, not blame,
> New birth of our new soil, the first American."

With Oliver Wendell Holmes comes the last of this brief
American list of honor. No other American has so combined
delicacy with New England humor. We should be poorer
by many a smile without "My Aunt" and "The Deacon's
Masterpiece." But this is not his entire gift. "The Cham-
bered Nautilus" strikes the chord of noble sentiment sounded
in the last stanza of "Thanatopsis" and it will continue to
sing in our hearts "As the swift seasons roll." There is in
his poems the smile and the sigh of the well-loved stanza,

> "And if I should live to be
>   The last leaf upon the tree
>   In the Spring.
> Let them smile; as I do now,
>   At the old forsaken bough
>   Where I cling."

And is this all? Around these few names does all the
fragrance of American poetry hover? In the hurry, pros-
perity, and luxury of modern life is the care of the flower of
poetry lost? Surely not. The last half of the nineteenth
century and the beginning of the twentieth have brought
many beautiful flowers of poetry and hints of more perfect

blossoms. Lanier has sung of the life of the south he loved; Whitman and Miller have stirred us with enthusiasm for the progress of the nation; Field and Riley have made us laugh and cry in sympathy; Aldrich, Sill, Van Dyke, Burroughs, and Thoreau have shared with us their hoard of beauty. Among the present generation may there appear many men and women whose devotion to the delicate flower shall be repaid by the gratitude of posterity!

SELECTIONS FROM AMERICAN POETRY

ANNE BRADSTREET

CONTEMPLATIONS°

Some time now past in the Autumnal Tide,
   When Phœbus° wanted but one hour to bed,
The trees all richly clad, yet void of pride,
   Were gilded o'er by his rich golden head.
Their leaves and fruits seem'd painted, but was true   5
Of green, of red, of yellow, mixed hue,
Rapt were my senses at this delectable° view.

I wist not what to wish, yet sure, thought I,
   If so much excellence abide below,
How excellent is He that dwells on high!   10
   Whose power and beauty by his works we know;
Sure he is goodness, wisdom, glory, light,
That hath this underworld so richly dight°:
More Heaven than Earth was here, no winter and no night.

Then on a stately oak I cast mine eye,   15
   Whose ruffling top the clouds seem'd to aspire;
How long since thou wast in thine infancy?
   Thy strength, and stature, more thy years admire;

Hath hundred winters past since thou wast born,
Or thousand since thou breakest thy shell of horn?   20
If so, all these as naught Eternity doth scorn.

*   *   *   *   *   *   *

I heard the merry grasshopper then sing,
  The black-clad cricket bear a second part,
They kept one tune, and played on the same string,
  Seeming to glory in their little art.   25
Shall creatures abject thus their voices raise?
And in their kind resound their Master's praise:
Whilst I, as mute, can warble forth no higher lays.

When I behold the heavens as in their prime,
  And then the earth (though old) still clad in green,   30
The stones and trees, insensible of time,
  Nor age nor wrinkle on their front are seen;
If winter come, and greenness then do fade,
A spring returns, and they more youthful made;
But Man grows old, lies down, remains where once he's laid.   35

MICHAEL WIGGLESWORTH

THE DAY OF DOOM°

SOUNDING OF THE LAST TRUMP

STILL was the night, Serene & Bright,
    when all Men sleeping lay;
Calm was the season, & carnal° reason
    thought so 'twould last for ay.
Soul, take thine ease, let sorrow cease,   5
    much good thou hast in store:
This was their Song, their Cups among,
    the Evening before.

Wallowing in all kind of sin,
    vile wretches lay secure: 10
The best of men had scarcely then
    their Lamps kept in good ure.
Virgins unwise, who through disguise
    amongst the best were number'd,
Had closed their eyes°; yea, and the wise   15
    through sloth and frailty slumber'd.

*   *   *   *   *   *   *

For at midnight brake forth a Light,
    which turn'd the night to day,
And speedily a hideous cry
    did all the world dismay.   20

3

Sinners awake, their hearts do ake,
    trembling their loynes surprizeth;
Amaz'd with fear, by what they hear,
    each one of them ariseth.

They rush from Beds with giddy heads,   25
    and to their windows run,
Viewing this light, which shines more bright
    than doth the Noon-day Sun.
Straightway appears (they see 't with tears)
    the Son of God most dread;   30
Who with his Train comes on amain
    to Judge both Quick and Dead.

Before his face the Heav'ns gave place,
    and Skies are rent asunder,
With mighty voice, and hideous noise,   35
    more terrible than Thunder.
His brightness damps heav'ns glorious lamps
    and makes them hang their heads,
As if afraid and quite dismay'd,
    they quit their wonted steads.°   40

*   *   *   *   *   *   *

No heart so bold, but now grows cold
    and almost dead with fear:
No eye so dry, but now can cry,
    and pour out many a tear.
Earth's Potentates and pow'rful States,   45
    Captains and Men of Might
Are quite abasht, their courage dasht
    at this most dreadful sight.

Mean men lament, great men do rent
   their Robes, and tear their hair:
They do not spare their flesh to tear
   through horrible despair.
All Kindreds wail: all hearts do fail:
   horror the world doth fill
With weeping eyes, and loud out-cries,
   yet knows not how to kill.

Some hide themselves in Caves and Delves,
   in places under ground:
Some rashly leap into the Deep,
   to scape by being drown'd:
Some to the Rocks (O senseless blocks!)
   and woody Mountains run,
That there they might this fearful sight,
   and dreaded Presence shun.

In vain do they to Mountains say,
   fall on us and us hide
From Judges ire, more hot than fire,
   for who may it abide?
No hiding place can from his Face
   sinners at all conceal,
Whose flaming Eye hid things doth 'spy
   and darkest things reveal.

The Judge draws nigh, exalted high,
   upon a lofty Throne,
Amidst a throng of Angels strong,
   lo, Israel's Holy One!

The excellence of whose presence
  and awful Majesty,
Amazeth Nature, and every Creature,
  doth more than terrify.   80

The Mountains smoak, the Hills are shook,
  the Earth is rent and torn,
As if she should be clear dissolv'd,
  or from the Center born.
The Sea doth roar, forsakes the shore,   85
  and shrinks away for fear;
The wild beasts flee into the Sea,
  so soon as he draws near.

*   *   *   *   *   *   *

Before his Throne a Trump is blown,
  Proclaiming the day of Doom: 90
Forthwith he cries, Ye dead arise,
  and unto Judgment come.
No sooner said, but 'tis obey'd;
  Sepulchres opened are:
Dead bodies all rise at his call,   95
  and 's mighty power declare.

*   *   *   *   *   *   *

His winged Hosts flie through all Coasts,
  together gathering
Both good and bad, both quick and dead,
  and all to Judgment bring.   100
Out of their holes those creeping Moles,
  that hid themselves for fear,
By force they take, and quickly make
  before the Judge appear.

Thus every one before the Throne   105
   of Christ the Judge is brought,
Both righteous and impious
   that good or ill hath wrought.
A separation, and diff'ring station
   by Christ appointed is   110
(To sinners sad) 'twixt good and bad,
   'twixt Heirs of woe and bliss.

PHILIP FRENEAU

THE WILD HONEYSUCKLE

FAIR flower, that dost so comely grow,
  Hid in this silent, dull retreat,
Untouched thy honied blossoms blow,
  Unseen thy little branches greet:
      No roving foot shall crush thee here,   5
      No busy hand provoke a tear.

By Nature's self in white arrayed,
  She bade thee shun the vulgar eye,
And planted here the guardian shade,
  And sent soft waters murmuring by;   10
      Thus quietly thy summer goes,
      Thy days declining to repose.

Smit with those charms, that must decay,
  I grieve to see your future doom;
They died — nor were those flowers more gay,   15
  The flowers that did in Eden bloom;
      Unpitying frosts, and Autumn's power,
      Shall leave no vestige of this flower.

From morning suns and evening dews
  At first thy little being came;   20

If nothing once, you nothing lose,
  For when you die you are the same;
    The space between is but an hour,
    The frail duration of a flower.

TO A HONEY BEE

THOU, born to sip the lake or spring,
  Or quaff the waters of the stream,
Why hither come on vagrant wing?
  Does Bacchus tempting seem, —
    Did he for you this glass prepare?   5
    Will I admit you to a share?

Did storms harass or foes perplex,
  Did wasps or king-birds bring dismay —
Did wars distress, or labors vex,
  Or did you miss your way?   10
    A better seat you could not take
    Than on the margin of this lake.

Welcome! — I hail you to my glass:
  All welcome, here, you find;
Here, let the cloud of trouble pass,   15
  Here, be all care resigned.
    This fluid never fails to please,
    And drown the griefs of men or bees.

What forced you here we cannot know,
  And you will scarcely tell,   20

But cheery we would have you go
   And bid a glad farewell:
      On lighter wings we bid you fly,
      Your dart will now all foes defy.

Yet take not, oh! too deep a drink,   25
   And in this ocean die;
Here bigger bees than you might sink,
    Even bees full six feet high.
      Like Pharaoh, then, you would be said
      To perish in a sea of red.°   30

Do as you please, your will is mine;
   Enjoy it without fear,
And your grave will be this glass of wine,
    Your epitaph° — a tear —
      Go, take your seat in Charon's° boat;   35
      We'll tell the hive, you died afloat.

THE INDIAN BURYING–GROUND

In spite of all the learned have said,
   I still my old opinion keep;
The posture that we give the dead
   Points out the soul's eternal sleep.

Not so the ancients of these lands; —   5
   The Indian, when from life released,
Again is seated with his friends,
   And shares again the joyous feast.

His imaged birds, and painted bowl,
   And venison, for a journey dressed,   10
Bespeak the nature of the soul,
   Activity, that wants no rest.

His bow for action ready bent,
   And arrows, with a head of stone,
Can only mean that life is spent,   15
   And not the old ideas gone.

Thou, stranger, that shalt come this way,
   No fraud upon the dead commit, —
Observe the swelling turf, and say,
   They do not *lie*, but here they *sit*.   20

Here still a lofty rock remains,
   On which the curious eye may trace
(Now wasted half by wearing rains)
   The fancies of a ruder race.

Here still an aged elm aspires,   25
   Beneath whose far projecting shade
(And which the shepherd still admires)
   The children of the forest played.

There oft a restless Indian queen
   (Pale Shebah with her braided hair),   30
And many a barbarous form is seen
   To chide the man that lingers there.

By midnight moons, o'er moistening dews,
   In habit for the chase arrayed,

The hunter still the deer pursues,   35
    The hunter and the deer — a shade!

And long shall timorous Fancy see
    The painted chief, and pointed spear,
And Reason's self shall bow the knee
    To shadows and delusions here.   40

EUTAW SPRINGS°

At Eutaw Springs the valiant died:
    Their limbs with dust are covered o'er;
Weep on, ye springs, your tearful tide;
    How many heroes are no more!

If in this wreck of ruin, they   5
    Can yet be thought to claim a tear,
O smite thy gentle breast, and say
    The friends of freedom slumber here!

Thou, who shalt trace this bloody plain,
    If goodness rules thy generous breast,   10
Sigh for the wasted rural reign;
    Sigh for the shepherds sunk to rest!

Stranger, their humble groves adorn;
    You too may fall, and ask a tear:
'Tis not the beauty of the morn   15
    That proves the evening shall be clear.

They saw their injured country's woe,
    The flaming town, the wasted field;

Then rushed to meet the insulting foe;
   They took the spear — but left the shield.   20

Led by thy conquering standards, Greene,°
   The Britons they compelled to fly:
None distant viewed the fatal plain,
   None grieved in such a cause to die —

But, like the Parthian,° famed of old,   25
   Who, flying, still their arrows threw,
These routed Britons, full as bold,
   Retreated, and retreating slew.

Now rest in peace, our patriot band;
   Though far from nature's limits **thrown,**   30
We trust they find a happier land,
   A bright Phœbus of their **own.**

FRANCIS HOPKINSON

THE BATTLE OF THE KEGS

GALLANTS attend and hear a friend
  Trill forth harmonious ditty,
Strange things I'll tell which late befell
  In Philadelphia city.

'Twas early day, as poets say,   5
  Just when the sun was rising,
A soldier stood on a log of wood,
  And saw a thing surprising.

As in amaze he stood to gaze,
  The truth can't be denied, sir,   10
He spied a score of kegs or more
  Come floating down the tide, sir.

A sailor too in jerkin blue,
  This strange appearance viewing,
First damned his eyes, in great surprise,   15
  Then said, "Some mischief's brewing.

"These kegs, I'm told, the rebels hold,
  Packed up like pickled herring;
And they're come down to attack the town,
  In this new way of ferrying."   20

14

The soldier flew, the sailor too,
  And scared almost to death, sir,
Wore out their shoes, to spread the news,
  And ran till out of breath, sir.

Now up and down throughout the town,   25
  Most frantic scenes were acted;
And some ran here, and others there,
  Like men almost distracted.

Some fire cried, which some denied,
  But said the earth had quaked;   30
And girls and boys, with hideous noise,
  Ran through the streets half naked.

Sir William he, snug as a flea,
  Lay all this time a snoring,
Nor dreamed of harm as he lay warm,   35
  In bed with Mrs. Loring.

Now in a fright, he starts upright,
  Awaked by such a clatter;
He rubs both eyes, and boldly cries,
  "For God's sake, what's the matter?"   40

At his bedside he then espied,
  Sir Erskine at command, sir,
Upon one foot he had one boot,
  And th' other in his hand, sir.

"Arise, arise," Sir Erskine cries,   45
  "The rebels — more's the pity,

Without a boat are all afloat,
  And ranged before the city.

"The motley crew, in vessels new,
  With Satan for their guide, sir,   50
Packed up in bags, or wooden kegs,
  Come driving down the tide, sir.

"Therefore prepare for bloody war,
  These kegs must all be routed,
Or surely we despised shall be,   55
  And British courage doubted."

The royal band now ready stand
  All ranged in dread array, sir,
With stomach° stout to see it out,
  And make a bloody day, sir.   60

The cannons roar from shore to shore.
  The small arms make a rattle;
Since wars began I'm sure no man
  E'er saw so strange a battle.

The rebel dales, the rebel vales,   65
  With rebel trees surrounded,
The distant woods, the hills and floods,
  With rebel echoes sounded.

The fish below swam to and fro,
  Attacked from every quarter;   70
Why sure, thought they, the devil's to pay,
  'Mongst folks above the water.

The kegs, 'tis said, though strongly made,
  Of rebel staves and hoops, sir,
Could not oppose their powerful foes,   75
  The conquering British troops, sir.

From morn to night these men of might
  Displayed amazing courage;
And when the sun was fairly down,
  Retired to sup their porridge.   80

A hundred men with each a pen,
  Or more upon my word, sir,
It is most true would be too few,
  Their valor to record, sir.

Such feats did they perform that day,   85
  Against these wicked kegs, sir,
That years to come, if they get home,
  They'll make their boasts and brags, sir.

c

JOSEPH HOPKINSON

HAIL COLUMBIA

Hail, Columbia! happy land!
Hail, ye heroes! heaven-born band!
  Who fought and bled in Freedom's cause,
  Who fought and bled in Freedom's cause,
And when the storm of war was gone,   5
Enjoyed the peace your valor won.
    Let independence be our boast,
    Ever mindful what it cost;
    Ever grateful for the prize,
    Let its altar reach the skies.   10

      Firm, united, let us be,
      Rallying round our Liberty;
      As a band of brothers joined,
      Peace and safety we shall find.

Immortal patriots! rise once more: 15
Defend your rights, defend your shore:
  Let no rude foe, with impious hand,
  Let no rude foe, with impious hand,
Invade the shrine where sacred lies
Of toil and blood the well-earned prize.   20
    While offering peace sincere and just,
    In Heaven we place a manly trust,

18

That truth and justice will prevail,
And every scheme of bondage fail.

      Firm, united, let us be,   25
      Rallying round our Liberty ;
      As a band of brothers joined,
      Peace and safety we shall find.

Sound, sound, the trump of Fame !
Let WASHINGTON'S great name   30
    Ring through the world with loud applause,
    Ring through the world with loud applause ;
Let every clime to Freedom dear,
Listen with a joyful ear.
    With equal skill, and godlike power,   35
    He governed in the fearful hour
Of horrid war ; or guides, with ease,
The happier times of honest peace.

      Firm, united, let us be,
      Rallying round our Liberty ;   40
      As a band of brothers joined,
      Peace and safety we shall find.

Behold the chief who now commands,
Once more to serve his country, stands —
    The rock on which the storm will beat,   45
    The rock on which the storm will beat ;
But, armed in virtue firm and true,
His hopes are fixed on Heaven and you.
    When hope was sinking in dismay,
    And glooms obscured Columbia's day,   50

His steady mind, from changes free,
Resolved on death or liberty.

Firm, united, let us be,
Rallying round our Liberty;
As a band of brothers joined,   55
Peace and safety we shall find.

The guards of the ... the dark ... very night,
Had a mind ... ... rows will
They took him and bore him afar from the shore,
To a ... on the hill; to a ... on the hill.

ANONYMOUS

THE BALLAD OF NATHAN HALE°

THE breezes went steadily through the tall pines,
A-saying "oh! hu-ush!" a-saying "oh! hu-ush!"
As stilly stole by a bold legion of horse,
For Hale in the bush, for Hale in the bush.

"Keep still!" said the thrush as she nestled her young,   5
In a nest by the road; in a nest by the road.
"For the tyrants are near, and with them appear
What bodes us no good, what bodes us no good."

The brave captain heard it, and thought of his home
In a cot by the brook; in a cot by the brook.   10
With mother and sister and memories dear,
He so gayly forsook; he so gayly forsook.

Cooling shades of the night were coming apace,
The tattoo had beat; the tattoo had beat.
The noble one sprang from his dark lurking-place,   15
To make his retreat; to make his retreat.

He warily trod on the dry rustling leaves,
As he passed through the wood; as he passed through the wood;
And silently gained his rude launch on the shore,
As she played with the flood; as she played with the flood.   20

21

The guards of the camp, on that dark, dreary night,
Had a murderous will; had a murderous will.
They took him and bore him afar from the shore,
To a hut on the hill; to a hut on the hill.

No mother was there, nor a friend who could cheer,   25
In that little stone cell; in that little stone cell.
But he trusted in love, from his Father above.
In his heart, all was well; in his heart, all was well.

An ominous owl, with his solemn bass voice,
Sat moaning hard by; sat moaning hard by: 30
"The tyrant's proud minions° most gladly rejoice,
For he must soon die; for he must soon die."

The brave fellow told them, no thing he restrained, —
The cruel general! the cruel general! —
His errand from camp, of the ends to be gained,   35
And said that was all; and said that was all.

They took him and bound him and bore him away,
Down the hill's grassy side; down the hill's grassy side.
'Twas there the base hirelings, in royal array,
His cause did deride; his cause did deride.   40

Five minutes were given, short moments, no more,
For him to repent; for him to repent.
He prayed for his mother, he asked not another,
To Heaven he went; to Heaven he went.

The faith of a martyr the tragedy showed,   45
As he trod the last stage; as he trod the last stage.

And Britons will shudder at gallant Hale's blood,
As his words do presage,° as his words do presage.

"Thou pale king of terrors, thou life's gloomy foe,
Go frighten the slave; go frighten the slave; 50
Tell tyrants, to you their allegiance they owe.
No fears for the brave; no fears for the brave."

A FABLE

Rejoice, Americans, rejoice!
Praise ye the Lord with heart and voice!
The treaty's signed with faithful France,
And now, like Frenchmen, sing and dance!

But when your joy gives way to reason, 5
And friendly hints are not deemed treason,
Let me, as well as I am able,
Present your Congress with a fable.

Tired out with happiness, the frogs
Sedition croaked through all their bogs; 10
And thus to Jove the restless race,
Made out their melancholy case.

"Famed, as we are, for faith and prayer,
We merit sure peculiar care;
But can we think great good was meant us, 15
When logs for Governors were sent us?

"Which numbers crushed they fell upon,
And caused great fear, — till one by one,

As courage came, we boldly faced 'em,
Then leaped upon 'em, and disgraced 'em!   20

"Great Jove," they croaked, "no longer fool us,
None but ourselves are fit to rule us;
We are too large, too free a nation,
To be encumbered with taxation!

"We pray for peace, but wish confusion,   25
Then right or wrong, a — revolution!
Our hearts can never bend to obey;
Therefore no king — and more we'll pray."

Jove smiled, and to their fate resigned
The restless, thankless, rebel kind;   30
Left to themselves, they went to work,
First signed a treaty with king Stork.

He swore that they, with his alliance,
To all the world might bid defiance;
Of lawful rule there was an end on't,   35
And frogs were henceforth — independent.

At which the croakers, one and all!
Proclaimed a feast, and festival!
But joy to-day brings grief to-morrow;
Their feasting o'er, now enter sorrow!   40

The Stork grew hungry, longed for fish;
The monarch could not have his wish;
In rage he to the marshes flies,
And makes a meal of his allies.

Then grew so fond of well-fed frogs,   45
He made a larder of the bogs!
Say, Yankees, don't you feel compunction,
At your unnatural rash conjunction?

Can love for you in him take root,
Who's Catholic, and absolute?   50
I'll tell these croakers how he'll treat 'em;
Frenchmen, like storks, love frogs — to eat 'em.

TIMOTHY DWIGHT

LOVE TO THE CHURCH

I LOVE thy kingdom, Lord,
   The house of thine abode,
The church our blest Redeemer saved
   With his own precious blood.

I love thy church, O God!   5
   Her walls before thee stand,
Dear as the apple of thine eye,
   And graven on thy hand.

If e'er to bless thy sons
   My voice or hands deny,   10
These hands let useful skill forsake,
   This voice in silence die.

For her my tears shall fall,
   For her my prayers ascend;
To her my cares and toils be given   15
   Till toils and cares shall end.

Beyond my highest joy
   I prize her heavenly ways,
Her sweet communion, solemn vows,
   Her hymns of love and praise.   20

Jesus, thou friend divine,
  Our Saviour and our King,
Thy hand from every snare and foe
  Shall great deliverance bring.

Sure as thy truth shall last,   25
  To Zion shall be given
The brightest glories earth can yield,
  And brighter bliss of heaven.

SAMUEL WOODWORTH

THE OLD OAKEN BUCKET

How dear to this heart are the scenes of my childhood,
  When fond recollection presents them to view!
The orchard, the meadow, the deep-tangled wild-wood,
  And every loved spot which my infancy knew!
The wide-spreading pond, and the mill that stood by it,   5
  The bridge, and the rock where the cataract fell,
The cot of my father, the dairy-house nigh it,
  And e'en the rude bucket that hung in the well —
The old oaken bucket, the iron-bound bucket,
The moss-covered bucket which hung in the well.   10

That moss-covered vessel I hailed as a treasure,
  For often at noon, when returned from the field,
I found it the source of an exquisite pleasure,
  The purest and sweetest that nature can yield.
How ardent I seized it, with hands that were glowing,   15
  And quick to the white-pebbled bottom it fell;
Then soon, with the emblem of truth overflowing,
  And dripping with coolness, it rose from the well —
The old oaken bucket, the iron-bound bucket,
The moss-covered bucket arose from the well.   20

How sweet from the green mossy brim to receive it,
  As poised on the curb it inclined to my lips!

Not a full blushing goblet could tempt me to leave it,
   The brightest that beauty or revelry sips.
And now, far removed from the loved habitation,   25
   The tear of regret will intrusively swell,
As fancy reverts to my father's plantation,
   And sighs for the bucket that hangs in the well —
The old oaken bucket, the iron-bound bucket,
The moss-covered bucket that hangs in the well!   30

WILLIAM CULLEN BRYANT

THANATOPSIS

To him who in the love of Nature holds
Communion with her visible forms, she speaks
A various language; for his gayer hours
She has a voice of gladness, and a smile
And eloquence of beauty, and she glides   5
Into his darker musings, with a mild
And healing sympathy, that steals away
Their sharpness, ere he is aware.   When thoughts
Of the last bitter hour come like a blight
Over thy spirit, and sad images   10
Of the stern agony, and shroud, and pall,
And breathless darkness, and the narrow house,
Make thee to shudder and grow sick at heart; —
Go forth, under the open sky, and list
To Nature's teachings, while from all around —   15
Earth and her waters, and the depths of air —
Comes a still voice: —

                 Yet a few days, and thee
The all-beholding sun shall see no more
In all his course; nor yet in the cold ground
Where thy pale form was laid with many tears,   20

Nor in the embrace of ocean, shall exist
Thy image. Earth, that nourished thee, shall claim
Thy growth, to be resolved to earth again,
And, lost each human trace, surrendering up
Thine individual being, shalt thou go   25
To mix forever with the elements,
To be a brother to the insensible rock
And to the sluggish clod, which the rude swain
Turns with his share, and treads upon. The oak
Shall send his roots abroad, and pierce thy mould.   30

   Yet not to thine eternal resting place
Shalt thou retire alone, nor couldst thou wish
Couch more magnificent. Thou shalt lie down
With patriarchs of the infant world ° — with kings,
The powerful of the earth — the wise, the good,   35
Fair forms, and hoary seers of ages past,
All in one mighty sepulchre. The hills
Rock-ribbed and ancient as the sun, — the vales
Stretching in pensive quietness between ;
The venerable woods — rivers that move   40
In majesty, and the complaining brooks
That make the meadows green ; and, poured round all,
Old Ocean's gray and melancholy waste, —
Are but the solemn decorations all
Of the great tomb of man. The golden sun,   45
The planets, all the infinite host of heaven,
Are shining on the sad abodes of death
Through the still lapse of ages. All that tread
The globe are but a handful to the tribes
That slumber in its bosom. — Take the wings   50
Of morning, pierce the Barcan wilderness,°

Or lose thyself in the continuous woods
Where rolls the Oregon, and hears no sound,
Save his own dashing° — yet the dead are there;
And millions in those solitudes, since first   55
The flight of years began, have laid them down
In their last sleep — the dead reign there alone.
So shalt thou rest, and what if thou withdraw
In silence from the living, and no friend
Take note of thy departure? All that breathe   60
Will share thy destiny. The gay will laugh
When thou art gone, the solemn brood of care
Plod on, and each one as before will chase
His favorite phantom; yet all these shall leave
Their mirth and their employments, and shall come   65
And make their bed with thee. As the long train
Of ages glides away, the sons of men —
The youth in life's green spring, and he who goes
In the full strength of years, matron and maid,
The speechless babe, and the gray-headed man —   70
Shall one by one be gathered to thy side,
By those who in their turn shall follow them.

So live, that when thy summons comes to join
The innumerable caravan, which moves
To that mysterious realm, where each shall take   75
His chamber in the silent halls of death,
Thou go not, like the quarry-slave at night,
Scourged to his dungeon, but, sustained and soothed
By an unfaltering trust, approach thy grave
Like one who wraps the drapery of his couch   80
About him, and lies down to pleasant dreams.

THE YELLOW VIOLET

WHEN beechen buds begin to swell,
  And woods the blue-bird's warble know,
The yellow violet's modest bell
  Peeps from the last year's leaves below.

Ere russet fields their green resume,   5
  Sweet flower, I love, in forest bare,
To meet thee, when thy faint perfume
  Alone is in the virgin air.

Of all her train, the hands of Spring
  First plant thee in the watery mould,   10
And I have seen thee blossoming
  Beside the snow-bank's edges cold.

Thy parent sun, who bade thee view
  Pale skies, and chilling moisture sip,
Has bathed thee in his own bright hue,   15
  And streaked with jet thy glowing lip.

Yet slight thy form, and low thy seat,
  And earthward bent thy gentle eye,
Unapt the passing view to meet,
  When loftier flowers are flaunting nigh.   20

Oft, in the sunless April day,
  Thy early smile has stayed my walk;
But midst the gorgeous blooms of May,
  I passed thee on thy humble stalk.

D

So they, who climb to wealth, forget   25
    The friends in darker fortunes tried.
I copied them — but I regret
    That I should ape° the ways of pride.

And when again the genial hour
    Awakes the painted tribes of light,   30
I'll not o'erlook the modest flower
    That made the woods of April bright.

TO A WATERFOWL°

Whither, midst falling dew,
While glow the heavens with the last steps of day,
Far, through their rosy depths, dost thou pursue
    Thy solitary way?

    Vainly the fowler's eye   5
Might mark thy distant flight to do thee wrong,
As, darkly painted on the crimson sky,
    Thy figure floats along.

    Seek'st thou the plashy° brink
Of weedy lake, or marge of river wide,   10
Or where the rocking billows rise and sink
    On the chafed ocean-side?

    There is a Power whose care
Teaches thy way along that pathless coast —
The desert and illimitable° air —   15
    Lone wandering, but not lost.

All day thy wings have fanned,
At that far height, the cold, thin atmosphere,
Yet stoop not, weary, to the welcome land,
    Though the dark night is near.   20

And soon that toil shall end;
Soon shalt thou find a summer home, and rest,
And scream among thy fellows; reeds shall bend,
    Soon, o'er thy sheltered nest.

Thou'rt gone, the abyss of heaven   25
Hath swallowed up thy form; yet, in my heart
Deeply has sunk the lesson thou hast given,
    And shall not soon depart.

He who, from zone to zone,
Guides through the boundless sky thy certain flight, 30
In the long way that I must tread alone,
    Will lead my steps aright.

GREEN RIVER°

WHEN breezes are soft and skies are fair,
I steal an hour from study and care,
And hie me away to the woodland scene,
Where wanders the stream with waters of green,
As if the bright fringe of herbs on its brink   5
Had given their stain to the waves they drink;
And they, whose meadows it murmurs through,
Have named the stream from its own fair hue.

Yet pure its waters — its shallows are bright
With colored pebbles and sparkles of light,   10
And clear the depths where its eddies play,
And dimples deepen and whirl away,
And the plane-tree's speckled arms o'ershoot
The swifter current that mines its root,
Through whose shifting leaves, as you walk the hill, 15
The quivering glimmer of sun and rill
With a sudden flash on the eye is thrown,
Like the ray that streams from the diamond-stone.
Oh, loveliest there the spring days come,
With blossoms, and birds, and wild-bees' hum ;   20
The flowers of summer are fairest there,
And freshest the breath of the summer air ;
And sweetest the golden autumn day
In silence and sunshine glides away.

Yet, fair as thou art, thou shunnest to glide,   25
Beautiful stream ! by the village side ;
But windest away from haunts of men,
To quiet valley and shaded glen ;
And forest, and meadow, and slope of hill,
Around thee, are lonely, lovely, and still,   30
Lonely — save when, by thy rippling tides,
From thicket to thicket the angler glides ;
Or the simpler° comes, with basket and book,
For herbs of power on thy banks to look ;
Or haply, some idle dreamer, like me,   35
To wander, and muse, and gaze on thee.
Still — save the chirp of birds that feed
On the river cherry and seedy reed,
And thy own wild music gushing out

With mellow murmur of fairy shout,⠀⠀⠀⠀⠀⠀⠀⠀⠀40
From dawn to the blush of another day,
Like traveller singing along his way.

⠀⠀That fairy music I never hear,
Nor gaze on those waters so green and clear,
And mark them winding away from sight,⠀⠀⠀⠀45
Darkened with shade or flashing with light,
While o'er them the vine to its thicket clings,
And the zephyr stoops to freshen his wings,
But I wish that fate had left me free
To wander these quiet haunts with thee,⠀⠀⠀⠀50
Till the eating cares of earth should depart,
And the peace of the scene pass into my heart;
And I envy thy stream, as it glides along
Through its beautiful banks in a trance of song.

⠀⠀Though forced to drudge for the dregs of men,⠀⠀55
And scrawl strange words with the barbarous pen,
And mingle among the jostling crowd,
Where the sons of strife are subtle and loud ° —
I often come to this quiet place,
To breathe the airs that ruffle thy face,⠀⠀⠀⠀60
And gaze upon thee in silent dream,
For in thy lonely and lovely stream
An image of that calm life appears
That won my heart in my greener years.

THE WEST WIND°

Beneath the forest's skirt I rest,
  Whose branching pines rise dark and high,
And hear the breezes of the West
  Among the thread-like foliage sigh.

Sweet Zephyr! why that sound of woe?   5
  Is not thy home among the flowers?
Do not the bright June roses blow,
  To meet thy kiss at morning hours?

And lo! thy glorious realm outspread —
  Yon stretching valleys, green and gay,   10
And yon free hill-tops, o'er whose head
  The loose white clouds are borne away.

And there the full broad river runs,
  And many a fount wells fresh and sweet,
To cool thee when the mid-day suns   15
  Have made thee faint beneath their heat.

Thou wind of joy, and youth, and love;
  Spirit of the new-wakened year!
The sun in his blue realm above
  Smooths a bright path when thou art here.   20

In lawns the murmuring bee is heard,
  The wooing ring-dove in the shade;
On thy soft breath, the new-fledged bird
  Takes wing, half happy, half afraid.

Ah! thou art like our wayward race; —   25
  When not a shade of pain or ill
Dims the bright smile of Nature's face,
  Thou lov'st to sigh and murmur still.

"I BROKE THE SPELL THAT HELD ME LONG"

I BROKE the spell that held me long,
The dear, dear witchery of song.
I said, the poet's idle lore
Shall waste my prime of years no more,
For Poetry, though heavenly born,   5
Consorts with poverty and scorn.

I broke the spell — nor deemed its power
Could fetter me another hour.
Ah, thoughtless! how could I forget
Its causes were around me yet?   10
For wheresoe'er I looked, the while,
Was Nature's everlasting smile.

Still came and lingered on my sight
Of flowers and streams the bloom and light,
And glory of the stars and sun; —   15
And these and poetry are one.
They, ere the world had held me long,
Recalled me to the love of song.

A FOREST HYMN

THE groves were God's first temples.   Ere man learned
To hew the shaft, and lay the architrave,°
And spread the roof above them — ere he framed
The lofty vault, to gather and roll back
The sound of anthems° ; in the darkling° wood,   5
Amid the cool and silence, he knelt down,
And offered to the Mightiest solemn thanks
And supplication.   For his simple heart
Might not resist the sacred influences
Which, from the stilly twilight of the place,   10
And from the gray old trunks that high in heaven
Mingled their mossy boughs, and from the sound
Of the invisible breath that swayed at once
All their green tops, stole over him, and bowed
His spirit with the thought of boundless power   15
And inaccessible majesty.   Ah, why
Should we, in the world's riper years, neglect
God's ancient sanctuaries, and adore
Only among the crowd, and under roofs
That our frail hands have raised?   Let me, at least,   20
Here, in the shadow of this aged wood,
Offer one hymn — thrice happy, if it find
Acceptance in His ear.°

Father, thy hand
Hath reared these venerable columns, thou
Didst weave this verdant roof.   Thou didst look down   25
Upon the naked earth, and, forthwith, rose
All these fair ranks of trees.   They, in thy sun,

Budded, and shook their green leaves in thy breeze,
And shot toward heaven. The century-living crow
Whose birth was in their tops, grew old and died   30
Among their branches, till, at last, they stood,
As now they stand, massy, and tall, and dark,
Fit shrine for humble worshipper to hold
Communion with his Maker. These dim vaults,°
These winding aisles, of human pomp or pride   35
Report not. No fantastic carvings show
The boast of our vain race to change the form
Of thy fair works. But thou art here — thou fill'st
The solitude. Thou art in the soft winds
That run along the summit of these trees   40
In music; thou art in the cooler breath
That from the inmost darkness of the place
Comes, scarcely felt; the barky trunks, the ground,
The fresh moist ground, are all instinct° with thee.
Here is continual worship; — Nature, here,   45
In the tranquillity that thou dost love,
Enjoys thy presence. Noiselessly, around,
From perch to perch, the solitary bird
Passes; and yon clear spring, that, midst its herbs
Wells softly forth and wandering steeps the roots   50
Of half the mighty forest, tells no tale
Of all the good it does. Thou hast not left
Thyself without a witness, in the shades,
Of thy perfections. Grandeur, strength, and grace
Are here to speak of thee. This mighty oak —   55
By whose immovable stem I stand and seem
Almost annihilated — not a prince,
In all that proud old world beyond the deep,
E'er wore his crown as loftily as he

Wears the green coronal of leaves with which   60
Thy hand has graced him.   Nestled at his root
Is beauty, such as blooms not in the glare
Of the broad sun.   That delicate forest flower,
With scented breath and look so like a smile,
Seems, as it issues from the shapeless mould,   65
An emanation° of the indwelling Life,
A visible token of the upholding Love,
That are the soul of this great universe.

My heart is awed within me when I think
Of the great miracle that still goes on,   70
In silence, round me — the perpetual work
Of thy creation, finished, yet renewed
Forever.   Written on thy works I read
The lesson of thy own eternity.
Lo! all grow old and die — but see again,   75
How on the faltering footsteps of decay
Youth presses — ever gay and beautiful youth
In all its beautiful forms.   These lofty trees
Wave not less proudly that their ancestors
Moulder beneath them.   Oh, there is not lost   80
One of earth's charms: upon her bosom yet,
After the flight of untold centuries,
The freshness of her far beginning lies
And yet shall lie.   Life mocks the idle hate
Of his arch-enemy Death — yea, seats himself   85
Upon the tyrant's throne — the sepulchre,
And of the triumphs of his ghastly foe
Makes his own nourishment.   For he came forth
From thine own bosom, and shall have no end.°

There have been holy men who hid themselves 90
Deep in the woody wilderness, and gave
Their lives to thought and prayer, till they outlived
The generation born with them, nor seemed
Less aged than the hoary trees and rocks
Around them; — and there have been holy men 95
Who deemed it were not well to pass life thus.°
But let me often to these solitudes
Retire, and in thy presence reassure
My feeble virtue.   Here its enemies,
The passions, at thy plainer footsteps shrink 100
And tremble and are still.   O God! when thou
Dost scare the world with tempest, set on fire
The heavens with falling thunderbolts, or fill,
With all the waters of the firmament,
The swift dark whirlwind that uproots the woods 105
And drowns the villages; when, at thy call,
Uprises the great deep and throws himself
Upon the continent, and overwhelms
Its cities — who forgets not, at the sight
Of these tremendous tokens of thy power, 110
His pride, and lays his strifes and follies by?
Oh, from these sterner aspects of thy face
Spare me and mine, nor let us need the wrath
Of the mad unchained elements to teach
Who rules them.   Be it ours to meditate, 115
In these calm shades, thy milder majesty,
And to the beautiful order of thy works
Learn to conform the order of our lives.

THE DEATH OF THE FLOWERS

The melancholy days are come, the saddest of the year,
Of wailing winds, and naked woods, and meadows brown and
    sere.
Heaped in the hollows of the grove, the autumn leaves lie
    dead;
They rustle to the eddying gust, and to the rabbit's tread;
The robin and the wren are flown, and from the shrubs the
    jay,   5
And from the wood-top calls the crow through all the gloomy
    day.

Where are the flowers, the fair young flowers, that lately
    sprang and stood
In brighter light and softer airs, a beauteous sisterhood?
Alas! they all are in their graves, the gentle race of flowers
Are lying in their lowly beds, with the fair and good of ours. 10
The rain is falling where they lie, but the cold November rain
Calls not from out the gloomy earth the lovely ones again.

The wind-flower and the violet, they perished long ago,
And the brier-rose and the orchis died amid the summer
    glow;
But on the hills the golden-rod, and the aster in the wood, 15
And the yellow sun-flower by the brook, in autumn beauty
    stood,
Till fell the frost from the clear cold heaven, as falls the plague
    on men,
And the brightness of their smile was gone, from upland,
    glade, and glen.

And now, when comes the calm mild day, as still such days
    will come,
To call the squirrel and the bee from out their winter home; 20
When the sound of dropping nuts is heard, though all the
    trees are still,
And twinkle in the smoky light the waters of the rill,
The south wind searches for the flowers whose fragrance late
    he bore,
And sighs to find them in the wood and by the stream no
    more.

And then I think of one who in her youthful beauty died,   25
The fair meek blossom that grew up and faded by my side.°
In the cold moist earth we laid her, when the forests cast the
    leaf,
And we wept that one so lovely should have a life so brief:
Yet not unmeet° it was that one, like that young friend of
    ours,
So gentle and so beautiful, should perish with the flowers. 30

THE GLADNESS OF NATURE

Is this a time to be cloudy and sad,
    When our mother Nature laughs around;
When even the deep blue heavens look glad,
    And gladness breathes from the blossoming ground?

There are notes of joy from the hang-bird° and wren,   5
    And the gossip of swallows through all the sky;
The ground-squirrel gayly chirps by his den,
    And the wilding° bee hums merrily by.

The clouds are at play in the azure space
    And their shadows at play on the bright-green vale, 10
And here they stretch to the frolic chase,
    And there they roll on the easy gale.

There's a dance of leaves in that aspen bower,
    There's a titter of winds in that beechen tree,
There's a smile on the fruit, and a smile on the flower, 15
    And a laugh from the brook that runs to the sea.

And look at the broad-faced sun, how he smiles
    On the dewy earth that smiles in his ray,
On the leaping waters and gay young isles;
    Ay, look, and he'll smile thy gloom away.   20

TO THE FRINGED GENTIAN°

Thou blossom bright with autumn dew,
And colored with the heaven's own blue,
That openest when the quiet light
Succeeds the keen and frosty night.

Thou comest not when violets lean   5
O'er wandering brooks and springs unseen,
Or columbines, in purple dressed,
Nod o'er the ground-bird's hidden nest.

Thou waitest late and com'st alone,
When woods are bare and birds are flown,   **10**
And frosts and shortening days portend°
The aged year is near his end.

Then doth thy sweet and quiet eye
Look through its fringes to the sky,
Blue — blue — as if that sky let fall　　　15
A flower from its cerulean° wall.

I would that thus, when I shall see
The hour of death draw near to me,
Hope, blossoming within my heart,
May look to heaven as I depart.　　　20

SONG OF MARION'S MEN

Our band is few but true and tried,
　　Our leader frank and bold ;
The British soldier trembles
　　When Marion's° name is told.
Our fortress is the good greenwood,　　　5
　　Our tent the cypress-tree ;
We know the forest round us,
　　As seamen know the sea.
We know its walls of thorny vines,
　　Its glades of reedy grass,　　　10
Its safe and silent islands
　　Within the dark morass.

Woe to the English soldiery
　　That little dread us near !
On them shall light at midnight　　　15
　　A strange and sudden fear :
When, waking to their tents on fire,
　　They grasp their arms in vain,

And they who stand to face us
   Are beat to earth again;   20
And they who fly in terror deem°
   A mighty host behind,
And hear the tramp of thousands
   Upon the hollow wind.

Then sweet the hour that brings release   25
   From danger and from toil :
We talk the battle over,
   And share the battle's spoil.
The woodland rings with laugh and shout,
   As if a hunt were up,°   30
And woodland flowers are gathered
   To crown the soldier's cup.
With merry songs we mock the wind
   That in the pine-top grieves,
And slumber long and sweetly   35
   On beds of oaken leaves.

Well knows the fair and friendly moon
   The band that Marion leads —
The glitter of their rifles,
   The scampering of their steeds.   40
'Tis life to guide the fiery barb°
   Across the moonlight plain ;
'Tis life to feel the night-wind
   That lifts the tossing mane.
A moment in the British camp —   45
   A moment — and away
Back to the pathless forest,
   Before the peep of day.

Grave men there are by broad Santee,°
    Grave men with hoary hairs;   50
Their hearts are all with Marion,
    For Marion are their prayers.
And lovely ladies greet our band
    With kindliest welcoming,
With smiles like those of summer,   55
    And tears like those of spring.
For them we wear these trusty arms,
    And lay them down no more
Till we have driven the Briton,
    Forever, from our shore.   60

THE CROWDED STREET

LET me move slowly through the street,
    Filled with an ever-shifting train,
Amid the sound of steps that beat
    The murmuring walks like autumn rain.

How fast the flitting figures come!   5
    The mild, the fierce, the stony face;
Some bright with thoughtless smiles, and some
    Where secret tears have left their trace.

They pass — to toil, to strife, to rest;
    To halls in which the feast is spread;   10
To chambers where the funeral guest
    In silence sits beside the dead.

And some to happy homes repair,
    Where children, pressing cheek to cheek,

E

With mute caresses shall declare   15
    The tenderness they cannot speak.

And some, who walk in calmness here,
    Shall shudder as they reach the door
Where one who made their dwelling dear,
    Its flower, its light, is seen no more.   20

Youth, with pale cheek and slender frame,
    And dreams of greatness in thine eye!
Go'st thou to build an early name,
    Or early in the task to die?

Keen son of trade, with eager brow!   25
    Who is now fluttering in thy snare?
Thy golden fortunes, tower they now,
    Or melt the glittering spires in air?

Who of this crowd to-night shall tread
    The dance till daylight gleam again?   30
Who sorrow o'er the untimely dead?
    Who writhe in throes° of mortal pain?

Some, famine-struck, shall think how long
    The cold dark hours, how slow the light;
And some, who flaunt amid the throng,   35
    Shall hide in dens of shame to-night.

Each, where his tasks or pleasures call,
    They pass, and heed each other not.
There is who heeds, who holds them all,
    In His large love and boundless thought.   40

These struggling tides of life that seem
   In wayward, aimless course to tend,
Are eddies of the mighty stream
   That rolls to its appointed end.°

THE SNOW-SHOWER°

STAND here by my side and turn, I pray,
   On the lake below thy gentle eyes;
The clouds hang over it, heavy and gray,
   And dark and silent the water lies;
And out of that frozen mist the snow   5
In wavering flakes begins to flow;
            Flake after flake
They sink in the dark and silent lake.

See how in a living swarm° they come
   From the chambers beyond that misty veil;   10
Some hover awhile in air, and some
   Rush prone° from the sky like summer hail.
All, dropping swiftly or settling slow,
Meet, and are still in the depths below;
            Flake after flake   15
Dissolved in the dark and silent lake.

Here delicate snow-stars,° out of the cloud,
   Come floating downward in airy play,
Like spangles dropped from the glistening crowd
   That whiten by night the milky way°;   20

There broader and burlier° masses fall;
The sullen water buries them all —
                    Flake after flake —
All drowned in the dark and silent lake.

And some, as on tender wings they glide   25
    From their chilly birth-cloud, dim and gray,
Are joined in their fall, and, side by side,
    Come clinging along their unsteady way;
As friend with friend, or husband with wife,
Makes hand in hand the passage of life;   30
                    Each mated flake
Soon sinks in the dark and silent lake.

Lo! while we are gazing, in swifter haste
    Stream down the snows, till the air is white,
As, myriads by myriads° madly chased,   35
    They fling themselves from their shadowy height.
The fair, frail creatures of middle° sky,
What speed they make, with their grave so nigh;
                    Flake after flake,
To lie in the dark and silent lake!   40

I see in thy gentle eyes a tear;
    They turn to me in sorrowful thought;
Thou thinkest of friends, the good and dear,
    Who were for a time, and now are not;
Like these fair children of cloud and frost,   45
That glisten a moment and then are lost,
                    Flake after flake —
All lost in the dark and silent lake.

Yet look again, for the clouds divide;
   A gleam of blue on the water lies; 50
And far away, on the mountain-side,
   A sunbeam falls from the opening skies,
But the hurrying host that flew between
The cloud and the water, no more is seen;
        Flake after flake, 55
At rest in the dark and silent lake.

ROBERT OF LINCOLN°

MERRILY swinging on brier and weed,
   Near to the nest of his little dame,
Over the mountain-side or mead,
   Robert of Lincoln is telling his name:
      Bob-o'-link, bob-o'-link, 5
      Spink, spank, spink;
Snug and safe is that nest of ours,
Hidden among the summer flowers,
      Chee, chee, chee.

Robert of Lincoln is gayly drest, 10
   Wearing a bright black wedding-coat;
White are his shoulders and white his crest
   Hear him call in his merry note:
      Bob-o'-link, bob-o'-link,
      Spink, spank, spink; 15
Look, what a nice new coat is mine.
Sure there was never a bird so fine.
      Chee, chee, chee.

Robert of Lincoln's Quaker wife,
  Pretty and quiet, with plain brown wings,   20
Passing at home a patient life,
  Broods in the grass while her husband sings:
     Bob-o'-link, bob-o'-link,
     Spink, spank, spink;
Brood, kind creature; you need not fear   25
Thieves and robbers while I am here.
     Chee, chee, chee.

Modest and shy as a nun is she;
  One weak chirp is her only note.
Braggart and prince of braggarts is he,   30
  Pouring boasts from his little throat:
     Bob-o'-link, bob-o'-link,
     Spink, spank, spink;
Never was I afraid of man;
Catch me, cowardly knaves, if you can!   35
     Chee, chee, chee.

Six white eggs on a bed of hay,
  Flecked with purple, a pretty sight!
There as the mother sits all day,
  Robert is singing with all his might: 40
     Bob-o'-link, bob-o'-link,
     Spink, spank, spink;
Nice good wife, that never goes out,
Keeping house while I frolic about.
     Chee, chee, chee.   45

Soon as the little ones chip the shell,
  Six wide mouths are open for food;

Robert of Lincoln bestirs him well,
 Gathering seeds for the hungry brood.
  Bob-o'-link, bob-o'-link,   50
  Spink, spank, spink;
This new life is likely to be
Hard for a gay young fellow like me.
  Chee, chee, chee.

Robert of Lincoln at length is made 55
 Sober with work, and silent with care;
Off is his holiday garment laid,
 Half forgotten that merry air:
  Bob-o'-link, bob-o'-link,
  Spink, spank, spink;   60
Nobody knows but my mate and I
Where our nest and our nestlings lie.
  Chee, chee, chee.

Summer wanes; the children are grown;
 Fun and frolic no more he knows; 65
Robert of Lincoln's a humdrum crone;
 Off he flies, and we sing as he goes:
  Bob-o'-link, bob-o'-link,
  Spink, spank, spink;
When you can pipe that merry old strain, 70
Robert of Lincoln, come back again.
  Chee, chee, chee.°

THE POET

THOU, who wouldst wear the name
　　Of poet mid thy brethren of mankind,
And clothe in words of flame
　　Thoughts that shall live within the general mind!
Deem° not the framing of a deathless lay   5
The pastime of a drowsy summer day.

But gather all thy powers,
　　And wreak° them on the verse that thou dost weave,
And in thy lonely hours,
　　At silent morning or at wakeful eve,   10
While the warm current tingles through thy veins,
Set forth the burning words in fluent strains.

No smooth array of phrase,
　　Artfully sought and ordered though it be,
Which the cold rhymer lays   15
　　Upon his page with languid industry,
Can wake the listless pulse to livelier speed,
Or fill with sudden tears the eyes that read.

The secret wouldst thou know
　　To touch the heart or fire the blood at will?   20
Let thine own eyes o'erflow;
　　Let thy lips quiver with the passionate thrill;
Seize the great thought, ere yet its power be past,
And bind, in words, the fleet emotion fast.

Then, should thy verse appear   25
　　Halting and harsh, and all unaptly° wrought,

Touch the crude line with fear,
   Save in the moment of impassioned thought;
Then summon back the original glow, and mend
The strain with rapture that with fire was penned.°   30

Yet let no empty gust
   Of passion find an utterance in thy lay,
A blast that whirls the dust
   Along the howling street and dies away;
But feelings of calm power and mighty sweep,   35
Like currents journeying through the windless deep.

Seek'st thou, in living lays,
   To limn° the beauty of the earth and sky?
Before thine inner gaze
   Let all that beauty in clear vision lie;   40
Look on it with exceeding love, and write
The words inspired by wonder and delight.

Of tempests wouldst thou sing,
   Or tell of battles — make thyself a part
Of the great tumult; cling   45
   To the tossed wreck with terror in thy heart;
Scale, with the assaulting host, the rampart's height,
And strike and struggle in the thickest fight.

So shalt thou frame a lay
   That haply may endure from age to age,   50
And they who read shall say:
   "What witchery hangs upon this poet's page!
What art is his the written spells to find
That sway from mood to mood the willing mind!"°

ABRAHAM LINCOLN

Oh, slow to smite and swift to spare,
    Gentle and merciful and just!
Who, in the fear of God, didst bear
    The sword of power, a nation's trust!

In sorrow by thy bier we stand,   5
    Amid the awe that hushes all,
And speak the anguish of a land
    That shook with horror at thy fall.

Thy task is done; the bond are free:
    We bear thee to an honored grave   10
Whose proudest monument shall be
    The broken fetters of the slave.

Pure was thy life; its bloody close
    Hath placed thee with the sons of light,
Among the noble host of those   15
    Who perished in the cause of Right.

FRANCIS SCOTT KEY

THE STAR-SPANGLED BANNER°

O SAY, can you see, by the dawn's early light,
What so proudly we hailed at the twilight's last gleaming?
Whose broad stripes and bright stars through the perilous
    fight,
O'er the ramparts we watched were so gallantly streaming;
And the rocket's red glare, the bombs bursting in air,   5
Gave proof through the night that our flag was still there;
O say, does that star-spangled banner yet wave
O'er the land of the free, and the home of the brave?

On the shore dimly seen through the mists of the deep,
Where the foe's haughty host in dread silence reposes,   10
What is that which the breeze, o'er the towering steep,
As it fitfully blows, now conceals, now discloses?
Now it catches the gleam of the morning's first beam,
In full glory reflected now shines on the stream;
'Tis the star-spangled banner; O long may it wave   15
O'er the land of the free, and the home of the brave!

And where is that band who so vauntingly swore
That the havoc of war and the battle's confusion
A home and a country should leave us no more?
Their blood has washed out their foul footsteps' pollution.   20
No refuge could save the hireling and slave,

From the terror of flight and the gloom of the grave;
And the star-spangled banner in triumph doth wave
O'er the land of the free, and the home of the brave!

O! thus be it ever, when freemen shall stand   25
Between their loved homes and the war's desolation:
Blest with victory and peace, may the heav'n-rescued land,
Praise the power that hath made and preserved us a nation.
Then conquer we must, for our cause it is just.
And this be our motto — "In God is our trust°";   30
And the star-spangled banner in triumph shall wave
O'er the land of the free, and the home of the brave.

JOSEPH RODMAN DRAKE

THE AMERICAN FLAG

WHEN Freedom from her mountain height
 Unfurled her standard to the air,
She tore the azure robe of night,
 And set the stars of glory there.
And mingled with its gorgeous dyes   5
The milky baldric° of the skies,
And striped its pure celestial white
With streakings of the morning light;
Then from his mansion in the sun
She called her eagle bearer down,   10
And gave into his mighty hand
The symbol of her chosen land.

Majestic monarch of the cloud,
 Who rear'st aloft thy regal form,
To hear the tempest trumpings loud   15
And see the lightning lances driven,
 When strive the warriors of the storm,
And rolls the thunder-drum of heaven,
Child of the sun! to thee 'tis given
 To guard the banner of the free,   20
To hover in the sulphur smoke,
To ward away the battle stroke,
And bid its blendings shine afar,
Like rainbows on the cloud of war,
 The harbingers of victory!°   25

Flag of the brave! thy folds shall fly,
The sign of hope and triumph high,
When speaks the signal trumpet tone,
And the long line comes gleaming on.
Ere yet the life-blood, warm and wet,   30
Has dimmed the glistening bayonet,
Each soldier eye shall brightly turn
To where thy sky-born glories burn,
And, as his springing steps advance,
Catch war and vengeance from the glance.   35
And when the cannon-mouthings loud
Heave in wild wreaths the battle shroud,
And gory sabres rise and fall
Like shoots of flame on midnight's pall,
　Then shall thy meteor glances glow,   40
And cowering foes shall shrink beneath
　Each gallant arm that strikes below
That lovely messenger of death.

Flag of the seas! on ocean wave
Thy stars shall glitter o'er the brave;   45
When death, careering° on the gale,
Sweeps darkly round the bellied° sail,
And frighted waves rush wildly back
Before the broadside's reeling rack,
Each dying wanderer of the sea   50
Shall look at once to heaven and thee,
And smile to see thy splendors fly
In triumph o'er his closing eye.

Flag of the free heart's hope and home!
　By angel hands to valor given;   55

Thy stars have lit the welkin° dome,
   And all thy hues were born in heaven.
Forever float that standard sheet!
   Where breathes the foe but falls before us,
With Freedom's soil beneath our feet,   60
   And Freedom's banner streaming o'er us?

THE CULPRIT FAY   (Selection)

*   *   *   *   *   *   *

'Tis the hour of fairy ban and spell:
The wood-tick has kept the minutes well;
He has counted them all with click and stroke,
Deep in the heart of the mountain oak,
And he has awakened the sentry elve   5
   Who sleeps with him in the haunted tree,
To bid him ring the hour of twelve,
   And call the fays to their revelry;
Twelve small strokes on his tinkling bell—
('Twas made of the white snail's pearly shell)   10
"Midnight comes, and all is well!
Hither, hither, wing your way!
'Tis the dawn of the fairy-day."

They come from beds of lichen green,
They creep from the mullen's velvet screen;   15
   Some on the backs of beetles fly
From the silver tops of moon-touched trees,
   Where they swung in their cobweb hammocks high,

And rocked about in the evening breeze;
   Some from the hum-bird's downy nest —   20
They had driven him out by elfin power,
   And, pillowed on plumes of his rainbow breast,
Had slumbered there till the charméd hour;
   Some had lain in the scoop of the rock,
With glittering ising-stars° inlaid;   25
   And some had opened the four-o'clock,
And stole within its purple shade.
   And now they throng the moonlight glade,
Above, below, on every side,
   Their little minim° forms arrayed   30
In the tricksy pomp of fairy pride.

They come not now to print the lea,
In freak and dance around the tree,
Or at the mushroom board to sup
And drink the dew from the buttercup.   35
A scene of sorrow waits them now,
For an Ouphe° has broken his vestal vow:
He has loved an earthly maid,
And left for her his woodland shade;
He has lain upon her lip of dew,   40
And sunned him in her eye of blue,
Fanned her cheek with his wing of air,
Played in the ringlets of her hair,
And, nestling on her snowy breast,
Forgot the lily-king's behest.°   45
For this the shadowy tribes of air
   To the elfin court must haste away;
And now they stand expectant there,
   To hear the doom of the Culprit Fay.

The throne was reared upon the grass,   50
Of spice-wood and of sassafras ;
On pillars of mottled tortoise-shell
    Hung the burnished canopy, —
And over it gorgeous curtains fell
    Of the tulip's crimson drapery.   55
The monarch sat on his judgment-seat,
    On his brow the crown imperial shone,
The prisoner Fay was at his feet,
    And his peers were ranged around the throne.
He waved his sceptre in the air,   60
    He looked around and calmly spoke ;
His brow was grave and his eye severe,
    But his voice in a softened accent broke :

"Fairy ! Fairy ! list and mark !
    Thou hast broke thine elfin chain ;   65
Thy flame-wood lamp is quenched and dark,
    And thy wings are dyed with a deadly stain ;
Thou hast sullied thine elfin purity
    In the glance of a mortal maiden's eye :
Thou hast scorned our dread decree,   70
    And thou shouldst pay the forfeit high,
But well I know her sinless mind
    Is pure as the angel forms above,
Gentle and meek and chaste and kind,
    Such as a spirit well might love.   75
Fairy ! had she spot or taint,
Bitter had been thy punishment :
Tied to the hornet's shardy° wings,
Tossed on the pricks of nettles' stings,
Or seven long ages doomed to dwell   80

F

With the lazy worm in the walnut-shell;
Or every night to writhe and bleed
Beneath the tread of the centipede;
Or bound in a cobweb dungeon dim,
Your jailer a spider huge and grim,   85
Amid the carrion bodies to lie
Of the worm, and the bug and the murdered fly:
These it had been your lot to bear,
Had a stain been found on the earthly fair.
Now list and mark our mild decree: 90
Fairy, this your doom must be:

"Thou shalt seek the beach of sand
Where the water bounds the elfin land;
Thou shalt watch the oozy° brine
Till the sturgeon leaps in the bright moonshine;   95
Then dart the glistening arch below,
And catch a drop from his silver bow.
The water-sprites will wield their arms,
    And dash around with roar and rave;
And vain are the woodland spirits' charms —   100
    They are the imps that rule the wave.
Yet trust thee in thy single might:
If thy heart be pure and thy spirit right,
Thou shalt win the warlock fight." . . .

*   *   *   *   *   *   *

The goblin marked his monarch well;   105
    He spake not, but he bowed him low;
Then plucked a crimson colen-bell,°
    And turned him round in act to go.
The way is long, he cannot fly,

His soiled wing has lost its power;   110
And he winds adown the mountain high
  For many a sore and weary hour:
Through dreary beds of tangled fern,
Through groves of nightshade° dark and dern,°
Over the grass and through the brake,   115
Where toils the ant and sleeps the snake;
  Now over the violet's azure flush
He skips along in lightsome mood;
  And now he thrids° the bramble-bush,
Till its points are dyed in fairy blood;   120
He has leaped the bog, he has pierced the brier,
He has swum the brook, and waded the mire,
Till his spirits sank and his limbs grew weak,
And the red waxed fainter in his cheek.
He had fallen to the ground outright,   125
  For rugged and dim was his onward track,
But there came a spotted toad in sight,
  And he laughed as he jumped upon her back;
He bridled her mouth with a silkweed twist,
  He lashed her sides with an osier thong;   130
And now through evening's dewy mist
  With leap and spring they bound along,
Till the mountain's magic verge is past,
And the beach of sand is reached at last.

Soft and pale is the moony beam,   135
Moveless still the glassy stream;
The wave is clear, the beach is bright
  With snowy shells and sparkling stones;
The shore-surge comes in ripples light,
  In murmurings faint and distant moans;   140

And ever afar in the silence deep
Is heard the splash of the sturgeon's leap,
And the bend of his graceful bow is seen —
A glittering arch of silver sheen,
Spanning the wave of burnished blue,   145
And dripping with gems of the river-dew.

The elfin cast a glance around,
    As he lighted down from his courser toad,
Then round his breast his wings he wound,
    And close to the river's brink he strode;   150
He sprang on a rock, he breathed a prayer,
    Above his head his arms he threw,
Then tossed a tiny curve in air,
    And headlong plunged in the waters blue.

Up sprung the spirits of the waves,   155
From the sea-silk beds in their coral caves;
With snail-plate armor snatched in haste,
They speed their way through the liquid waste.
Some are rapidly borne along
On the mailéd shrimp or the prickly prong,°   160
Some on the blood-red leeches glide,
Some on the stony star-fish ride,
Some on the back of the lancing squab,
Some on the sideling soldier-crab,
And some on the jellied quarl° that flings   165
At once a thousand streamy stings.
They cut the wave with the living oar,
And hurry on to the moonlight shore,
To guard their realms and chase away
The footsteps of the invading Fay.   170

Fearlessly he skims along;
His hope is high and his limbs are strong;
He spreads his arms like the swallow's wing,
And throws his feet with a frog-like fling;
His locks of gold on the waters shine,   175
   At his breast the tiny foam-beads rise,
His back gleams bright above the brine,
   And the wake-line° foam behind him lies.
But the water-sprites are gathering near
   To check his course along the tide;   180
Their warriors come in swift career
   And hem him round on every side:
On his thigh the leech has fixed his hold,
The quarl's long arms are round him rolled,
The prickly prong has pierced his skin,   185
And the squab has thrown his javelin,
The gritty star has rubbed him raw,
And the crab has struck with his giant claw.
He howls with rage, and he shrieks with pain;
He strikes around, but his blows are vain;   190
Hopeless is the unequal fight:
Fairy, naught is left but flight.

He turned him round and fled amain,°
With hurry and dash, to the beach again;
He twisted over from side to side,   195
And laid his cheek to the cleaving tide;
The strokes of his plunging arms are fleet,
And with all his might he flings his feet.
But the water-sprites are round him still,
To cross his path and work him ill: 200
They bade the wave before him rise;

They flung the sea-fire in his eyes;
And they stunned his ears with the scallop-stroke,
With the porpoise heave and the drum-fish croak.
Oh, but a weary wight was he   205
When he reached the foot of the dog-wood tree.
Gashed and wounded, and stiff and sore,
He laid him down on the sandy shore;
He blessed the force of the charméd line,
    And he banned° the water-goblins' spite   210
For he saw around in the sweet moonshine
Their little wee faces above the brine,
    Giggling and laughing with all their might
    At the piteous hap of the Fairy wight.

Soon he gathered the balsam dew   215
    From the sorrel-leaf and the henbane° bud;
Over each wound the balm he drew,
    And with cobweb lint he stanched the blood.
The mild west wind was soft and low;
It cooled the heat of his burning brow,   220
And he felt new life in his sinews shoot
As he drank the juice of the calamus root.
And now he treads the fatal° shore
As fresh and vigorous as before.

Wrapped in musing stands the sprite: 225
'Tis the middle wane of night;
    His task is hard, his way is far,
But he must do his errand right
    Ere dawning mounts her beamy car,
And rolls her chariot wheels of light;   230
And vain are the spells of fairy-land,
He must work with a human hand.

He cast a saddened look around;
   But he felt new joy his bosom swell,
When glittering on the shadowed ground   235
   He saw a purple mussel-shell;
Thither he ran, and he bent him low,
He heaved at the stern and he heaved at the bow,
And he pushed her over the yielding sand
Till he came to the verge of the haunted land.   240
She was as lovely a pleasure-boat
   As ever fairy had paddled in,
For she glowed with purple paint without,
   And shone with silvery pearl within:
A sculler's notch° in the stern he made,   245
An oar he shaped of the bootle-blade;
Then sprung to his seat with a lightsome leap,
And launched afar on the calm, blue deep.

The imps of the river yell and rave:
They had no power above the wave,   250
But they heaved the billow before the prow,
   And they dashed the surge against her side,
And they struck her keel with jerk and blow,
   Till the gunwale bent to the rocking tide.
She wimpled° about to the pale moonbeam,   255
Like a feather that floats on a wind-tossed stream;
And momently athwart° her track
The quarl upreared his island back,
And the fluttering scallop behind would float,
And patter the water about the boat;   260
But he bailed her out with his colen-bell,
   And he kept her trimmed with a wary tread,
While on every side like lightning fell
   The heavy strokes of his bootle-blade.

Onward still he held his way,   265
Till he came where the column of moonshine lay,
And saw beneath the surface dim
The brown-backed sturgeon slowly swim.
Around him were the goblin train;
But he sculled with all his might and main,   270
And followed wherever the sturgeon led,
Till he saw him upward point his head;
Then he dropped his paddle-blade,
And held his colen-goblet up
To catch the drop in its crimson cup.   275

With sweeping tail and quivering fin
    Through the wave the sturgeon flew,
And like the heaven-shot javelin
    He sprung above the waters blue.
Instant as the star-fall light,   280
    He plunged him in the deep again,
But left an arch of silver bright,
    The rainbow of the moony main.
It was a strange and lovely sight
    To see the puny goblin there: 285
He seemed an angel form of light,
    With azure wing and sunny hair,
    Throned on a cloud of purple fair,
Circled with blue and edged with white,
And sitting at the fall of even   290
Beneath the bow of summer heaven.

A moment, and its lustre fell;
    But ere it met the billow blue

He caught within his crimson bell
  A droplet of its sparkling dew. 295
Joy to thee, Fay! thy task is done;
Thy wings are pure, for the gem is won.
Cheerly ply thy dripping oar,
And haste away to the elfin shore!

He turns, and lo on either side 300
The ripples on his path divide;
And the track o'er which his boat must pass
Is smooth as a sheet of polished glass.
Around, their limbs the sea-nymphs lave,
  With snowy arms half swelling out, 305
While on the glossed° and gleamy wave
  Their sea-green ringlets loosely float:
They swim around with smile and song;
  They press the bark with pearly hand,
And gently urge her course along, 310
  Toward the beach of speckled sand;
  And as he lightly leaped to land
They bade adieu with nod and bow,
  Then gaily kissed each little hand,
And dropped in the crystal deep below. 31£

A moment stayed the fairy there:
He kissed the beach and breathed a prayer;
Then spread his wings of gilded blue,
And on to the elfin court he flew.
As ever ye saw a bubble rise, 3°
And shine with a thousand changing dyes,
Till, lessening far, through ether driven,
It mingles with the hues of heaven;

As, at the glimpse of morning pale,
The lance-fly spreads his silken sail
And gleams with blendings soft and bright
Till lost in the shades of fading night;
So rose from earth the lovely Fay,
So vanished far in heaven away! °

325

FITZ-GREENE HALLECK

MARCO BOZZARIS°

At midnight, in his guarded tent,
  The Turk was dreaming of the hour
When Greece, her knee in suppliance bent,
  Should tremble at his power;
In dreams, through camp and court he bore   5
The trophies of a conqueror;
  In dreams his song of triumph heard;
Then wore his monarch's signet ring;
Then pressed that monarch's throne — a king:
As wild his thoughts and gay of wing   10
  As Eden's garden bird.

At midnight, in the forest shades,
  Bozzaris ranged his Suliote° band,
True as the steel of their tried blades,
  Heroes in heart and hand.   15
There had the Persian's thousands stood,
There had the glad earth drunk their blood
  On old Platæa's day;
And now there breathed that haunted air
The sons of sires who conquered there,   20
With arm to strike, and soul to dare,
  As quick, as far as they.°

75

An hour passed on — the Turk awoke;
   That bright dream was his last;
He woke — to hear his sentries shriek,   25
"To arms! they come! the Greek! the Greek!"
He woke — to die midst flame and smoke,
And shout and groan and sabre-stroke,
   And death-shots falling thick and fast
As lightnings from the mountain-cloud;   30
And heard, with voice as trumpet loud,
   Bozzaris cheer his band:
"Strike — till the last armed foe expires!
Strike — for your altars and your fires!
Strike — for the green graves of your sires,   35
   God, and your native land!"

They fought like brave men, long and well;
   They piled that ground with Moslem slain;
They conquered — but Bozzaris fell,
   Bleeding at every vein.   40
His few surviving comrades saw
His smile when rang their proud hurrah,
   And the red field was won;
Then saw in death his eyelids close
Calmly, as to a night's repose,   45
   Like flowers at set of sun.

Come to the bridal chamber, Death!
   Come to the mother's when she feels,
For the first time, her first-born's breath;
   Come when the blessed seals   50
That close the pestilence are broke,
And crowded cities wail its stroke;

Come in consumption's ghastly form,
The earthquake shock, the ocean storm;
Come when the heart beats high and warm   55
  With banquet-song and dance and wine;
And thou art terrible — the tear,
The groan, the knell, the pall, the bier,
And all we know or dream or fear
  Of agony, are thine.   60

But to the hero, when his sword
  Has won the battle for the free,
Thy voice sounds like a prophet's word,
And in its hollow tones are heard
  The thanks of millions yet to be.   65
Come when his task of fame is wrought,
Come with her laurel-leaf, blood-bought,
  Come in her crowning hour, and then
Thy sunken eye's unearthly light
To him is welcome as the sight   70
  Of sky and stars to prisoned men;
Thy grasp is welcome as the hand
Of brother in a foreign land;
Thy summons welcome as the cry
That told the Indian isles were nigh   75
  To the world-seeking Genoese,
When the land-wind, from woods of palm
And orange-groves and fields of balm,
  Blew o'er the Haytian seas.°

Bozzaris, with the storied brave   80
  Greece nurtured in her glory's time,

Rest thee — there is no prouder grave,
    Even in her own proud clime.
She wore no funeral-weeds for thee,
    Nor bade the dark hearse wave its plume,   85
Like torn branch from death's leafless tree,
In sorrow's pomp and pageantry,
    The heartless luxury of the tomb.
But she remembers thee as one
Long loved and for a season gone;   90
For thee her poet's lyre is wreathed,
Her marble wrought, her music breathed;
For thee she rings the birthday bells;
Of thee her babes' first lisping tells;
For thine her evening prayer is said   95
At palace-couch and cottage-bed;
Her soldier, closing with the foe,
Gives for thy sake a deadlier blow;
His plighted maiden, when she fears
For him, the joy of her young years,   100
Thinks of thy fate and checks her tears;
    And she, the mother of thy boys,
Though in her eye and faded cheek
Is read the grief she will not speak,
    The memory of her buried joys,   105
And even she who gave thee birth,
Will, by their pilgrim-circled° hearth,
    Talk of thy doom without a sigh,
For thou art Freedom's now and Fame's,
One of the few, the immortal names,   110
    That were not born to die.

ON THE DEATH OF JOSEPH RODMAN DRAKE

GREEN be the turf above thee,
    Friend of my better days!
None knew thee but to love thee,
    Nor named thee but to praise.

Tears fell, when thou wert dying,   5
    From eyes unused to weep,
And long where thou art lying,
    Will tears the cold turf steep.

When hearts, whose truth was proven,
    Like thine, are laid in earth,   10
There should a wreath be woven
    To tell the world their worth;

And I, who woke each morrow
    To clasp thy hand in mine,
Who shared thy joy and sorrow,   15
    Whose weal and woe were thine;

It should be mine to braid it
    Around thy faded brow,
But I've in vain essayed it,
    And feel I cannot now.   20

While memory bids me weep thee,
    Nor thoughts nor words are free,
The grief is fixed too deeply
    That mourns a man like thee.

JOHN HOWARD PAYNE

HOME, SWEET HOME!

Mɪᴅ pleasures and palaces though we may roam,
Be it ever so humble, there's no place like home;
A charm from the sky seems to hallow us there,
Which, seek through the world, is ne'er met with elsewhere.
    Home, Home, sweet, sweet Home!   5
There's no place like Home! there's no place like Home!

An exile from home, splendor dazzles in vain;
O, give me my lowly thatched cottage again!
The birds singing gayly, that came at my call, —
Give me them, — and the peace of mind, dearer than all!   10
    Home, Home, sweet, sweet Home!
There's no place like Home! there's no place like Home!

How sweet 'tis to sit 'neath a fond father's smile,
And the cares of a mother to soothe and beguile!
Let others delight mid new pleasures to roam,   15
But give me, oh, give me, the pleasures of home!
    Home, Home, sweet, sweet Home!
There's no place like Home! there's no place like Home!

To thee I'll return, overburdened with care;
The heart's dearest solace will smile on me there;   20
No more from that cottage again will I roam;
Be it ever so humble, there's no place like home.
    Home, Home, sweet, sweet Home!
There's no place like Home! there's no place like Home!

EDGAR ALLAN POE

TO HELEN

HELEN,° thy beauty is to me
  Like those Nicéan° barks of yore,
That gently, o'er a perfumed sea,
  The weary, way-worn wanderer bore
  To his own native shore.   5

On desperate seas long wont to roam,
  Thy hyacinth° hair, thy classic face,
Thy Naiad° airs have brought me home
  To the glory that was Greece,
  And the grandeur that was Rome.   10

Lo! in yon brilliant window-niche
  How statue-like I see thee stand,
  The agate lamp within thy hand!
Ah, Psyche,° from the regions which
  Are Holy-Land!   15

ISRAFEL°

In Heaven a spirit doth dwell
  "Whose heart-strings are a lute°;"
None sing so wildly well
As the angel Israfel,
And the giddy stars (so legends tell)   5
Ceasing their hymns, attend the spell
  Of his voice, all mute.

Tottering above
  In her highest noon,
  The enamoured moon   10
Blushes with love,
  While, to listen, the red levin°
  (With the rapid Pleiads, even,
  Which were seven,)
  Pauses in Heaven.   15

And they say (the starry choir
  And the other listening things)
That Israfeli's fire
Is owing to that lyre
  By which he sits and sings—   20
The trembling living wire
  Of those unusual strings.

But the skies that angel trod,
Where deep thoughts are a duty—
Where Love's a grown-up God—   25
  Where the Houri° glances are

Imbued with all the beauty
  Which we worship in a star.

Therefore, thou art not wrong,
  Israfeli, who despisest   30
An unimpassioned song;
To thee the laurels belong,
  Best bard, because the wisest!
Merrily live, and long!

The ecstasies above   35
  With thy burning measures suit —
Thy grief, thy joy, thy hate, thy love,
  With the fervour of thy lute —
  Well may the stars be mute!

Yes, Heaven is thine; but this   40
  Is a world of sweets and sours;
  Our flowers are merely — flowers,
And the shadow of thy perfect bliss
  Is the sunshine of ours.

If I could dwell   45
Where Israfel
  Hath dwelt, and he where I,
He might not sing so wildly well
  A mortal melody,
While a bolder note than this might swell   50
  From my lyre within the sky.

LENORE

AH, broken is the golden bowl! the spirit flown forever!
Let the bell toll! — a saintly soul floats on the Stygian river;
And, Guy De Vere, hast *thou* no tear? — weep now or never
    more!
See! on yon drear and rigid bier low lies thy love, Lenore!
Come! let the burial rite be read — the funeral song be
    sung! —   5
An anthem for the queenliest dead that ever died so young —
A dirge for her the doubly dead in that she died so young.

"Wretches! ye loved her for her wealth and hated her for her
    pride,
"And when she fell in feeble health, ye blessed her — that
    she died!
"How *shall* the ritual, then, be read? — the requiem how be
    sung   10
"By you — by yours, the evil eye, — by yours, the slander-
    ous tongue
"That did to death the innocence that died, and died so
    young?"

Peccavimus°; but rave not thus! and let a Sabbath song
Go up to God so solemnly the dead may feel no wrong!
The sweet Lenore hath "gone before," with Hope, that flew
    beside,   15
Leaving thee wild for the dear child that should have been
    thy bride —
For her, the fair and *debonair*, that now so lowly lies,
The life upon her yellow hair but not within her eyes —
The life still there, upon her hair — the death upon her eyes.

"Avaunt° ! — avaunt ! from fiends below, the indignant
    ghost is riven — 20
"From Hell unto a high estate far up within the Heaven —
"From grief and groan, to a golden throne, beside the King
    of Heaven."
Let no bell toll then ! — lest her soul, amid its hallowed mirth,
Should catch the note as it doth float up from the damnéd
    Earth ! —
And I ! — to-night my heart is light !   No dirge will I upraise, 25
But waft the angel on her flight with a Pæan° of old days !

THE COLISEUM

Type of the antique Rome ! Rich reliquary
Of lofty contemplation left to Time
By buried centuries of pomp and power !
At length — at length — after so many days
Of weary pilgrimage and burning thirst, 5
(Thirst for the springs of lore that in thee lie,)
I kneel, an altered and an humble man,
Amid thy shadows, and so drink within
My very soul thy grandeur, gloom, and glory !

Vastness ! and Age ! and Memories of Eld !° 10
Silence ! and Desolation ! and dim Night !
I feel ye now — I feel ye in your strength —
O spells more sure than e'er Judæan king
Taught in the gardens of Gethsemane !°
O charms more potent than the rapt Chaldee 15
Ever drew down from out the quiet stars !°

Here, where a hero fell, a column falls!
Here, where the mimic eagle glared in gold,
A midnight vigil holds the swarthy bat!
Here, where the dames of Rome their gilded hair   20
Waved to the wind, now wave the reed and thistle!
Here, where on golden throne the monarch lolled,
Glides, spectre-like, unto his marble home,
Lit by the wan light of the hornéd moon,
The swift and silent lizard of the stones!   25

But stay! these walls — these ivy-clad arcades —
These mouldering plinths — these sad and blackened shafts —
These vague entablatures — this crumbling frieze —
These shattered cornices° — this wreck — this ruin —
These stones — alas! these gray stones — are they all —   30
All of the famed, and the colossal left
By the corrosive° Hours to Fate and me?

"Not all" — the Echoes answer me — "not all!
"Prophetic sounds and loud, arise forever
"From us, and from all Ruin, unto the wise,   35
"As melody from Memnon to the Sun.°
"We rule the hearts of mightiest men — we rule
"With a despotic sway all giant minds.
"We are not impotent — we pallid stones.
"Not all our power is gone — not all our fame —   40
"Not all the magic of our high renown —
"Not all the wonder that encircles us —
"Not all the mysteries that in us lie —
"Not all the memories that hang upon
"And cling around about us as a garment,   45
"Clothing us in a robe of more than glory."

THE HAUNTED PALACE

In the greenest of our valleys
   By good angels tenanted,
Once a fair and stately palace —
   Radiant palace — reared its head.
In the monarch Thought's dominion —   5
   It stood there!
Never seraph spread a pinion
   Over fabric half so fair!

Banners yellow, glorious, golden,
   On its roof did float and flow,   10
(This — all this — was in the olden
   Time long ago,)
And every gentle air that dallied,
   In that sweet day,
Along the ramparts plumed and pallid,   15
   A wingéd odor went away.

Wanderers in that happy valley,
   Through two luminous windows, saw
Spirits moving musically,
   To a lute's well-tunéd law,   20
Round about a throne where, sitting,
   (Porphyrogene!)
In state his glory well befitting,
   The ruler of the realm was seen.

And all with pearl and ruby glowing   25
   Was the fair palace door,

Through which came flowing, flowing, flowing
  And sparkling evermore,
A troop of Echoes, whose sweet duty
  Was but to sing,   30
In voices of surpassing beauty,
  The wit and wisdom of their king.

But evil things, in robes of sorrow,
  Assailed the monarch's high estate.
(Ah, let us mourn! — for never morrow   35
  Shall dawn upon him desolate!)
And round about his home the glory
  That blushed and bloomed,
Is but a dim-remembered story
  Of the old time entombed.   40

And travellers, now, within that valley,
  Through the red-litten windows see
Vast forms, that move fantastically
  To a discordant melody,
While, like a ghastly rapid river,   45
  Through the pale door
A hideous throng rush out forever
  And laugh — but smile no more.

TO ONE IN PARADISE

Thou wast all that to me, love,
  For which my soul did pine —
A green isle in the sea, love,
  A fountain and a shrine,

All wreathed with fairy fruits and flowers,   5
  And all the flowers were mine.

Ah, dream too bright to last!
  Ah, starry Hope! that didst arise
But to be overcast!
  A voice from out the Future cries,   10
"On! on!" — but o'er the Past
  (Dim gulf!) my spirit hovering lies
Mute, motionless, aghast!

For, alas! alas! with me
  The light of Life is o'er!   15
"No more — no more — no more —"
(Such language holds the solemn sea
  To the sands upon the shore)
Shall bloom the thunder-blasted tree,
  Or the stricken eagle soar!   20

And all my days are trances,
  And all my nightly dreams
Are where thy grey eye glances,
  And where thy footstep gleams —
In what ethereal dances,   25
  By what eternal streams.

EULALIE. — A SONG

I DWELT alone
  In a world of moan,
And my soul was a stagnant tide,

Till the fair and gentle Eulalie became my blushing bride —
Till the yellow-haired young Eulalie became my smiling
    bride.   5

        Ah, less — less bright
        The stars of the night
    Than the eyes of the radiant girl!
        And never a flake
        That the vapor can make   10
    With the moon-tints of purple and pearl,
Can vie with the modest Eulalie's most unregarded curl —
Can compare with the bright-eyed Eulalie's most humble
    and careless curl.

        Now Doubt — now Pain
        Come never again,   15
    For her soul gives me sigh for sigh,
        And all day long
        Shines, bright and strong,
    Astarté° within the sky,
While ever to her dear Eulalie upturns her matron eye —   20
While ever to her young Eulalie upturns her violet eye.

THE RAVEN

Once upon a midnight dreary, while I pondered, weak and
    weary,
Over many a quaint and curious volume of forgotten lore —
While I nodded, nearly napping, suddenly there came a tap-
    ping,

As of some one gently rapping, rapping at my chamber door.
"'Tis some visitor," I muttered, "tapping at my chamber
   door —
                        Only this and nothing more." 5

Ah, distinctly I remember it was in the bleak December;
And each separate dying ember wrought its ghost upon the
   floor.
Eagerly I wished the morrow; — vainly I had sought to
   borrow
From my books surcease of sorrow — sorrow for the lost
   Lenore — 10
For the rare and radiant maiden whom the angels name
   Lenore —
                        Nameless *here* for evermore.

And the silken, sad, uncertain rustling of each purple curtain
Thrilled me — filled me with fantastic terrors never felt
   before;
So that now, to still the beating of my heart, I stood repeat-
   ing 15
"'Tis some visitor entreating entrance at my chamber door —
Some late visitor entreating entrance at my chamber door; —
                        This it is and nothing more."

Presently my soul grew stronger; hesitating then no longer,
"Sir," said I, "or Madam, truly your forgiveness I implore; 20
But the fact is I was napping, and so gently you came rapping
And so faintly you came tapping, tapping at my chamber door,
That I scarce was sure I heard you" — here I opened wide
   the door; —
                        Darkness there and nothing more.

Deep into that darkness peering, long I stood there wonder-
 ing, fearing,   25
Doubting, dreaming dreams no mortal ever dared to dream
 before;
But the silence was unbroken, and the stillness gave no token,
And the only word there spoken was the whispered word,
 "Lenore!"
This I whispered, and an echo murmured back the word
 "Lenore!"
        Merely this and nothing more. 30

Back into the chamber turning, all my soul within me burning,
Soon again I heard a tapping somewhat louder than before.
"Surely," said I, "surely that is something at my window
 lattice;
Let me see, then, what thereat is, and this mystery explore—
Let my heart be still a moment and this mystery explore;—35
      'Tis the wind and nothing more!"

Open here I flung the shutter, when, with many a flirt and
 flutter
In there stepped a stately Raven of the saintly days of yore.
Not the least obeisance made he; not a minute stopped or
 stayed he;
But, with mien of lord or lady, perched above my chamber
 door —   40
Perched upon a bust of Pallas° just above my chamber door —
      Perched, and sat, and nothing more.

Then this ebony bird beguiling my sad fancy into smiling,
By the grave and stern decorum of the countenance it wore,

"Though thy crest be shorn and shaven, thou," I said, "art
   sure no craven,   45
Ghastly grim and ancient Raven wandering from the Nightly
   shore —
Tell me what thy lordly name is on the Night's Plutonian
   shore° !"
                             Quoth the Raven, "Nevermore."

Much I marvelled this ungainly fowl to hear discourse so
   plainly,
Though its answer little meaning — little relevancy° bore ; 50
For we cannot help agreeing that no living human being
Ever yet was blessed with seeing bird above his chamber
   door —
Bird or beast upon the sculptured bust above his chamber
   door,
                    With such name as "Nevermore."

But the Raven, sitting lonely on the placid bust, spoke only 55
That one word, as if his soul in that one word he did outpour.
Nothing farther then he uttered — not a feather then he
   fluttered —
Till I scarcely more than muttered "Other friends have
   flown before —
On the morrow *he* will leave me, as my hopes have flown
   before."
               Then the bird said "Nevermore." 60

Startled at the stillness broken by reply so aptly spoken,
"Doubtless," said I, "what it utters is its only stock and
   store,
Caught from some unhappy master whom unmerciful Disaster

Followed fast and followed faster till his songs one burden
    bore —
Till the dirges of his Hope that melancholy burden bore   65
               Of 'Never — nevermore.'"

But the Raven still beguiling all my fancy into smiling,
Straight I wheeled a cushioned seat in front of bird, and bust
    and door;
Then, upon the velvet sinking, I betook myself to linking
Fancy unto fancy, thinking what this ominous bird of yore — 70
What this grim, ungainly, ghastly, gaunt, and ominous bird
    of yore
               Meant in croaking "Nevermore."

Thus I sat engaged in guessing, but no syllable expressing
To the fowl whose fiery eyes now burned into my bosom's
    core;
This and more I sat divining, with my head at ease reclining 75
On the cushion's velvet lining that the lamp-light gloated
    o'er,
But whose velvet violet lining with the lamp-light gloating
    o'er,
               She shall press, ah, nevermore!

Then, methought, the air grew denser, perfumed from an
    unseen censer
Swung by Seraphim° whose foot-falls tinkled on the tufted
    floor.   80
"Wretch," I cried, "thy God hath lent thee — by these
    angels he hath sent thee
Respite — respite and nepenthe° from thy memories of
    Lenore;

Quaff, oh quaff this kind nepenthe and forget this lost Le-
    nore!"
                  Quoth the Raven, "Nevermore."

"Prophet!" said I, "thing of evil! prophet still, if bird or
    devil! —   85
Whether Tempter sent, or whether tempest tossed thee here
    ashore,
Desolate yet all undaunted, on this desert land enchanted —
On this home by Horror haunted — tell me truly, I implore —
Is there — *is* there balm in Gilead°? — tell me — tell me, I
    implore!"
                  Quoth the Raven, "Nevermore." 90

"Prophet!" said I, "thing of evil! — prophet still, if bird or
    devil!
By that Heaven that bends above us — by that God we both
    adore —
Tell this soul with sorrow laden if, within the distant
    Aidenn,°
It shall clasp a sainted maiden whom the angels name
    Lenore:
Clasp a rare and radiant maiden whom the angels name
    Lenore."   95
                  Quoth the Raven, "Nevermore."

"Be that word our sign of parting, bird or fiend!" I shrieked,
    upstarting —
"Get thee back into the tempest and the Night's Plutonian
    shore!
Leave no black plume as a token of that lie thy soul hath
    spoken!

Leave my loneliness unbroken! — quit the bust above my
    door!
Take thy beak from out my heart, and take thy form from off
    my door!"

                    Quoth the Raven, "Nevermore."

And the Raven, never flitting, still is sitting, *still* is sitting
On the pallid bust of Pallas just above my chamber door;
And his eyes have all the seeming of a demon's that is dream-
    ing,   105
And the lamp-light o'er him streaming throws his shadow on
    the floor°;
And my soul from out that shadow that lies floating on the
    floor

                    Shall be lifted — nevermore!°

TO HELEN°

I saw thee once — once only — years ago:
I must not say *how* many — but *not* many.
It was a July midnight; and from out
A full-orbed moon, that, like thine own soul, soaring,
Sought a precipitate pathway up through heaven,   5
There fell a silvery-silken veil of light,
With quietude and sultriness and slumber,
Upon the upturn'd faces of a thousand
Roses that grew in an enchanted garden,
Where no wind dared to stir, unless on tiptoe —   10
Fell on the upturn'd faces of these roses
That gave out, in return for the love-light,

Their odorous souls in an ecstatic death —
Fell on the upturn'd faces of these roses
That smiled and died in this parterre,° enchanted   15
By thee, and by the poetry of thy presence.

Clad all in white, upon a violet bank
I saw thee half reclining; while the moon
Fell on the upturn'd faces of the roses,
And on thine own, upturn'd — alas, in sorrow!   20

Was it not Fate, that, on this July midnight —
Was it not Fate, (whose name is also Sorrow),
That bade me pause before that garden-gate,
To breathe the incense of those slumbering roses?
No footstep stirred: the hated world all slept,   25
Save only thee and me. (Oh, heaven! — oh, God!
How my heart beats in coupling those two words!)
Save only thee and me. I paused — I looked —
And in an instant all things disappeared.
(Ah, bear in mind this garden was enchanted!)   30
The pearly lustre of the moon went out:
The mossy banks and the meandering paths,
The happy flowers and the repining trees,
Were seen no more: the very roses' odors
Died in the arms of the adoring airs.   35
All — all expired save thee — save less than thou:
Save only the divine light in thine eyes —
Save but the soul in thine uplifted eyes.
I saw but them — they were the world to me.
I saw but them — saw only them for hours —   40
Saw only them until the moon went down.
What wild heart-histories seemed to lie enwritten

H

Upon those crystalline, celestial spheres!
How dark a wo! yet how sublime a hope!
How silently serene a sea of pride!   45
How daring an ambition! yet how deep —
How fathomless a capacity for love!

But now, at length, dear Dian° sank from sight,
Into a western couch of thunder-cloud;
And thou, a ghost, amid the entombing trees   50
Didst glide away. *Only thine eyes remained.*
They *would not* go — they never yet have gone.
Lighting my lonely pathway home that night,
They have not left me (as my hopes have) since.
They follow me — they lead me through the years — 55
They are my ministers — yet I their slave.
Their office is to illumine and enkindle —
My duty, *to be saved* by their bright light,
And purified in their electric fire,
And sanctified in their elysian° fire.   60
They fill my soul with Beauty (which is Hope),
And are far up in Heaven — the stars I kneel to
In the sad, silent watches of my night;
While even in the meridian glare of day
I see them still — two sweetly scintillant°   65
Venuses,° unextinguished by the sun!

ANNABEL LEE

It was many and many a year ago,
  In a kingdom by the sea
That a maiden there lived whom you may know
  By the name of ANNABEL LEE;
And this maiden she lived with no other thought   5
  Than to love and be loved by me.

I was a child and *she* was a child,
  In this kingdom by the sea,
But we loved with a love that was more than love—
  I and my ANNABEL LEE—   10
With a love that the winged seraphs of heaven
  Coveted her and me.

And this was the reason that, long ago,
  In this kingdom by the sea,
A wind blew out of a cloud, chilling   15
  My beautiful ANNABEL LEE;
So that her highborn kinsmen came
  And bore her away from me,
To shut her up in a sepulchre
  In this kingdom by the sea.   20

The angels, not half so happy in heaven,
  Went envying her and me—
Yes!—that was the reason (as all men know,
  In this kingdom by the sea)
That the wind came out of the cloud by night,   25
  Chilling and killing my ANNABEL LEE.

But our love it was stronger by far than the love
    Of those who were older than we —
    Of many far wiser than we —
And neither the angels in heaven above,   30
    Nor the demons down under the sea,
Can ever dissever my soul from the soul
    Of the beautiful ANNABEL LEE:

For the moon never beams, without bringing me dreams
    Of the beautiful ANNABEL LEE;   35
And the stars never rise, but I feel the bright eyes
    Of the beautiful ANNABEL LEE:
And so, all the night-tide, I lie down by the side
Of my darling — my darling — my life and my bride,
    In the sepulchre there by the sea —   40
    In her tomb by the sounding sea.

THE BELLS

I

    HEAR the sledges with the bells —
        Silver bells!
What a world of merriment their melody foretells!
    How they tinkle, tinkle, tinkle,
        In the icy air of night!   5
    While the stars that oversprinkle
    All the heavens, seem to twinkle
        With a crystalline delight:
        Keeping time, time, time,
        In a sort of Runic° rhyme,   10

To the tintinnabulation° that so musically wells
      From the bells, bells, bells, bells,
            Bells, bells, bells —
From the jingling and the tinkling of the bells.

II

      Hear the mellow wedding bells,   15
            Golden bells!
What a world of happiness their harmony foretells!
      Through the balmy air of night
      How they ring out their delight!
            From the molten-golden notes,   20
                  And all in tune,
            What a liquid ditty floats,
To the turtle-dove that listens, while she gloats
                  On the moon!

      Oh, from out the sounding cells,   25
What a gush of euphony° voluminously wells!
                  How it swells!
                  How it dwells
            On the Future! — how it tells
            Of the rapture that impels   30
      To the swinging and the ringing
            Of the bells, bells, bells —
      Of the bells, bells, bells, bells,
            Bells, bells, bells —
To the rhyming and the chiming of the bells!   35

III

Hear the loud alarum bells —
      Brazen bells!
What a tale of terror, now their turbulency tells!
    In the startled ear of night
    How they scream out their affright!   40
      Too much horrified to speak,
      They can only shriek, shriek,
        Out of tune,
In a clamorous appealing to the mercy of the fire,
In a mad expostulation with the deaf and frantic fire, 45
      Leaping higher, higher, higher,
      With a desperate desire,
    And a resolute endeavor
  Now — now to sit, or never,
By the side of the pale-faced moon.   50
    Oh, the bells, bells, bells!
    What a tale their terror tells
        Of Despair!
How they clang, and clash, and roar!
What a horror they outpour   55
On the bosom of the palpitating air!

    Yet the ear, it fully knows,
      By the twanging,
      And the clanging,
   How the danger ebbs and flows;   60
    Yet the ear distinctly tells,
      In the jangling,
      And the wrangling,
How the danger sinks and swells,

By the sinking or the swelling in the anger of the bells —
Of the bells — 66
Of the bells, bells, bells, bells,
Bells, bells, bells —
In the clamor and the clangor of the bells!

IV

Hear the tolling of the bells — 70
Iron bells!
What a world of solemn thought their monody° compels!
In the silence of the night,
How we shiver with affright
At the melancholy menace of their tone: 75
For every sound that floats
From the rust within their throats
Is a groan.
And the people — ah, the people —
They that dwell up in the steeple, 80
All alone,
And who, tolling, tolling, tolling,
In that muffled monotone,
Feel a glory in so rolling
On the human heart a stone — 85
They are neither man or woman —
They are neither brute nor human —
They are Ghouls°: —

And their king it is who tolls: —
And he rolls, rolls, rolls, 90
Rolls
A pæan from the bells!

And his merry bosom swells
   With the pæan of the bells!
And he dances, and he yells;   95
Keeping time, time, time,
In a sort of Runic rhyme,
To the pæan of the bells: —
      Of the bells:
Keeping time, time, time,   100
In a sort of Runic rhyme,
   To the throbbing of the bells —
Of the bells, bells, bells —
   To the sobbing of the bells: —
Keeping time, time, time,   105
   As he knells, knells, knells,
In a happy Runic rhyme,
   To the rolling of the bells —
Of the bells, bells, bells: —
   To the tolling of the bells —   110
Of the bells, bells, bells, bells,
   Bells, bells, bells —
To the moaning and the groaning of the bells.

ELDORADO

Gaily bedight,
  A gallant knight,
In sunshine and in shadow,
  Had journeyed long,
  Singing a song,   5
In search of Eldorado.°

But he grew old —
This knight so bold —
And o'er his heart a shadow
Fell as he found
No spot of ground
That looked like Eldorado.

And, as his strength
Failed him at length,
He met a pilgrim shadow —
"Shadow," said he,
"Where can it be —
This land of Eldorado?"

"Over the Mountains
Of the Moon,
Down the Valley of the Shadow,°
Ride, boldly ride,"
The shade replied, —
"If you seek for Eldorado."

HENRY WADSWORTH LONGFELLOW

HYMN TO THE NIGHT

Ἀσπασίη, τρίλλιστος.°

I HEARD the trailing garments of the Night
   Sweep through her marble halls!
I saw her sable skirts all fringed with light
   From the celestial walls!

I felt her presence, by its spell of might,   5
   Stoop o'er me from above;
The calm, majestic presence of the Night,
   As of the one I love.

I heard the sounds of sorrow and delight,
   The manifold, soft chimes,   10
That fill the haunted chambers of the Night,
   Like some old poet's rhymes.

From the cool cisterns of the midnight air
   My spirit drank repose;
The fountain of perpetual peace flows there —   15
   From those deep cisterns flows.

O holy Night! from thee I learn to bear
   What man has borne before!
Thou layest thy finger on the lips of Care,
   And they complain no more.   20

Peace! Peace! Orestes-like° I breathe this prayer!
   Descend with broad-winged flight,
The welcome, the thrice-prayed for, the most fair,
   The best-beloved Night!

A PSALM OF LIFE

WHAT THE HEART OF THE YOUNG MAN SAID TO THE PSALMIST

   TELL me not, in mournful numbers,
      "Life is but an empty dream!"
   For the soul is dead that slumbers,
      And things are not what they seem.

   Life is real! Life is earnest!   5
      And the grave is not its goal;
   "Dust thou art,° to dust returnest,"
      Was not spoken of the soul.

   Not enjoyment, and not sorrow,
      Is our destined end or way°;   10
   But to act, that each to-morrow
      Find us farther than to-day.

   Art is long, and Time is fleeting,
      And our hearts, though stout and brave,
   Still, like muffled drums, are beating   15
      Funeral marches to the grave.

In the world's broad field of battle,
  In the bivouac of Life,
Be not like dumb, driven cattle;
  Be a hero in the strife!   20

Trust no Future, howe'er pleasant!
  Let the dead Past bury its dead!
Act, — act in the living Present!
  Heart within, and God o'erhead!

Lives of great men all remind us   25
  We can make our lives sublime,
And, departing, leave behind us
  Footprints on the sands of time;

Footprints, that perhaps another,
  Sailing o'er life's solemn main,   30
A forlorn and shipwrecked brother,
  Seeing, shall take heart again.

Let us, then, be up and doing,
  With a heart for any fate;
Still achieving, still pursuing,   35
  Learn to labor and to wait.

THE SKELETON IN ARMOR°

"SPEAK! speak! thou fearful guest!
Who, with thy hollow breast
Still in rude armor drest,
  Comest to daunt me!

Wrapt not in Eastern balms,   5
But with thy fleshless palms
Stretched, as if asking alms,
    Why dost thou haunt me?"

Then, from those cavernous eyes
Pale flashes seemed to rise,   10
As when the Northern skies
    Gleam in December;
And, like the water's flow
Under December's snow,
Came a dull voice of woe   15
    From the heart's chamber.

"I was a Viking old!
My deeds, though manifold,
No Skald° in song has told,
    No Saga° taught thee!   20
Take heed, that in thy verse
Thou dost the tale rehearse,
Else dread a dead man's curse;
    For this I sought thee.

"Far in the Northern Land,   25
By the wild Baltic's strand,
I, with my childish hand,
    Tamed the ger-falcon°;
And, with my skates fast-bound,
Skimmed the half-frozen Sound,   30
That the poor whimpering hound
    Trembled to walk on.

"Oft to his frozen lair
Tracked I the grisly bear,
While from my path the hare   35
    Fled like a shadow;
Oft through the forest dark
Followed the were-wolf's° bark,
Until the soaring lark
    Sang from the meadow.   40

"But when I older grew,
Joining a corsair's° crew,
O'er the dark sea I flew
    With the marauders.
Wild was the life we led;   45
Many the souls that sped,
Many the hearts that bled,
    By our stern orders.

"Many a wassail-bout°
Wore the long Winter out;   50
Often our midnight shout
    Set the cocks crowing,
As we the Berserk's° tale
Measured in cups of ale,
Draining the oaken pail,   55
    Filled to o'erflowing.

"Once as I told in glee
Tales of the stormy sea,
Soft eyes did gaze on me,
    Burning yet tender;   60

And as the white stars shine
On the dark Norway pine,
On that dark heart of mine
    Fell their soft splendor.

"I wooed the blue-eyed maid,   65
Yielding, yet half afraid,
And in the forest's shade
    Our vows were plighted.
Under its loosened vest
Fluttered her little breast,   70
Like birds within their nest
    By the hawk frighted.

"Bright in her father's hall
Shields gleamed upon the wall,
Loud sang the minstrels all,   75
    Chaunting his glory;
When of old Hildebrand
I asked his daughter's hand,
Mute did the minstrels stand
    To hear my story.   80

"While the brown ale he quaffed,
Loud then the champion laughed,
And as the wind-gusts waft
    The sea-foam brightly,
So the loud laugh of scorn,   85
Out of those lips unshorn,
From the deep drinking-horn
    Blew the foam lightly.

"She was a Prince's child,
I but a Viking wild,   90
And though she blushed and smiled,
   I was discarded!
Should not the dove so white
Follow the sea-mew's° flight,
Why did they leave that night   95
   Her nest unguarded?

"Scarce had I put to sea,
Bearing the maid with me, —
Fairest of all was she
   Among the Norsemen! —   100
When on the white sea-strand,
Waving his armèd hand,
Saw we old Hildebrand,
   With twenty horsemen.

"Then launched they to the blast,   105
Bent like a reed each mast,
Yet we were gaining fast,
   When the wind failed us;
And with a sudden flaw
Come round the gusty Skaw,°   110
So that our foe we saw
   Laugh as he hailed us.

"And as to catch the gale
Round veered the flapping sail,
Death! was the helmsman's hail   115
   Death without quarter!

Mid-ships with iron keel
Struck we her ribs of steel;
Down her black hulk did reel
   Through the black water!   120

"As with his wings aslant,
Sails the fierce cormorant,
Seeking some rocky haunt,
   With his prey laden,
So toward the open main,   125
Beating to sea again,
Through the wild hurricane,
   Bore I the maiden.

"Three weeks we westward bore,
And when the storm was o'er,   130
Cloud-like we saw the shore
   Stretching to lee-ward;
There for my lady's bower
Built I the lofty tower,
Which, to this very hour,   135
   Stands looking sea-ward.

"There lived we many years;
Time dried the maiden's tears;
She had forgot her fears,
   She was a mother;   140
Death closed her mild blue eyes,
Under that tower she lies;
Ne'er shall the sun arise
   On such another!

I

"Still grew my bosom then,   145
Still as a stagnant fen!
Hateful to me were men,
    The sun-light hateful.
In the vast forest here,
Clad in my warlike gear,   150
Fell I upon my spear,
    O, death was grateful!

"Thus, seamed with many scars
Bursting these prison bars,
Up to its native stars   155
    My soul ascended!
There from the flowing bowl
Deep drinks the warrior's soul,
Skoal! to the Northland! *skoal!*"°
— Thus the tale ended.   160

THE WRECK OF THE HESPERUS°

It was the schooner Hesperus,
    That sailed the wintry sea;
And the skipper had taken his little daughtèr,
    To bear him company.

Blue were her eyes as the fairy-flax,   5
    Her cheeks like the dawn of day,
And her bosom white as the hawthorn buds,
    That ope in the month of May.

The skipper he stood beside the helm,
    His pipe was in his mouth,   10

And he watched how the veering flaw° did blow
  The smoke now West, now South.

Then up and spake an old Sailòr,
  Had sailed the Spanish Main,°
"I pray thee, put into yonder port,   15
  For I fear a hurricane.

"Last night, the moon had a golden ring,
  And to-night no moon we see!"
The skipper, he blew a whiff from his pipe,
  And a scornful laugh laughed he.   20

Colder and louder blew the wind,
  A gale from the Northeast;
The snow fell hissing in the brine,
  And the billows frothed like yeast.

Down came the storm, and smote amain,   25
  The vessel in its strength;
She shuddered and paused, like a frighted steed,
  Then leaped her cable's length.

"Come hither! come hither! my little daughtèr,
  And do not tremble so;   30
For I can weather the roughest gale,
  That ever wind did blow."°

He wrapped her warm in his seaman's coat
  Against the stinging blast;
He cut a rope from a broken spar,   35
  And bound her to the mast.

"O father!° I hear the church-bells ring,
    O say, what may it be?"
"'Tis a fog-bell on a rock-bound coast!" —
    And he steered for the open sea.   40

"O father! I hear the sound of guns,
    O say, what may it be?"
"Some ship in distress, that cannot live
    In such an angry sea!"

"O father! I see a gleaming light,   45
    O say, what may it be?"
But the father answered never a word,
    A frozen corpse was he.

Lashed to the helm, all stiff and stark,
    With his face turned to the skies,   50
The lantern gleamed through the gleaming snow
    On his fixed and glassy eyes.

Then the maiden clasped her hands and prayed
    That savèd she might be;
And she thought of Christ, who stilled the wave, 55
    On the Lake of Galilee.°

And fast through the midnight dark and drear,
    Through the whistling sleet and snow,
Like a sheeted ghost, the vessel swept
    Towards the reef of Norman's Woe.°   60

And ever the fitful gusts between,
    A sound came from the land;

It was the sound of the trampling surf,
  On the rocks and the hard sea-sand.

The breakers were right beneath her bows,   65
  She drifted a dreary wreck,
And a whooping billow swept the crew
  Like icicles from her deck.

She struck where the white and fleecy waves
  Looked soft as carded wool,°   70
But the cruel rocks, they gored her side
  Like the horns of an angry bull.

Her rattling shrouds, all sheathed in ice,
  With the masts went by the board;
Like a vessel of glass, she stove and sank,   75
  Ho! ho! the breakers roared!

At daybreak, on the bleak sea-beach,
  A fisherman stood aghast,
To see the form of a maiden fair,
  Lashed close to a drifting mast.   80

The salt sea was frozen on her breast,
  The salt tears in her eyes;
And he saw her hair, like the brown sea-weed,
  On the billows fall and rise.

Such was the wreck of the Hesperus,   85
  In the midnight and the snow!
Christ save us all from a death like this,
  On the reef of Norman's Woe!

THE VILLAGE BLACKSMITH

UNDER a spreading chestnut tree
  The village smithy stands;
The smith, a mighty man is he,
  With large and sinewy hands;
And the muscles of his brawny arms   5
  Are strong as iron bands.

His hair is crisp, and black, and long,
  His face is like the tan;
His brow is wet with honest sweat,
  He earns whate'er he can,   10
And looks the whole world in the face,
  For he owes not any man.

Week in, week out, from morn till night,
  You can hear his bellows blow;
You can hear him swing his heavy sledge,   15
  With measured beat and slow,
Like a sexton ringing the village bell,
  When the evening sun is low.

And children coming home from school
  Look in at the open door;   20
They love to see the flaming forge,
  And hear the bellows roar,
And catch the burning sparks that fly
  Like chaff from a threshing-floor.

He goes on Sunday to the church,   25
  And sits among his boys;

He hears the parson pray and preach,
 He hears his daughter's voice,
Singing in the village choir,
 And it makes his heart rejoice.   30

It sounds to him like her mother's voice,
 Singing in Paradise!
He needs must think of her once more,
 How in the grave she lies;
And with his hard, rough hand he wipes   35
 A tear out of his eyes.

Toiling, — rejoicing, — sorrowing,
 Onward through life he goes;
Each morning sees some task begin,
 Each evening sees it close;   40
Something attempted, something done,
 Has earned a night's repose.°

Thanks, thanks to thee, my worthy friend,
 For the lesson thou hast taught!
Thus at the flaming forge of life   45
 Our fortunes must be wrought;
Thus on its sounding anvil shaped
 Each burning deed and thought!

IT IS NOT ALWAYS MAY

NO HAY PÁJAROS EN LOS NIDOS DE ANTAÑO°

Spanish Proverb.

THE sun is bright, — the air is clear,
    The darting swallows soar and sing,
And from the stately elms I hear
    The bluebird prophesying Spring.

So blue yon winding river flows,   5
    It seems an outlet from the sky,
Where, waiting till the west wind blows,
    The freighted° clouds at anchor lie.

All things are new; — the buds, the leaves,
    That gild the elm tree's nodding crest,   10
And even the nest beneath the eaves; —
    There are no birds in last year's nest!

All things rejoice in youth and love,
    The fulness of their first delight!
And learn from the soft heavens above   15
    The melting tenderness of night.

Maiden, that read'st this simple rhyme,
    Enjoy thy youth, it will not stay;
Enjoy the fragrance of thy prime,
    For O! it is not always May!   20

Enjoy the Spring of Love and Youth,
  To some good angel leave the rest;
For Time will teach thee soon the truth,
  There are no birds in last year's nest!

EXCELSIOR.°

THE shades of night were falling fast,
As through an Alpine village passed
A youth, who bore, 'mid snow and ice,
A banner with the strange device,
        Excelsior!   5

His brow was sad; his eye beneath,
Flashed like a falchion° from its sheath,
And like a silver clarion rung
The accents of that unknown tongue,
        Excelsior!   10

In happy homes he saw the light
Of household fires gleam warm and bright;
Above, the spectral glaciers shone,
And from his lips escaped a groan,
        Excelsior!   15

"Try not the Pass!" the old man said;
"Dark lowers the tempest overhead,
The roaring torrent is deep and wide!"
And loud that clarion voice replied,
        Excelsior!   20

"O stay," the maiden said, "and rest
Thy weary head upon this breast!"
A tear stood in his bright blue eye,
But still he answered, with a sigh,
     Excelsior!
                                25

"Beware the pine tree's withered branch!
Beware the awful avalanche!"
This was the peasant's last Good-night,
A voice replied, far up the height,
     Excelsior!
                                30

At break of day, as heavenward
The pious monks of Saint Bernard
Uttered the oft-repeated prayer,
A voice cried through the startled air,
     Excelsior!
                                35

A traveller, by the faithful hound,
Half-buried in the snow was found,
Still grasping in his hand of ice
That banner with the strange device,
     Excelsior!
                                40

There in the twilight cold and gray,
Lifeless, but beautiful, he lay,
And from the sky, serene and far,
A voice fell, like a falling star,
     Excelsior!
                                45

THE RAINY DAY

THE day is cold, and dark, and dreary;
It rains, and the wind is never weary;
The vine still clings to the mouldering wall,
But at every gust the dead leaves fall,
 And the day is dark and dreary.   5

My life is cold, and dark, and dreary;
It rains, and the wind is never weary;
My thoughts still cling to the mouldering Past,
But the hopes of youth fall thick in the blast,
 And the days are dark and dreary.   10

Be still, sad heart! and cease repining;
Behind the clouds is the sun still shining;
Thy fate is the common fate of all,
Into each life some rain must fall,
 Some days must be dark and dreary.   15

THE ARROW AND THE SONG

I SHOT an arrow into the air,
It fell to earth, I knew not where;
For, so swiftly it flew, the sight
Could not follow it in its flight.

I breathed a song into the air,   5
It fell to earth, I knew not where;
For who has sight so keen and strong,
That it can follow the flight of song?

Long, long afterward, in an oak
I found the arrow, still unbroke;   10
And the song, from beginning to end,
I found again in the heart of a friend.

THE DAY IS DONE

THE day is done, and the darkness
    Falls from the wings of Night,
As a feather is wafted downward
    From an eagle in his flight.

I see the lights of the village   5
    Gleam through the rain and the mist,
And a feeling of sadness comes o'er me,
    That my soul cannot resist:

A feeling of sadness and longing,
    That is not akin to pain,   10
And resembles sorrow only
    As the mist resembles the rain.

Come, read to me some poem,
    Some simple and heartfelt lay,
That shall soothe this restless feeling,   15
    And banish the thoughts of day.

Not from the grand old masters,
    Not from the bards sublime,
Whose distant footsteps echo
    Through the corridors of Time.   20

For, like strains of martial music,
   Their mighty thoughts suggest
Life's endless toil and endeavor;
   And to-night I long for rest.

Read from some humbler poet,°   25
   Whose songs gushed from his heart,
As showers from the clouds of summer,
   Or tears from the eyelids start;

Who, through long days of labor,
   And nights devoid of ease,   30
Still heard in his soul the music
   Of wonderful melodies.

Such songs have power to quiet
   The restless pulse of care,
And come like the benediction   35
   That follows after prayer.

Then read from the treasured volume
   The poem of thy choice,
And lend to the rhyme of the poet
   The beauty of thy voice.   40

And the night shall be filled with music,
   And the cares, that infest the day,
Shall fold their tents, like the Arabs,
   And as silently steal away.

WALTER VON DER VOGELWEIDE°

VOGELWEID, the Minnesinger,
    When he left this world of ours,
Laid his body in the cloister,
    Under Würtzburg's minster towers.°

And he gave the monks his treasures,   5
    Gave them all with this behest:
They should feed the birds at noontide
    Daily on his place of rest;

Saying, "From these wandering minstrels
    I have learned the art of song°;   10
Let me now repay the lessons
    They have taught so well and long."

Thus the bard of love departed;
    And, fulfilling his desire,
On his tomb the birds were feasted   15
    By the children of the choir.

Day by day, o'er tower and turret,
    In foul weather and in fair,
Day by day, in vaster numbers,
    Flocked the poets of the air.   20

On the tree whose heavy branches
    Overshadowed all the place,
On the pavement, on the tombstone,
    On the poet's sculptured face,

On the cross-bars of each window,   25
    On the lintel of each door,
They renewed the War of Wartburg,°
    Which the bard had fought before.

There they sang their merry carols,
    Sang their lauds on every side;   30
And the name their voices uttered
    Was the name of Vogelweid.

Till at length the portly abbot
    Murmured, "Why this waste of food?
Be it changed to loaves henceforward   35
    For our fasting brotherhood."

Then in vain o'er tower and turret,
    From the walls and woodland nests,
When the minster bells rang noontide,
    Gathered the unwelcome guests.   40

Then in vain, with cries discordant,
    Clamorous round the Gothic spire,°
Screamed the feathered Minnesingers
    For the children of the choir.

Time has long effaced the inscriptions   45
    On the cloister's funeral stones,
And tradition only tells us
    Where repose the poet's bones.

But around the vast cathedral,
    By sweet echoes multiplied,   50
Still the birds repeat the legend,
    And the name of Vogelweid.

THE BUILDERS

ALL are architects of Fate,
   Working in these walls of Time;
Some with massive deeds and great,
   Some with ornaments of rhyme.

Nothing useless is, or low;   5
   Each thing in its place is best;
And what seems but idle show
   Strengthens and supports the rest.

For the structure that we raise,
   Time is with materials filled;   10
Our to-days and yesterdays
   Are the blocks with which we build.

Truly shape and fashion these;
   Leave no yawning gaps between:
Think not, because no man sees,   15
   Such things will remain unseen.

In the elder days of Art,
   Builders wrought with greatest care
Each minute and unseen part!°
   For the Gods see everywhere.   20

Let us do our work as well,
   Both the unseen and the seen;
Make the house, where Gods may dwell,
   Beautiful, entire, and clean.

Else our lives are incomplete,   25
   Standing in these walls of Time,
Broken stairways, where the feet
   Stumble as they seek to climb.

Build to-day, then, strong and sure,
   With a firm and ample base;   30
And ascending and secure
   Shall to-morrow find its place.

Thus alone can we attain
   To those turrets, where the eye
Sees the world as one vast plain,   35
   And one boundless reach of sky.

SANTA FILOMENA°

Whene'er a noble deed is wrought,
Whene'er is spoken a noble thought,
   Our hearts, in glad surprise,
   To higher levels rise.

The tidal wave of deeper souls   5
Into our inmost being rolls,
   And lifts us unawares
   Out of all meaner cares.

Honor to those whose words or deeds
Thus help us in our daily needs,   10
   And by their overflow
   Raise us from what is low!

K

Thus thought I, as by night I read
Of the great army of the dead,
 The trenches cold and damp,   15
 The starved and frozen camp, —

The wounded from the battle-plain,
In dreary hospitals of pain,
 The cheerless corridors,
 The cold and stony floors.   20

Lo! in that house of misery
A lady with a lamp I see
 Pass through the glimmering gloom,
 And flit from room to room.

And slow, as in a dream of bliss,   25
The speechless sufferer turns to kiss
 Her shadow, as it falls
 Upon the darkening walls.

As if a door in heaven should be
Opened and then closed suddenly,   30
 The vision came and went,
 The light shone and was spent.

On England's annals, through the long
Hereafter of her speech and song,
 That light its rays shall cast   35
 From portals of the past.

A Lady with a Lamp shall stand
In the great history of the land,

A noble type of good,
Heroic womanhood.   40

Nor even shall be wanting here
The palm, the lily, and the spear,°
    The symbols that of yore
    Saint Filomena bore.

THE DISCOVERER OF THE NORTH CAPE

A Leaf from King Alfred's Orosius°

OTHERE, the old sea-captain,
    Who dwelt in Helgoland,°
To King Alfred, the Lover of Truth,
Brought a snow-white walrus-tooth,
    Which he held in his brown right hand.   5

His figure was tall and stately,
    Like a boy's his eye appeared;
His hair was yellow as hay,
But threads of a silvery gray
    Gleamed in his tawny beard.   10

Hearty and hale was Othere,
    His cheek had the color of oak;
With a kind of laugh in his speech,
Like the sea-tide on a beach,
    As unto the King he spoke.   15

And Alfred, King of the Saxons,
    Had a book upon his knees,
And wrote down the wondrous tale
Of him who was first to sail
    Into the Arctic seas.   20

"So far I live to the northward,
    No man lives north of me;
To the east are wild mountain-chains,
And beyond them meres and plains;
    To the westward all is sea.   25

"So far I live to the northward,
    From the harbor of Skeringes-hale,
If you only sailed by day,
With a fair wind all the way,
    More than a month would you sail.   30

"I own six hundred reindeer,
    With sheep and swine beside;
I have tribute from the Finns,
Whalebone and reindeer-skins,
    And ropes of walrus-hide.   35

"I ploughed the land with horses,
    But my heart was ill at ease,
For the old seafaring men
Came to me now and then,
    With their sagas of the seas; —   40

"Of Iceland and of Greenland,
    And the stormy Hebrides,°

And the undiscovered deep; —
I could not eat nor sleep
    For thinking of those seas.   45

"To the northward stretched the desert,
    How far I fain would know;
So at last I sallied forth,
And three days sailed due north,
    As far as the whale-ships go.   50

"To the west of me was the ocean,
    To the right the desolate shore,
But I did not slacken sail
For the walrus or the whale,
    Till after three days more.   55

"The days grew longer and longer,
    Till they became as one,
And southward through the haze
I saw the sullen blaze
    Of the red midnight sun.   60

"And then uprose before me,
    Upon the water's edge,
The huge and haggard shape
Of that unknown North Cape,
    Whose form is like a wedge.   65

"The sea was rough and stormy,
    The tempest howled and wailed,
And the sea-fog, like a ghost,
Haunted that dreary coast,
    But onward still I sailed.   70

"Four days I steered to eastward,
    Four days without a night:
Round in a fiery ring
Went the great sun, O King,
    With red and lurid light."   75

Here Alfred, King of the Saxons,
    Ceased writing for a while;
And raised his eyes from his book,
With a strange and puzzled look,
    And an incredulous smile.   80

But Othere, the old sea-captain,
    He neither paused nor stirred,
Till the King listened, and then
Once more took up his pen,
    And wrote down every word.   85

"And now the land," said Othere,
    "Bent southward suddenly,
And I followed the curving shore
And ever southward bore
    Into a nameless sea.°   90

"And there we hunted the walrus,
    The narwhale, and the seal;
Ha! 't was a noble game!
And like the lightning's flame
    Flew our harpoons of steel.   95

"There were six of us all together,
    Norsemen of Helgoland;

In two days and no more
We killed of them threescore,
    And dragged them to the strand!"°   100

Here Alfred the Truth-Teller
    Suddenly closed his book,
And lifted his blue eyes,
With doubt and strange surmise
    Depicted in their look.   105

And Othere the old sea-captain
    Stared at him wild and weird,
Then smiled, till his shining teeth
Gleamed white from underneath
    His tawny, quivering beard.   110

And to the King of the Saxons,
    In witness of the truth,
Raising his noble head,
He stretched his brown hand, and said,
    "Behold this walrus-tooth!"°   115

SANDALPHON°

HAVE you read in the Talmud° of old,
In the Legends the Rabbins have told
    Of the limitless realms of the air, —
Have you read it, — the marvellous story
Of Sandalphon, the Angel of Glory,   5
    Sandalphon, the Angel of Prayer?

How, erect, at the outermost gates
Of the City Celestial he waits,
  With his feet on the ladder of light,
That, crowded with angels unnumbered,   **10**
By Jacob was seen as he slumbered
  Alone in the desert at night?°

The Angels of Wind and of Fire,
Chant only one hymn, and expire
  With the song's irresistible stress;   **15**
Expire in their rapture and wonder,
As harp-strings are broken asunder
  By music they throb to express.

But serene in the rapturous throng,
Unmoved by the rush of the song,   **20**
  With eyes unimpassioned and slow,
Among the dead angels, the deathless
Sandalphon stands listening breathless
  To sounds that ascend from below; —

From the spirits on earth that adore,   **25**
From the souls that entreat and implore
  In the fervor and passion of prayer;
From the hearts that are broken with losses,
And weary with dragging the crosses
  Too heavy for mortals to bear.   **30**

And he gathers the prayers as he stands,
And they change into flowers in his hands,
  Into garlands of purple and red;

And beneath the great arch of the portal,
Through the streets of the City Immortal   35
  Is wafted the fragrance they shed.

It is but a legend, I know, —
A fable, a phantom, a show,
  Of the ancient Rabbinical° lore;
Yet the old mediæval tradition,   40
The beautiful, strange superstition
  But haunts me and holds me the more.

When I look from my window at night,
And the welkin° above is all white,
  All throbbing and panting with stars,   45
Among them majestic is standing
Sandalphon the angel, expanding
  His pinions in nebulous° bars.

And the legend, I feel, is a part
Of the hunger and thirst of the heart,   50
  The frenzy and fire of the brain,
That grasps at the fruitage forbidden,
The golden pomegranates of Eden,
  To quiet its fever and pain.

THE LANDLORD'S TALE°

Paul Revere's Ride°

Listen, my children, and you shall hear
Of the midnight ride of Paul Revere,
On the eighteenth of April, in Seventy-five;
Hardly a man is now alive
Who remembers that famous day and year.

He said to his friend, "If the British march
By land or sea from the town to-night,
Hang a lantern aloft in the belfry arch
Of the North Church tower as a signal light, —
One, if by land, and two, if by sea;   10
And I on the opposite shore will be,
Ready to ride and spread the alarm
Through every Middlesex village and farm,
For the country-folk to be up and to arm."

Then he said, "Good night!" and with muffled oar   15
Silently rowed to the Charlestown shore,
Just as the moon rose over the bay,
Where swinging wide at her moorings lay
The Somerset, British man-of-war;
A phantom ship, with each mast and spar   20
Across the moon like a prison bar,
And a huge black hulk that was magnified
By its own reflection in the tide.

Meanwhile, his friend, through alley and street,
Wanders and watches with eager ears,   25

Till in the silence around him he hears
The muster of men at the barrack door,
The sound of arms, and the tramp of feet,
And the measured tread of the grenadiers,
Marching down to their boats on the shore.   30

Then he climbed to the tower of the church,
Up the wooden stairs, with stealthy tread,
To the belfry-chamber overhead,
And startled the pigeons from their perch
On the sombre rafters, that round him made   35
Masses and moving shapes of shade, —
Up the trembling ladder, steep and tall,
To the highest window in the wall,
Where he paused to listen and look down
A moment on the roofs of the town,   40
And the moonlight flowing over all.
Beneath, in the churchyard, lay the dead,
In their night-encampment on the hill,
Wrapped in silence so deep and still
That he could hear, like a sentinel's tread,   45
The watchful night-wind, as it went
Creeping along from tent to tent,
And seeming to whisper, "All is well!"
A moment only he feels the spell
Of the place and the hour, and the secret dread   50
Of the lonely belfry and the dead;
For suddenly all his thoughts are bent
On a shadowy something far away,
Where the river widens to meet the bay, —
A line of black that bends and floats   55
On the rising tide, like a bridge of boats.

Meanwhile, impatient to mount and ride,
Booted and spurred, with a heavy stride
On the opposite shore walked Paul Revere.
Now he patted his horse's side, **60**
Now gazed at the landscape far and near,
Then, impetuous, stamped the earth,
And turned and tightened his saddlegirth;
But mostly he watched with eager search
The belfry-tower of the Old North Church, **65**
As it rose above the graves on the hill,
Lonely and spectral and sombre and still.
And lo! as he looks, on the belfry's height
A glimmer, and then a gleam of light!
He springs to the saddle, the bridle he turns, **70**
But lingers and gazes, till full on his sight
A second lamp in the belfry burns!

A hurry of hoofs in a village street,
A shape in the moonlight, a bulk in the dark,
And beneath, from the pebbles, in passing, a spark **75**
Struck out by a steed flying fearless and fleet;
That was all! And yet, through the gloom and the light,
The fate of a nation was riding that night;
And the spark struck out by that steed, in his flight,
Kindled the land into flame with its heat. **80**

He has left the village and mounted the steep,
And beneath him, tranquil and broad and deep,
Is the Mystic, meeting the ocean tides;
And under the alders, that skirt its edge,
Now soft on the sand, now loud on the ledge, **85**
Is heard the tramp of his steed as he rides.

It was twelve by the village clock
When he crossed the bridge into Medford town.
He heard the crowing of the cock,
And the barking of the farmer's dog,   90
And felt the damp of the river fog,
That rises after the sun goes down.

It was one by the village clock,
When he galloped into Lexington.
He saw the gilded weathercock   95
Swim in the moonlight as he passed,
And the meeting-house windows, blank and bare,
Gaze at him with a spectral glare,
As if they already stood aghast
At the bloody work they would look upon.   100

It was two by the village clock,
When he came to the bridge in Concord town.
He heard the bleating of the flock,
And the twitter of birds among the trees,
And felt the breath of the morning breeze   105
Blowing over the meadows brown.
And one was safe and asleep in his bed
Who at the bridge would be first to fall,
Who that day would be lying dead,
Pierced by a British musket-ball.°   110

You know the rest.   In the books you have read,
How the British Regulars fired and fled, —
How the farmers gave them ball for ball,
From behind each fence and farmyard wall,

Chasing the red-coats down the lane,   115
Then crossing the fields to emerge again
Under the trees at the turn of the road,
And only pausing to fire and load.

So through the night rode Paul Revere;
And so through the night went his cry of alarm   120
To every Middlesex village and farm, —
A cry of defiance and not of fear,
A voice in the darkness, a knock at the door,
And a word that shall echo forevermore!
For, borne on the night-wind of the Past,   125
Through all our history, to the last,
In the hour of darkness and peril and need,
The people will waken and listen to hear
The hurrying hoof-beats of that steed,
And the midnight message of Paul Revere.   130

THE SICILIAN'S TALE

King Robert of Sicily°

Robert of Sicily, brother of Pope Urbane
And Valmond, Emperor of Allemaine,
Apparelled in magnificent attire,
With retinue of many a knight and squire,
On St. John's eve, at vespers, proudly sat   5
And heard the priests chant the Magnificat.
And as he listened, o'er and o'er again
Repeated, like a burden or refrain,
He caught the words, " *Deposuit potentes*
De sede, et exaltavit humiles; "   10

And slowly lifting up his kingly head
He to a learned clerk beside him said,
"What mean these words?" The clerk made answer meet,
"He has put down the mighty from their seat,
And has exalted them of low degree."   15
Thereat King Robert muttered scornfully,
"'Tis well that such seditious° words are sung
Only by priests and in the Latin tongue;
For unto priests and people be it known,
There is no power can push me from my throne!"   20
And leaning back, he yawned and fell asleep,
Lulled by the chant monotonous and deep.

When he awoke, it was already night;
The church was empty, and there was no light,
Save where the lamps, that glimmered few and faint, 25
Lighted a little space before some saint.
He started from his seat and gazed around,
But saw no living thing and heard no sound.
He groped towards the door, but it was locked;
He cried aloud, and listened, and then knocked,   30
And uttered awful threatenings and complaints,
And imprecations upon men and saints.
The sounds re-echoed from the roof and walls
As if dead priests were laughing in their stalls!

At length the sexton, hearing from without   35
The tumult of the knocking and the shout,
And thinking thieves were in the house of prayer,
Came with his lantern, asking, "Who is there?"
Half choked with rage, King Robert fiercely said,
"Open: 'tis I, the King! Art thou afraid?"   40

The frightened sexton, muttering, with a curse,
"This is some drunken vagabond, or worse!"
Turned the great key and flung the portal wide;
A man rushed by him at a single stride,
Haggard, half naked, without hat or cloak,   45
Who neither turned, nor looked at him, nor spoke,
But leaped into the blackness of the night,
And vanished like a spectre from his sight.

Robert of Sicily, brother of Pope Urbane
And Valmond, Emperor of Allemaine,   50
Despoiled of his magnificent attire,
Bare-headed, breathless, and besprent° with mire,
With sense of wrong and outrage desperate,
Strode on and thundered at the palace gate;
Rushed through the court-yard, thrusting in his rage   55
To right and left each seneschal° and page,
And hurried up the broad and sounding stair,
His white face ghastly in the torches' glare.
From hall to hall he passed with breathless speed;
Voices and cries he heard, but did not heed,   60
Until at last he reached the banquet-room,
Blazing with light, and breathing with perfume.

There on the dais sat another king,
Wearing his robes, his crown, his signet-ring,
King Robert's self in features, form, and height,   65
But all transfigured with angelic light!
It was an Angel; and his presence there
With a divine effulgence filled the air,
An exaltation, piercing the disguise,
Though none the hidden Angel recognize.   70

A moment speechless, motionless, amazed,
The throneless monarch on the Angel gazed,
Who met his looks of anger and surprise
With the divine compassion of his eyes;
Then said, "Who art thou? and why com'st thou here?" 75
To which King Robert answered with a sneer,
"I am the King, and come to claim my own
From an impostor, who usurps my throne!"
And suddenly, at these audacious words,
Up sprang the angry guests, and drew their swords; 80
The Angel answered, with unruffled brow,
"Nay, not the King, but the King's Jester, thou
Henceforth shalt wear the bells and scalloped cape,
And for thy counsellor shalt lead an ape;
Thou shalt obey my servants when they call, 85
And wait upon my henchmen in the hall!"

Deaf to King Robert's threats and cries and prayers,
They thrust him from the hall and down the stairs;
A group of tittering pages ran before,
And as they opened wide the folding-door, 90
His heart failed, for he heard, with strange alarms,
The boisterous laughter of the men-at-arms,
And all the vaulted chamber roar and ring
With the mock plaudits of "Long live the King!"

Next morning, waking with the day's first beam, 95
He said within himself, "It was a dream!"
But the straw rustled as he turned his head,
There were the cap and bells beside his bed,
Around him rose the bare, discolored walls,
Close by, the steeds were champing in their stalls, 100

L

And in the corner, a revolting shape,
Shivering and chattering sat the wretched ape.
It was no dream; the world he loved so much
Had turned to dust and ashes at his touch!

Days came and went; and now returned again   105
To Sicily the old Saturnian° reign;
Under the Angel's governance benign
The happy island danced with corn and wine,
And deep within the mountain's burning breast
Enceladus, the giant,° was at rest.   110

Meanwhile King Robert yielded to his fate,
Sullen and silent and disconsolate.
Dressed in the motley garb that Jesters wear,
With looks bewildered and a vacant stare,
Close shaven above the ears, as monks are shorn,   115
By courtiers mocked, by pages laughed to scorn,
His only friend the ape, his only food
What others left, — he still was unsubdued.
And when the Angel met him on his way,
And half in earnest, half in jest, would say,   120
Sternly, though tenderly, that he might feel
The velvet scabbard held a sword of steel,
"Art thou the King?" the passion of his woe
Burst from him in resistless overflow,
And, lifting high his forehead, he would fling   125
The haughty answer back, "I am, I am the King!"

Almost three years were ended; when there came
Ambassadors of great repute and name
From Valmond, Emperor of Allemaine,

Unto King Robert, saying that Pope Urbane   130
By letter summoned them forthwith to come
On Holy Thursday to his city of Rome.
The Angel with great joy received his guests,
And gave them presents of embroidered vests,
And velvet mantles with rich ermine lined,   135
And rings and jewels of the rarest kind.
Then he departed with them o'er the sea
Into the lovely land of Italy,
Whose loveliness was more resplendent made
By the mere passing of that cavalcade,   140
With plumes, and cloaks, and housings, and the stir
Of jewelled bridle and of golden spur.
And lo! among the menials, in mock state,
Upon a piebald steed, with shambling gait,
His cloak of fox-tails flapping in the wind,   145
The solemn ape demurely perched behind,
King Robert rode, making huge merriment
In all the country towns through which they went.

The Pope received them with great pomp and blare
Of bannered trumpets, on Saint Peter's square,   150
Giving his benediction and embrace,
Fervent, and full of apostolic grace.
While with congratulations and with prayers
He entertained the Angel unawares,
Robert, the Jester, bursting through the crowd,   155
Into their presence rushed, and cried aloud,
"I am the King! Look, and behold in me
Robert, your brother, King of Sicily!
This man, who wears my semblance to your eyes,
Is an impostor in a king's disguise.   160

Do you not know me? does no voice within
Answer my cry, and say we are akin?"
The Pope in silence, but with troubled mien,
Gazed at the Angel's countenance serene;
The Emperor, laughing, said, "It is strange sport   165
To keep a madman for thy Fool at court!"
And the poor, baffled Jester in disgrace
Was hustled back among the populace.

In solemn state the Holy Week went by,
And Easter Sunday gleamed upon the sky;   170
The presence of the Angel, with its light,
Before the sun rose, made the city bright,
And with new fervor filled the hearts of men,
Who felt that Christ indeed had risen again.
Even the Jester, on his bed of straw,   175
With haggard eyes the unwonted splendor saw,
He felt within a power unfelt before,
And, kneeling humbly on his chamber floor,
He heard the rushing garments of the Lord
Sweep through the silent air, ascending heavenward.   180

And now the visit ending, and once more
Valmond returning to the Danube's shore,
Homeward the Angel journeyed, and again
The land was made resplendent with his train,
Flashing along the towns of Italy   185
Unto Salerno, and from there by sea.
And when once more within Palermo's wall,
And, seated on the throne in his great hall,
He heard the Angelus from convent towers,
As if the better world conversed with ours,   190

He beckoned to King Robert to draw nigher,
And with a gesture bade the rest retire;
And when they were alone, the Angel said,
"Art thou the King?"   Then bowing down his head,
King Robert crossed both hands upon his breast,   195
And meekly answered him: "Thou knowest best!
My sins as scarlet are; let me go hence,
And in some cloister's school of penitence,
Across those stones, that pave the way to heaven,
Walk barefoot, till my guilty soul is shriven!"   200

The Angel smiled, and from his radiant face
A holy light illumined all the place,
And through the open window, loud and clear,
They heard the monks chant in the chapel near,
Above the stir and tumult of the street: 205
"He has put down the mighty from their seat,
And has exalted them of low degree!"
And through the chant a second melody
Rose like the throbbing of a single string:
"I am an Angel, and thou art the King!"   210

King Robert, who was standing near the throne,
Lifted his eyes, and lo! he was alone!
But all apparelled as in days of old,
With ermined mantle and with cloth of gold;
And when his courtiers came, they found him there   215
Kneeling upon the floor, absorbed in silent prayer.

THE THEOLOGIAN'S TALE

The Legend Beautiful

"Hadst thou stayed, I must have fled!"
That is what the Vision said.

In his chamber all alone,
Kneeling on the floor of stone,
Prayed the Monk in deep contrition   5
For his sins of indecision,
Prayed for greater self-denial
In temptation and in trial;
It was noonday by the dial,°
And the Monk was all alone.   10

Suddenly, as if it lightened,
An unwonted splendor brightened
All within him and without him
In that narrow cell of stone;
And he saw the Blessed Vision   15
Of our Lord, with light Elysian
Like a vesture wrapped about Him,
Like a garment round Him thrown.

Not as crucified and slain,
Not in agonies of pain,   20
Not with bleeding hands and feet,
Did the Monk his Master see;
But as in the village street,
In the house or harvest-field,
Halt and lame and blind He healed,   25
When He walked in Galilee.

In an attitude imploring,
Hands upon his bosom crossed,
Wondering, worshipping, adoring,
Knelt the Monk in rapture lost.   30
Lord, he thought, in heaven that reignest,
Who am I, that thus thou deignest
To reveal thyself to me?
Who am I, that from the centre
Of thy glory thou shouldst enter   35
This poor cell, my guest to be?

Then amid his exaltation,
Loud the convent bell appalling,
From its belfry calling, calling,
Rang through court and corridor   40
With persistent iteration°
He had never heard before.
It was now the appointed hour
When alike in shine or shower,
Winter's cold or summer's heat,   45
To the convent portals came
All the blind and halt and lame,
All the beggars of the street,
For their daily dole° of food
Dealt them by the brotherhood;   50
And their almoner° was he
Who upon his bended knee,
Rapt in silent ecstasy
Of divinest self-surrender,
Saw the Vision and the Splendor.   55
Deep distress and hesitation
Mingled with his adoration;

Should he go or should he stay?
Should he leave the poor to wait
Hungry at the convent gate,
Till the Vision passed away?   60
Should he slight his radiant guest,
Slight this visitant celestial,
For a crowd of ragged, bestial
Beggars at the convent gate?   65
Would the Vision there remain?
Would the Vision come again?
Then a voice within his breast
Whispered, audible and clear
As if to the outward ear: 70
"Do thy duty; that is best;
Leave unto thy Lord the rest!"

Straightway to his feet he started,
And with longing look intent
On the Blessed Vision bent,   75
Slowly from his cell departed,
Slowly on his errand went.

At the gate the poor were waiting,
Looking through the iron grating,
With that terror in the eye   80
That is only seen in those
Who amid their wants and woes
Hear the sound of doors that close,
And of feet that pass them by;
Grown familiar with disfavor,   85
Grown familiar with the savor
Of the bread by which men die!

But to-day, they know not why,
Like the gate of Paradise
Seemed the convent gate to rise,   90
Like a sacrament divine
Seemed to them the bread and wine.
In his heart the Monk was praying,
Thinking of the homeless poor,
What they suffer and endure;   95
What we see not, what we see;
And the inward voice was saying:
"Whatsoever thing thou doest
To the least of mine and lowest,
That thou doest unto me!"°   100

Unto me! but had the Vision
Come to him in beggar's clothing,
Come a mendicant imploring.
Would he then have knelt adoring,
Or have listened with derision,   105
And have turned away with loathing?

Thus his conscience put the question,
Full of troublesome suggestion,
As at length, with hurried pace,
Towards his cell he turned his face,   110
And beheld the convent bright
With a supernatural light,
Like a luminous cloud expanding
Over floor and wall and ceiling.

But he paused with awe-struck feeling   115
At the threshold of his door,

For the Vision still was standing
As he left it there before,
When the convent bell appalling,
From its belfry calling, calling,   120
Summoned him to feed the poor.
Through the long hour intervening
It had waited his return,
And he felt his bosom burn,
Comprehending all the meaning,   125
When the Blessed Vision said,
"Hadst thou stayed, I must have fled!"

JOHN GREENLEAF WHITTIER

PROEM°

To Edition of 1847

I LOVE the old melodious lays
Which softly melt the ages through,
    The songs of Spenser's° golden days,
    Arcadian Sidney's° silvery phrase,
Sprinkling our noon of time with freshest morning dew.

    Yet, vainly in my quiet hours
To breathe their marvellous notes I try;
    I feel them, as the leaves and flowers
    In silence feel the dewy showers,
And drink with glad, still lips the blessing of the sky.   **10**

    The rigor of a frozen clime,
The harshness of an untaught ear,
    The jarring words of one whose rhyme
    Beat often Labor's hurried time,
Or Duty's rugged march through storm and strife, are here. **15**

    Of mystic beauty, dreamy grace,
No rounded art the lack supplies;
    Unskilled the subtle lines to trace,
    Or softer shades of Nature's face,
I view her common forms with unanointed eyes.   **20**

    Nor mine the seer-like power to show
The secrets of the heart and mind;

To drop the plummet-line° below
Our common world of joy and woe,
A more intense despair or brighter hope to find.   25

Yet here at least an earnest sense
Of human right and weal is shown;
A hate of tyranny intense,
And hearty in its vehemence,
As if my brother's pain and sorrow were my own.°   30

O Freedom! if to me belong
Nor mighty Milton's gift divine,°
Nor Marvell's° wit and graceful song,
Still with a love as deep and strong
As theirs, I lay, like them, my best gifts on thy shrine!   35

THE FROST SPIRIT°

He comes, — he comes, — the Frost Spirit comes! You
    may trace his footsteps now
On the naked woods and the blasted fields and the brown
    hill's withered brow.
He has smitten the leaves of the gray old trees where their
    pleasant green came forth,
And the winds, which follow wherever he goes, have shaken
    them down to earth.

He comes, — he comes, — the Frost Spirit comes! — from
    the frozen Labrador, —   5
From the icy bridge of the Northern seas, which the white
    bear wanders o'er, —

Where the fisherman's sail is stiff with ice, and the luckless
forms below
In the sunless cold of the lingering night into marble statues
grow!

He comes, — he comes, — the Frost Spirit comes! — on the
rushing Northern blast,
And the dark Norwegian pines have bowed as his fearful
breath went past.   10
With an unscorched wing he has hurried on, where the fires
of Hecla° glow
On the darkly beautiful sky above and the ancient ice below.

He comes, — he comes, — the Frost Spirit comes! — and
the quiet lake shall feel
The torpid touch of his glazing breath, and ring to the skater's
heel;
And the streams which danced on the broken rocks, or sang
to the leaning grass,   15
Shall bow again to their winter chain, and in mournful silence
pass.

He comes, — he comes, — the Frost Spirit comes! — let us
meet him as we may,
And turn with the light of the parlor-fire his evil power away;
And gather closer the circle round, when that fire-light
dances high,
And laugh at the shriek of the baffled Fiend as his sounding
wing goes by!   20

SONGS OF LABOR

DEDICATION

I WOULD the gift I offer here
   Might graces from thy favor take,
And, seen through Friendship's atmosphere,
   On softened lines and coloring, wear
The unaccustomed light of beauty, for thy sake.   5

Few leaves of Fancy's spring remain:
   But what I have I give to thee, —
The o'er-sunned bloom of summer's plain,°
   And paler flowers, the latter rain
Calls from the westering slope of life's autumnal lea.   10

Above the fallen groves of green,
   Where youth's enchanted forest stood,
Dry root and mosséd trunk between,
   A sober after-growth is seen,
As springs the pine where falls the gay-leafed maple wood! 15

Yet birds will sing, and breezes play
   Their leaf-harps in the sombre tree,
And through the bleak and wintry day
   It keeps its steady green alway, —
So, even my after-thoughts may have a charm for thee.   20

Art's perfect forms no moral need,
   And beauty is its own excuse°;

But for the dull and flowerless weed
   Some healing virtue still must plead,
And the rough ore must find its honors in its use.   25

So haply these, my simple lays
   Of homely toil, may serve to show
The orchard bloom and tasseled maize
   That skirt and gladden duty's ways,
The unsung beauty hid life's common things below.   3¹

Haply from them the toiler, bent
   Above his forge or plough, may gain
A manlier spirit of content,
   And feel that life is wisest spent
Where the strong working hand makes strong the working
   brain.°   35

The doom which to the guilty pair°
   Without the walls of Eden came,
Transforming sinless ease to care
   And rugged toil, no more shall bear
The burden of old crime, or mark of primal shame.   4c

A blessing now, — a curse no more;
   Since He whose name we breathe with awe,
The coarse mechanic vesture wore,° —
   A poor man toiling with the poor,
In labor, as in prayer, fulfilling the same law.   45

THE LUMBERMEN

WILDLY round our woodland quarters,
    Sad-voiced Autumn grieves;
Thickly down these swelling waters
    Float his fallen leaves.
Through the tall and naked timber, 5
    Column-like and old,
Gleam the sunsets of November,
    From their skies of gold.

O'er us, to the southland heading,
    Screams the gray wild-goose;
On the night-frost sounds the treading 10
    Of the brindled moose.
Noiseless creeping, while we're sleeping,
    Frost his task-work plies;
Soon, his icy bridges heaping, 15
    Shall our log-piles rise.

When, with sounds of smothered thunder,
    On some night of rain,
Lake and river break asunder
    Winter's weakened chain, 20
Down the wild March flood shall bear them
    To the saw-mill's wheel,
Or where Steam, the slave, shall tear them
    With his teeth of steel.

Be it starlight, be it moonlight, 25
    In these vales below,

When the earliest beams of sunlight
  Streak the mountain's snow,
Crisps the hoar-frost, keen and early,
  To our hurrying feet,   30
And the forest echoes clearly
  All our blows repeat.

Where the crystal Ambijejis°
  Stretches broad and clear,
And Millnoket's° pine-black ridges   35
  Hide the browsing deer:
Where, through lakes and wide morasses,
  Or through rocky walls,
Swift and strong, Penobscot° passes
  White with foamy falls;   40

Where, through clouds, are glimpses given
  Of Katahdin's° sides, —
Rock and forest piled to heaven,
  Torn and ploughed by slides!
Far below, the Indian trapping,   45
  In the sunshine warm;
Far above, the snow-cloud wrapping
  Half the peak in storm!

Where are mossy carpets better
  Than the Persian weaves,   50
And than Eastern perfumes sweeter
  Seem the fading leaves;
And a music wild and solemn
  From the pine-tree's height,

M

Rolls its vast and sea-like volume   55
  On the wind of night ;

*   *   *   *   *   *   *

Not for us the measured ringing
  From the village spire,
Not for us the Sabbath singing
  Of the sweet-voiced choir :   60
Ours the old, majestic temple,
  Where God's brightness shines
Down the dome so grand and ample,
  Propped by lofty pines !

*   *   *   *   *   *   *

Keep who will the city's alleys,   65
  Take the smooth-shorn plain, —
Give to us the cedar valleys,
  Rocks and hills of Maine !
In our North-land, wild and woody,
  Let us still have part :   70
Rugged nurse and mother sturdy,
  Hold us to thy heart !

O, our free hearts beat the warmer
  For thy breath of snow ;
And our tread is all the firmer   75
  For thy rocks below.
Freedom, hand in hand with labor,
  Walketh strong and brave ;
On the forehead of his neighbor
  No man writeth Slave !   80

Lo, the day breaks! old Katahdin's
　　Pine-trees show its fires,
While from these dim forest gardens
　　Rise their blackened spires.
Up, my comrades! up and doing!　　85
　　Manhood's rugged play
Still renewing, bravely hewing
　　Through the world our way!

BARCLAY OF URY°

Up the streets of Aberdeen,°
By the kirk and college green,
　　Rode the Laird of Ury;
Close behind him, close beside,
Foul of mouth and evil-eyed,　　5
　　Pressed the mob in fury.

Flouted him the drunken churl,°
Jeered at him the serving-girl,
　　Prompt to please her master;
And the begging carlin,° late　　10
Fed and clothed at Ury's gate,
　　Cursed him as he passed her.

Yet, with calm and stately mien,
Up the streets of Aberdeen
　　Came he slowly riding;　　15
And, to all he saw and heard,
Answering not with bitter word,
　　Turning not for chiding.

Came a troop with broadswords swinging,
Bits and bridles sharply ringing,   20
    Loose and free and froward;
Quoth the foremost, "Ride him down!
Push him! prick him! through the town
    Drive the Quaker coward!"

But from out the thickening crowd   25
Cried a sudden voice and loud:
    "Barclay! Ho! a Barclay!"
And the old man at his side
Saw a comrade, battle tried,
    Scarred and sun-burned darkly;   30

Who with ready weapon bare,
Fronting to the troopers there,
    Cried aloud: "God save us,
Call ye coward him who stood
Ankle deep in Lützen's° blood,   35
    With the brave Gustavus?"°

"Nay, I do not need thy sword,
Comrade mine," said Ury's lord;
    "Put it up, I pray thee:
Passive to His holy will,   40
Trust I in my Master still,
    Even though He slay me.

"Pledges of thy love and faith,
Proved on many a field of death,
    Not by me are needed."   45
Marvelled much that henchman bold,

That his laird, so stout of old,
  Now so meekly pleaded.

"Woe's the day!" he sadly said,
With a slowly shaking head,   50
  And a look of pity;
"Ury's honest lord reviled,
Mock of knave and sport of child,
  In his own good city!

"Speak the word, and, master mine,   55
As we charged on Tilly's° line,
  And his Walloon° lancers,
Smiting through their midst we'll teach
Civil look and decent speech
  To these boyish prancers!"   60

"Marvel not, mine ancient friend,
Like beginning, like the end:"
  Quoth the Laird of Ury,
"Is the sinful servant more
Than his gracious Lord who bore   65
  Bonds and stripes in Jewry?°

"Give me joy that in His name
I can bear, with patient frame,
  All these vain ones offer;
While for them He suffereth long,   70
Shall I answer wrong with wrong,
  Scoffing with the scoffer?

"Happier I, with loss of all,
Hunted, outlawed, held in thrall,

    With few friends to greet me,   75
Than when reeve° and squire were seen,
Riding out from Aberdeen,
    With bared heads to meet me.

"When each goodwife, o'er and o'er,
Blessed me as I passed her door;   80
    And the snooded° daughter,
Through her casement glancing down,
Smiled on him who bore renown
    From red fields of slaughter.

"Hard to feel the stranger's scoff,   85
Hard the old friend's falling off,
    Hard to learn forgiving;
But the Lord His own rewards,
And His love with theirs accords,
    Warm and fresh and living.   90

"Through this dark and stormy night
Faith beholds a feeble light
    Up the blackness streaking;
Knowing God's own time is best,
In a patient hope I rest   95
    For the full day-breaking!"

So the Laird of Ury said,
Turning slow his horse's head
    Toward the Tolbooth° prison,
Where, through iron grates, he heard   100
Poor disciples of the Word
    Preach of Christ arisen!

Not in vain, Confessor old,
Unto us the tale is told
　Of thy day of trial;   105
Every age on him who strays
From its broad and beaten ways
　Pours its sevenfold vial.

Happy he whose inward ear
Angel comfortings can hear,   110
　O'er the rabble's laughter;
And, while Hatred's fagots burn,
Glimpses through the smoke discern
　Of the good hereafter.

Knowing this, that never yet   115
Share of Truth was vainly set
　In the world's wide fallow;
After hands shall sow the seed,
After hands from hill and mead
　Reap the harvest yellow.   120

Thus, with somewhat of the Seer,
Must the moral pioneer
　From the Future borrow;
Clothe the waste with dreams of grain,
And, on midnight's sky of rain,   125
　Paint the golden morrow!°

ALL'S WELL

THE clouds, which rise with thunder, slake
   Our thirsty souls with rain;
The blow most dreaded falls to break
   From off our limbs a chain;
And wrongs of man to man but make   5
   The love of God more plain.
As through the shadowy lens of even
The eye looks farthest into heaven
On gleams of star and depths of blue
The glaring sunshine never knew!   10

RAPHAEL°

I SHALL not soon forget that sight:
   The glow of autumn's westering day,
A hazy warmth, a dreamy light,
   On Raphael's picture lay.

It was a simple print I saw,   5
   The fair face of a musing boy°;
Yet, while I gazed, a sense of awe
   Seemed blending with my joy.

A simple print : — the graceful flow
   Of boyhood's soft and wavy hair,   10
And fresh young lip and cheek, and brow
   Unmarked and clear, were there.

Yet through its sweet and calm repose
  I saw the inward spirit shine;
It was as if before me rose   15
  The white veil of a shrine.

As if, as Gothland's sage° has told,
  The hidden life, the man within,
Dissevered from its frame and mould,
  By mortal eye were seen.   20

Was it the lifting of that eye,
  The waving of that pictured hand?
Loose as a cloud-wreath on the sky,
  I saw the walls expand.

The narrow room had vanished, — space,   25
  Broad, luminous, remained alone,
Through which all hues and shapes of grace
  And beauty looked or shone.

Around the mighty master came
  The marvels which his pencil wrought,   30
Those miracles of power whose fame
  Is wide as human thought.

There drooped thy more than mortal face,
  O Mother, beautiful and mild!
Enfolding in one dear embrace   35
  Thy Saviour and thy Child!°

The rapt brow of the Desert John°;
  The awful glory of that day

When all the Father's brightness shone
    Through manhood's veil of clay.°   40

And, midst gray prophet forms, and wild
    Dark visions of the days of old,°
How sweetly woman's beauty smiled
    Through locks of brown and gold!

There Fornarina's° fair young face   45
    Once more upon her lover shone,
Whose model of an angel's grace
    He borrowed from her own.

Slow passed that vision from my view,
    But not the lesson which it taught;   50
The soft, calm shadows which it threw
    Still rested on my thought:

The truth, that painter, bard, and sage,
    Even in Earth's cold and changeful clime,
Plant for their deathless heritage   55
    The fruits and flowers of time.

We shape ourselves the joy or fear
    Of which the coming life is made,
And fill our Future's atmosphere
    With sunshine or with shade.   60

The tissue of the Life to be
    We weave with colors all our own,
And in the field of Destiny
    We reap as we have sown.

Still shall the soul around it call   65
   The shadows which it gathered here,
And, painted on the eternal wall,
   The Past shall reappear.

Think ye the notes of holy song
   On Milton's tuneful ear have died?°   70
Think ye that Raphael's angel throng
   Has vanished from his side?

O no! — We live our life again:
   Or warmly touched, or coldly dim,
The pictures of the Past remain, —   75
   Man's works shall follow him!

SEED–TIME AND HARVEST

As o'er his furrowed fields which lie
Beneath a coldly-dropping sky,
Yet chill with winter's melted snow,
The husbandman goes forth to sow,

Thus, Freedom,° on the bitter blast   5
The ventures of thy seed we cast,
And trust to warmer sun and rain
To swell the germ, and fill the grain.

Who calls thy glorious service hard?
Who deems it not its own reward?   10
Who, for its trials, counts it less
A cause of praise and thankfulness?

It may not be our lot to wield
The sickle in the ripened field;
Nor ours to hear, on summer eves,   15
The reaper's song among the sheaves.

Yet where our duty's task is wrought
In unison with God's great thought,
The near and future blend in one,
And whatsoe'er is willed, is done!   20

And ours the grateful service whence
Comes, day by day, the recompense;
The hope, the trust, the purpose stayed,
The fountain and the noonday shade.

And were this life the utmost span,   25
The only end and aim of man,°
Better the toil of fields like these
Than waking dream and slothful ease.

But life, though falling like our grain,
Like that revives and springs again;   30
And, early called, how blest are they
Who wait in heaven their harvest-day!

THE PROPHECY OF SAMUEL SEWALL

1697

Up and down the village streets
Strange are the forms my fancy meets,
For the thoughts and things of to-day are **hid,**
And through the veil of a closéd lid
The ancient worthies I see again :   5
I hear the tap of the elder's cane,
And his awful periwig I see,
And the silver buckles of shoe and knee.
Stately and slow, with thoughtful air,
His black cap hiding his whitened hair,   10
Walks the Judge of the great Assize,
Samuel Sewall the good and wise.°
His face with lines of firmness wrought,
He wears the look of a man unbought,
Who swears to his hurt and changes not ;   15
Yet, touched and softened nevertheless
With the grace of Christian gentleness,
The face that a child would climb to kiss !
True and tender and brave and just,
That man might honor and woman trust.   20

Touching and sad, a tale is told,
Like a penitent hymn of the Psalmist old,
Of the fast which the good man lifelong kept
With a haunting sorrow that never slept,
As the circling year brought round the time   25
Of an error that left the sting of crime,

When he sat on the bench of the witchcraft courts,
With the laws of Moses and Hale's Reports,°
And spake, in the name of both, the word
That gave the witch's neck to the cord,   30
And piled the oaken planks that pressed
The feeble life from the warlock's° breast!
All the day long, from dawn to dawn,
His door was bolted, his curtain drawn;
No foot on his silent threshold trod,   35
No eye looked on him save that of God,
As he baffled the ghosts of the dead with charms
Of penitent tears, and prayers, and psalms,
And, with precious proofs from the sacred word
Of the boundless pity and love of the Lord,   40
His faith confirmed and his trust renewed
That the sin of his ignorance, sorely rued,
Might be washed away in the mingled flood
Of his human sorrow and Christ's dear blood!

   Green forever the memory be   45
Of the Judge of the old Theocracy,°
Whom even his errors glorified,
Like a far-seen, sunlit mountain-side
By the cloudy shadows which o'er it glide!
Honor and praise to the Puritan   50
Who the halting step of his age outran,
And, seeing the infinite worth of man
In the priceless gift the Father gave,
In the infinite love that stooped to save,
Dared not brand his brother a slave!   55
"Who doth such wrong," he was wont to say,
In his own quaint, picture-loving way,

"Flings up to Heaven a hand-grenade°
Which God shall cast down upon his head!"

    Widely as heaven and hell, contrast   60
That brave old jurist of the past
And the cunning trickster and knave of courts
Who the holy features of Truth distorts, —
Ruling as right the will of the strong,
Poverty, crime, and weakness wrong;   65
Wide-eared to power, to the wronged and weak
Deaf as Egypt's gods of leek;
Scoffing aside at party's nod,
Order of nature and law of God;
For whose dabbled ermine respect were waste,   70
Reverence folly, and awe misplaced;
Justice of whom 't were vain to seek
As from Koordish robber° or Syrian Sheik!°
O, leave the wretch to his bribes and sins;
Let him rot in the web of lies he spins!   75
To the saintly soul of the early day,
To the Christian judge, let us turn and say:
"Praise and thanks for an honest man! —
Glory to God for the Puritan!"

    I see, far southward, this quiet day,   80
The hills of Newbury° rolling away,
With the many tints of the season gay,
Dreamily blending in autumn mist
Crimson, and gold, and amethyst.
Long and low, with dwarf trees crowned,   85
Plum Island lies, like a whale aground,
A stone's toss over the narrow sound.

Inland, as far as the eye can go,
The hills curve round like a bended bow;
A silver arrow from out them sprung,   90
I see the shine of the Quasycung;
And, round and round, over valley and hill,
Old roads winding, as old roads will,
Here to a ferry, and there to a mill;
And glimpses of chimneys and gabled eaves,   95
Through green elm arches and maple leaves, —
Old homesteads sacred to all that can
Gladden or sadden the heart of man, —
Over whose thresholds of oak and stone
Life and Death have come and gone!   100
There pictured tiles in the fireplace show,
Great beams sag from the ceiling low,
The dresser glitters with polished wares,
The long clock ticks on the foot-worn stairs,
And the low, broad chimney shows the crack   105
By the earthquake made a century back.
Up from their midst springs the village spire
With the crest of its cock in the sun afire;
Beyond are orchards and planting lands,
And great salt marshes and glimmering sands,   110
And, where north and south the coast-lines run,
The blink of the sea in breeze and sun!

    I see it all like a chart unrolled,
But my thoughts are full of the past and old,
I hear the tales of my boyhood told;   115
And the shadows and shapes of early days
Flit dimly by in the veiling haze,
With measured movement and rhythmic chime

Weaving like shuttles my web of rhyme.
I think of the old man wise and good   120
Who once on yon misty hillsides stood,
(A poet who never measured rhyme,
A seer unknown to his dull-eared time,)
And, propped on his staff of age, looked down,
With his boyhood's love, on his native town,   125
Where, written, as if on its hills and plains,
His burden of prophecy yet remains,
For the voices of wood, and wave, and wind
To read in the ear of the musing mind: —

"As long as Plum Island, to guard the coast   130
As God appointed, shall keep its post;
As long as a salmon shall haunt the deep
Of Merrimack River, or sturgeon leap;
As long as pickerel swift and slim,
Or red-backed perch, in Crane Pond swim;   135
As long as the annual sea-fowl know
Their time to come and their time to go;
As long as cattle shall roam at will
The green, grass meadows by Turkey Hill;
As long as sheep shall look from the side   140
Of Oldtown Hill on marishes wide,
And Parker River, and salt-sea tide;
As long as a wandering pigeon shall search
The fields below from his white-oak perch,
When the barley-harvest is ripe and shorn,   145
And the dry husks fall from the standing corn;
As long as Nature shall not grow old,
Nor drop her work from her doting hold,
And her care for the Indian corn forget,

N

And the yellow rows in pairs to set; —   150
So long shall Christians here be born,
Grow up and ripen as God's sweet corn! —
By the beak of bird, by the breath of frost
Shall never a holy ear be lost,
But, husked by Death in the Planter's sight,   155
Be sown again in the fields of light!"°

The Island still is purple with plums,
Up the river the salmon comes,
The sturgeon leaps, and the wild-fowl feeds
On hillside berries and marish seeds, —   160
All the beautiful signs remain,
From spring-time sowing to autumn rain
The good man's vision returns again!
And let us hope, as well we can,
That the Silent Angel who garners man   165
May find some grain as of old he found
In the human cornfield ripe and sound,
And the Lord of the Harvest deign to own
The precious seed by the fathers sown!

SKIPPER IRESON'S RIDE°

Of all the rides since the birth of time,
Told in story or sung in rhyme,—
On Apuleius's Golden Ass,°
Or one-eyed Calendar's horse of brass,°
Witch astride of a human hack,   5
Islam's prophet on Al-Borák,°—
The strangest ride that ever was sped

Was Ireson's, out from Marblehead!
 Old Floyd Ireson, for his hard heart,
  Tarred and feathered and carried in a cart 10
 By the women of Marblehead!°

Body of turkey, head of owl,
Wings a-droop like a rained-on fowl,
Feathered and ruffled in every part,
Skipper Ireson stood in the cart. 15
Scores of women, old and young,
Strong of muscle, and glib of tongue,
Pushed and pulled up the rocky lane,
Shouting and singing the shrill refrain:
 "Here's Flud Oirson, fur his horrd horrt, 20
 Torr'd an' futherr'd an' corr'd in a corrt
  By the women o' Morble'ead!"

Wrinkled scolds with hands on hips,
Girls in bloom of cheek and lips,
Wild-eyed, free-limbed, such as chase 25
Bacchus round some antique vase,
Brief of skirt, with ankles bare,
Loose of kerchief and loose of hair,
With conch-shells blowing and fish-horns' twang.
Over and over the Mænads° sang: 30
 "Here's Flud Oirson, fur his horrd horrt,
 Torr'd an' futherr'd an' corr'd in a corrt
  By the women o' Morble'ead!"

Small pity for him! — He sailed away
From a leaking ship, in Chaleur Bay,° — 35
Sailed away from a sinking wreck,

With his own town's-people on her deck!
"Lay by! lay by!" they called to him.
Back he answered, "Sink or swim!
Brag of your catch of fish again!"   40
And off he sailed through the fog and rain!
  Old Floyd Ireson, for his hard heart,
    Tarred and feathered and carried in a cart
      By the women of Marblehead!

Fathoms deep in dark Chaleur   45
That wreck shall lie forevermore.
Mother and sister, wife and maid,
Looked from the rocks of Marblehead
Over the moaning and rainy sea,—
Looked for the coming that might not be!   50
What did the winds and the sea-birds say
Of the cruel captain who sailed away?—
  Old Floyd Ireson, for his hard heart,
    Tarred and feathered and carried in a cart
      By the women of Marblehead!   55

Through the street, on either side,
Up flew windows, doors swung wide;
Sharp-tongued spinsters, old wives gray,
Treble lent the fish-horn's bray.
Sea-worn grandsires, cripple-bound,   60
Hulks of old sailors run aground,
Shook head, and fist, and hat, and cane,
And cracked with curses the old refrain:
  "Here's Flud Oirson, fur his horrd horrt,
    Torr'd an' futherr'd an' corr'd in a corrt   65
      By the women o' Morble'ead!"

Sweetly along the Salem road
Bloom of orchard and lilac showed.
Little the wicked skipper knew
Of the fields so green and the sky so blue.　　70
Riding there in his sorry trim,
Like an Indian idol glum and grim,
Scarcely he seemed the sound to hear
Of voices shouting, far and near:
　　"Here's Flud Oirson, fur his horrd horrt,　　75
　　Torr'd an' futherr'd an' corr'd in a corrt
　　　　By the women o' Morble'ead!"

"Hear me, neighbors!" at last he cried,—
"What to me is this noisy ride?
What is the shame that clothes the skin　　80
To the nameless horror that lives within?
Waking or sleeping, I see a wreck,
And hear a cry from a reeling deck!
Hate me and curse me, — I only dread
The hand of God and the face of the dead!"　　85
　　Said old Floyd Ireson, for his hard heart,
　　Tarred and feathered and carried in a cart
　　　　By the women of Marblehead!

Then the wife of the skipper lost at sea
Said, "God has touched him! — why should we?"　　90
Said an old wife mourning her only son,
"Cut the rogue's tether and let him run!"
So with soft relentings and rude excuse,
Half scorn, half pity, they cut him loose,
And gave him a cloak to hide him in,　　95

And left him alone with his shame and sin.
 Poor Floyd Ireson, for his hard heart,
 Tarred and feathered and carried in a cart
  By the women of Marblehead!

THE DOUBLE-HEADED SNAKE OF NEWBURY

FAR away in the twilight time
Of every people, in every clime,
Dragons and griffins and monsters dire,
Born of water, and air, and fire,
Or nursed, like the Python, in the mud   5
And ooze of the old Deucalion flood,°
Crawl and wriggle and foam with rage,
Through dusk tradition and ballad age.
So from the childhood of Newbury town°
And its time of fable the tale comes down 10
Of a terror which haunted bush and brake,
The Amphisbæna, the Double Snake!

Thou who makest the tale thy mirth,
Consider that strip of Christian earth
On the desolate shore of a sailless sea, 15
Full of terror and mystery,
Half-redeemed from the evil hold
Of the wood so dreary, and dark, and old,
Which drank with its lips of leaves the dew
When Time was young, and the world was new, 20
And wove its shadows with sun and moon,
Ere the stones of Cheops° were squared and hewn.

Think of the sea's dread monotone,
Of the mournful wail from the pine-wood blown,
Of the strange, vast splendors that lit the North, 25
Of the troubled throes of the quaking earth,
And the dismal tales the Indian told,
Till the settler's heart at his hearth grew cold,
And he shrank from the tawny wizard's boasts,
And the hovering shadows seemed full of ghosts, 30
And above, below, and on every side,
The fear of his creed seemed verified; —
And think, if his lot were now thine own,
To grope with terrors nor named nor known,
How laxer muscle and weaker nerve 35
And a feebler faith thy need might serve;
And own to thyself the wonder more
That the snake had two heads, and not a score!

Whether he lurked in the Oldtown fen
Or the gray earth-flax of the Devil's Den, 40
Or swam in the wooded Artichoke,
Or coiled by the Northman's Written Rock,
Nothing on record is left to show;
Only the fact that he lived, we know,
And left the cast of a double head 45
In the scaly mask which he yearly shed.
For he carried a head where his tail should be,
And the two, of course, could never agree,
But wriggled about with main and might,
Now to the left and now to the right; 50
Pulling and twisting this way and that,
Neither knew what the other was at.

A snake with two heads, lurking so near!—
Judge of the wonder, guess at the fear!
Think what ancient gossips might say,   55
Shaking their heads in their dreary way,
Between the meetings on Sabbath-day;
How urchins, searching at day's decline
The Common Pasture° for sheep or kine,
The terrible double-ganger° heard   60
In the leafy rustle or whir of bird!
Think what a zest it gave to the sport,
In berry-time, of the younger sort,
As over pastures blackberry-twined,
Reuben and Dorothy lagged behind,   65
And closer and closer, for fear of harm,
The maiden clung to her lover's arm;
And how the spark, who was forced to stay,
By his sweetheart's fears, till the break of day,
Thanked the snake for the fond delay!   70

Far and wide the tale was told,
Like a snowball growing while it rolled.
The nurse hushed with it the baby's cry;
And it served, in the worthy minister's eye,
To paint the primitive serpent by.   75
Cotton Mather° came galloping down
All the way to Newbury town,
With his eyes agog and his ears set wide,
And his marvellous inkhorn at his side;
Stirring the while in the shallow pool   80
Of his brains for the lore he learned at school,
To garnish the story, with here a streak
Of Latin, and there another of Greek:

And the tales he heard and the notes he took,
Behold! are they not in his Wonder-Book?°   85

Stories, like dragons, are hard to kill.
If the snake does not, the tale runs still
In Byfield Meadows, on Pipestave Hill.
And still, whenever husband and wife
Publish the shame of their daily strife,   90
And, with mad cross-purpose, tug and strain
At either end of the marriage-chain,
The gossips say, with a knowing shake
Of their gray heads, "Look at the Double Snake!
One in body and two in will,   95
The Amphisbæna is living still!"

MAUD MULLER

MAUD MULLER, on a summer's day,
Raked the meadow sweet with hay.

Beneath her torn hat glowed the wealth
Of simple beauty and rustic health.

Singing, she wrought, and her merry glee   5
The mock-bird echoed from his tree.

But when she glanced to the far-off town,
White from its hill-slope looking down,

The sweet song died, and a vague unrest
And a nameless longing filled her breast,—   10

A wish, that she hardly dared to own,
For something better than she had known.

The Judge rode slowly down the lane,
Smoothing his horse's chestnut mane.

He drew his bridle in the shade   15
Of the apple-trees, to greet the maid,

And ask a draught from the spring that flowed
Through the meadow across the road.

She stooped where the cool spring bubbled up,
And filled for him her small tin cup,   20

And blushed as she gave it, looking down
On her feet so bare, and her tattered gown.

"Thanks!" said the Judge; "a sweeter draught
From a fairer hand was never quaffed."

He spoke of the grass and flowers and trees,   25
Of the singing birds and the humming bees;

Then talked of the haying, and wondered whether
The cloud in the west would bring foul weather.

And Maud forgot her brier-torn gown,
And her graceful ankles bare and brown;   30

And listened, while a pleased surprise
Looked from her long-lashed hazel eyes.

At last, like one who for delay
Seeks a vain excuse, he rode away.

Maud Muller looked and sighed: "Ah me!   35
That I the Judge's bride might be!

"He would dress me up in silks so fine,
And praise and toast me at his wine.

"My father should wear a broadcloth coat;
My brother should sail a painted boat.   40

"I'd dress my mother so grand and gay,
And the baby should have a new toy each day.

"And I'd feed the hungry and clothe the poor
And all should bless me who left our door."

The Judge looked back as he climbed the hill,   45
And saw Maud Muller standing still.

"A form more fair, a face more sweet
Ne'er hath it been my lot to meet.

"And her modest answer and graceful air
Show her wise and good as she is fair.   50

"Would she were mine, and I to-day,
Like her, a harvester of hay:

"No doubtful balance of rights and wrongs,
Nor weary lawyers with endless tongues,

"But low of cattle and song of birds,   55
And health and quiet and loving words."

But he thought of his sisters, proud and cold,
And his mother, vain of her rank and gold.

So, closing his heart, the Judge rode on,
And Maud was left in the field alone.   60

But the lawyers smiled that afternoon,
When he hummed in court an old love-tune;

And the young girl mused beside the well,
Till the rain on the unraked clover fell.

He wedded a wife of richest dower,   65
Who lived for fashion, as he for power.

Yet oft, in his marble hearth's bright glow,
He watched a picture come and go;

And sweet Maud Muller's hazel eyes
Looked out in their innocent surprise.   70

Oft, when the wine in his glass was red,
He longed for the wayside well instead;

And closed his eyes on his garnished rooms
To dream of meadows and clover-blooms.

And the proud man sighed, with a secret pain,   75
"Ah, that I were free again!

"Free as when I rode that day,
Where the barefoot maiden raked her hay."

She wedded a man unlearned and poor,
And many children played round her door.　　80

But care and sorrow, and childbirth pain,
Left their traces on heart and brain.

And oft, when the summer sun shone hot
On the new-mown hay in the meadow lot,

And she heard the little spring brook fall　　85
Over the roadside, through the wall,

In the shade of the apple-tree again
She saw a rider draw his rein.

And gazing down with timid grace
She felt his pleased eyes read her face.　　90

Sometimes her narrow kitchen walls
Stretched away into stately halls;

The weary wheel to a spinnet turned,
The tallow candle an astral° burned,

And for him who sat by the chimney lug,　　95
Dozing and grumbling o'er pipe and mug,

A manly form at her side she saw,
And joy was duty and love was law.

Then she took up her burden of life again,
Saying only, "It might have been."   100

Alas for maiden, alas for Judge,
For rich repiner and household drudge!

God pity them both! and pity us all,
Who vainly the dreams of youth recall.

For of all sad words of tongue or pen,   105
The saddest are these: "It might have been!"

Ah, well! for us all some sweet hope lies
Deeply buried from human eyes;

And, in the hereafter, angels may
Roll the stone from its grave away!   110

BURNS°

ON RECEIVING A SPRIG OF HEATHER IN BLOSSOM

No more these simple flowers belong
    To Scottish maid and lover;
Sown in the common soil of song,
    They bloom the wide world over.

In smiles and tears, in sun and showers,   5
    The minstrel and the heather,
The deathless singer and the flowers
    He sang of live together.

Wild heather-bells and Robert Burns!
   The moorland flower and peasant!   10
How, at their mention, memory turns
   Her pages old and pleasant!

The gray sky wears again its gold
   And purple of adorning,
And manhood's noonday shadows hold   15
   The dews of boyhood's morning.

The dews that washed the dust and soil
   From off the wings of pleasure,
The sky, that flecked the ground of toil
   With golden threads of leisure.   20

I call to mind the summer day,
   The early harvest mowing,
The sky with sun and clouds at play,
   And flowers with breezes blowing.

I hear the blackbird in the corn,   25
   The locust in the haying;
And, like the fabled hunter's horn,
   Old tunes my heart is playing.

How oft that day, with fond delay,
   I sought the maple's shadow,   30
And sang with Burns the hours away,
   Forgetful of the meadow!

Bees hummed, birds twittered, overhead
   I heard the squirrels leaping;

The good dog listened while I read,   35
    And wagged his tail in keeping.

I watched him while in sportive mood
    I read " *The Twa Dogs* " story,
And half believed he understood
    The poet's allegory.°   40

Sweet day, sweet songs! — The golden hours
    Grew brighter for that singing,
From brook and bird and meadow flowers
    A dearer welcome bringing.

New light on home-seen Nature beamed,   45
    New glory over Woman;
And daily life and duty seemed
    No longer poor and common.

I woke to find the simple truth
    Of fact and feeling better   50
Than all the dreams that held my youth
    A still repining debtor:

That Nature gives her handmaid, Art,
    The themes of sweet discoursing;
The tender idyls of the heart   55
    In every tongue rehearsing.

Why dream of lands of gold and pearl,
    Of loving knight and lady,
When farmer boy and barefoot girl
    Were wandering there already?   60

I saw through all familiar things
   The romance underlying;
The joys and griefs that plume the wings
   Of Fancy skyward flying.

I saw the same blithe day return, 65
   The same sweet fall of even,
That rose on wooded Craigie-burn,
   And sank on crystal Devon.°

I matched with Scotland's heathery hills
   The sweet-brier and the clover; 70
With Ayr and Doon,° my native rills,
   Their wood-hymns chanting over.

O'er rank and pomp, as he had seen,
   I saw the Man uprising;
No longer common or unclean, 75
   The child of God's baptizing!

With clearer eyes I saw the worth
   Of life among the lowly;
The Bible at his Cotter's hearth
   Had made my own more holy. 80

And if at times an evil strain,
   To lawless love appealing,
Broke in upon the sweet refrain
   Of pure and healthful feeling,

It died upon the eye and ear, 85
   No inward answer gaining;

o

No heart had I to see or hear
    The discord and the staining.

Let those who never erred forget
    His worth, in vain bewailings;   90
Sweet Soul of Song! — I own my debt
    Uncancelled by his failings!°

Lament who will the ribald line
    Which tells his lapse from duty,
How kissed the maddening lips of wine   95
    Or wanton ones of beauty;

But think, while falls that shade between
    The erring one and Heaven,
That he who loved like Magdalen,°
    Like her may be forgiven.   100

Not his the song whose thunderous chime
    Eternal echoes render, —
The mournful Tuscan's° haunted rhyme,
    And Milton's starry splendor!

But who his human heart has laid   105
    To Nature's bosom nearer?
Who sweetened toil like him, or paid
    To love a tribute dearer?

Through all his tuneful art, how strong
    The human feeling gushes!   110
The very moonlight of his song
    Is warm with smiles and blushes!

Give lettered pomp to teeth of Time,
  So "Bonnie Doon" but tarry;
Blot out the Epic's stately rhyme,   115
  But spare his Highland Mary!

THE HERO

"O FOR a knight like Bayard°,
  Without reproach or fear;
My light glove on his casque of steel,
  My love-knot on his spear!

"O for the white plume floating   5
  Sad Zutphen's° field above, —
The lion heart in battle,
  The woman's heart in love!

"O that man once more were manly,
  Woman's pride, and not her scorn: 10
That once more the pale young mother
  Dared to boast 'a man is born°'!

"But, now life's slumberous current
  No sun-bowed cascade wakes;
No tall, heroic manhood   15
  The level dulness breaks.

"O for a knight like Bayard,
  Without reproach or fear!
My light glove on his casque of steel
  My love-knot on his spear!"   20

Then I said, my own heart throbbing
    To the time her proud pulse beat,
"Life hath its regal natures yet, —
    True, tender, brave, and sweet!

"Smile not, fair unbeliever!   25
    One man, at least, I know,
Who might wear the crest of Bayard
    Or Sidney's° plume of snow.

"Once, when over purple mountains
    Died away the Grecian sun,   30
And the far Cyllenian ranges°
    Paled and darkened, one by one, —

"Fell the Turk, a bolt of thunder,
    Cleaving all the quiet sky,
And against his sharp steel lightnings   35
    Stood the Suliote° but to die.

"Woe for the weak and halting!
    The crescent blazed behind
A curving line of sabres
    Like fire before the wind!   40

"Last to fly, and first to rally,
    Rode he of whom I speak,°
When, groaning in his bridle-path,
    Sank down a wounded Greek.

"With the rich Albanian° costume   45
    Wet with many a ghastly stain,

Gazing on earth and sky as one
   Who might not gaze again!

"He looked forward to the mountains,
   Back on foes that never spare,   50
Then flung him from his saddle,
   And placed the stranger there.

"'Allah! hu!' Through flashing sabres,
   Through a stormy hail of lead,
The good Thessalian charger   55
   Up the slopes of olives sped.

"Hot spurred the turbaned riders;
   He almost felt their breath,
Where a mountain stream rolled darkly down
   Between the hills and death.   60

"One brave and manful struggle, —
   He gained the solid land,
And the cover of the mountains,
   And the carbines of his band!"

"It was very great and noble,"   65
   Said the moist-eyed listener then,
"But one brave deed makes no hero;
   Tell me what he since hath been!"

"Still a brave and generous manhood,
   Still an honor without stain,   70
In the prison of the Kaiser,
   By the barricades of Seine.

"But dream not helm and harness
　　The sign of valor true;
Peace hath higher tests of manhood　　75
　　Than battle ever knew.

"Wouldst know him now?　Behold him,
　　The Cadmus° of the blind,
Giving the dumb lip language,
　　The idiot clay a mind.　　80

"Walking his round of duty
　　Serenely day by day,
With the strong man's hand of labor
　　And childhood's heart of play.

"True as the knights of story,　　85
　　Sir Lancelot° and his peers,
Brave in his calm endurance
　　As they in tilt of spears.

"As waves in stillest waters,
　　As stars in noonday skies,　　90
All that wakes to noble action
　　In his noon of calmness lies.

"Wherever outraged Nature
　　Asks word or action brave,
Wherever struggles labor,　　95
　　Wherever groans a slave, —

"Wherever rise the peoples,
　　Wherever sinks a throne,

The throbbing heart of Freedom finds
  An answer in his own.   100

"Knight of a better era,
  Without reproach or fear!
Said I not well that Bayards
  And Sidneys still are here?"

THE ETERNAL GOODNESS

O FRIENDS! with whom my feet have trod
  The quiet aisles of prayer,
Glad witness to your zeal for God
  And love of man I bear.

I trace your lines of argument;   5
  Your logic linked and strong
I weigh as one who dreads dissent,
  And fears a doubt as wrong.

But still my human hands are weak
  To hold your iron creeds;   10
Against the words ye bid me speak
  My heart within me pleads.

Who fathoms the Eternal Thought?
  Who talks of scheme and plan?
The Lord is God! He needeth not   15
  The poor device of man.

I walk with bare, hushed feet the ground
  Ye tread with boldness shod:

I dare not fix with mete and bound
  The love and power of God.   20

Ye praise His justice; even such
  His pitying love I deem:
Ye seek a king; I fain would touch
  The robe that hath no seam.°

Ye see the curse which overbroods   25
  A world of pain and loss;
I hear our Lord's beatitudes
  And prayer upon the cross.

    *   *   *   *   *

The wrong that pains my soul below
  I dare not throne above: 30
I know not of His hate, — I know
  His goodness and His love.

I dimly guess from blessings known
  Of greater out of sight,
And, with the chastened Psalmist, own   35
  His judgments too are right.°

I long for household voices gone,
  For vanished smiles I long,
But God hath led my dear ones on,
  And He can do no wrong.   40

I know not what the future hath
  Of marvel or surprise,
Assured alone that life and death
  His mercy underlies.

And if my heart and flesh are weak   45
   To bear an untried pain,
The bruised reed He will not break,
   But strengthen and sustain.

No offering of my own I have,
   Nor works my faith to prove;   50
I can but give the gifts He gave,
   And plead His love for love.

And so beside the Silent Sea
   I wait the muffled oar°;
No harm from Him can come to me   55
   On ocean or on shore.

I know not where His islands lift
   Their fronded palms in air;
I only know I cannot drift
   Beyond His love and care.   60

O brothers! if my faith is vain,
   If hopes like these betray,
Pray for me that my feet may gain
   The sure and safer way.

And Thou, O Lord! by whom are seen   65
   Thy creatures as they be,
Forgive me if too close I lean
   My human heart on Thee!

THE PIPES AT LUCKNOW

PIPES of the misty moorlands
  Voice of the glens and hills;
The droning of the torrents,
  The treble of the rills!
Not the braes of broom and heather,   5
  Nor the mountains dark with rain,
Nor maiden bower, nor border tower,
  Have heard your sweetest strain!

Dear to the Lowland° reaper,
  And plaided mountaineer, —   10
To the cottage and the castle
  The Scottish pipes are dear; —
Sweet sounds the ancient pibroch°
  O'er mountain, loch, and glade;
But the sweetest of all music   15
  The Pipes at Lucknow played.

Day by day the Indian tiger
  Louder yelled, and nearer crept°;
Round and round the jungle-serpent
  Near and nearer circles swept.   20
"Pray for rescue, wives and mothers, —
  Pray to-day!" the soldier said;
"To-morrow, death's between us
  And the wrong and shame we dread."

O, they listened, looked, and waited,   25
  Till their hope became despair;

And the sobs of low bewailing
   Filled the pauses of their prayer.
Then up spake a Scottish maiden,
   With her ear unto the ground :   30
"Dinna ye hear it ? — dinna ye hear it ?
   The pipes o' Havelock° sound !"

Hushed the wounded man his groaning ;
   Hushed the wife her little ones ;
Alone they heard the drum-roll   35
   And the roar of Sepoy° guns.
But to sounds of home and childhood
   The Highland ear was true ; —
As her mother's cradle-crooning
   The mountain pipes she knew.   40

Like the march of soundless music
   Through the vision of the seer,
More of feeling than of hearing,
   Of the heart than of the ear,
She knew the droning pibroch,   45
   She knew the Campbell's call :
"Hark ! hear ye no' MacGregor's, —
   The grandest o' them all !"

O, they listened, dumb and breathless,
   And they caught the sound at last ;   50
Faint and far beyond the Goomtee°
   Rose and fell the piper's blast !
Then a burst of wild thanksgiving
   Mingled woman's voice and man's :
"God be praised ! — the March of Havelock ! 55
   The piping of the clans !"

Louder, nearer, fierce as vengeance,
   Sharp and shrill as swords at strife,
Came the wild MacGregor's clan-call,
   Stinging all the air to life.   60
But when the far-off dust-cloud
   To plaided legions grew,
Full tenderly and blithesomely
   The pipes of rescue blew!

Round the silver domes of Lucknow,   65
   Moslem mosque and Pagan shrine,
Breathed the air to Britons dearest,
   The air of Auld Lang Syne.
O'er the cruel roll of war-drums
   Rose that sweet and homelike strain;   70
And the tartan clove the turban,
   As the Goomtee cleaves the plain.

Dear to the corn-land reaper
   And plaided mountaineer, —
To the cottage and the castle   75
   The piper's song is dear.
Sweet sounds the Gaelic° pibroch
   O'er mountain, glen, and glade,
But the sweetest of all music
   The Pipes at Lucknow played!   80

COBBLER KEEZAR'S VISION°

THE beaver cut his timber
  With patient teeth that day,
The minks were fish-wards, and the crows
  Surveyors of high way, —

When Keezar sat on the hillside   5
  Upon his cobbler's form,
With a pan of coals on either hand
  To keep his waxed-ends warm.

And there, in the golden weather,
  He stitched and hammered and sung;   10
In the brook he moistened his leather,
  In the pewter mug his tongue.

Well knew the tough old Teuton
  Who brewed the stoutest ale,
And he paid the good-wife's reckoning   15
  In the coin of song and tale.

The songs they still are singing
  Who dress the hills of vine,
The tales that haunt the Brocken°
  And whisper down the Rhine.   20

Woodsy and wild and lonesome,
  The swift stream wound away,
Through birches and scarlet maples
  Flashing in foam and spray, —

Down on the sharp-horned ledges   25
    Plunging in steep cascade,
Tossing its white-maned waters
    Against the hemlock's shade.

Woodsy and wild and lonesome,
    East and west and north and south;   30
Only the village of fishers
    Down at the river's mouth;

Only here and there a clearing,
    With its farm-house rude and new,
And tree-stumps, swart° as Indians,   35
    Where the scanty harvest grew.

No shout of home-bound reapers,
    No vintage-song he heard,
And on the green no dancing feet
    The merry violin stirred.   40

"Why should folk be glum," said Keezar,
    "When Nature herself is glad,
And the painted woods are laughing
    At the faces so sour and sad?"

Small heed had the careless cobbler   45
    What sorrow of heart was theirs
Who travailed in pain with the births of God
    And planted a state with prayers, —

Hunting of witches and warlocks,°
    Smiting the heathen horde, —   50

One hand on the mason's trowel,
   And one on the soldier's sword!°

But give him his ale and cider,
   Give him his pipe and song,
Little he cared for Church or State,   55
   Or the balance of right and wrong.

"'Tis work, work, work," he muttered —
   "And for rest a snuffle of psalms!"
He smote on his leathern apron
   With his brown and waxen palms.   60

"O for the purple harvests
   Of the days when I was young!
For the merry grape-stained maidens,
   And the pleasant songs they sung!

"O for the breath of vineyards,   65
   Of apples and nuts and wine!
For an oar to row and a breeze to blow
   Down the grand old river Rhine!"

A tear in his blue eye glistened
   And dropped on his beard so gray.   70
"Old, old am I," said Keezar,
   "And the Rhine flows far away!"

But a cunning man was the cobbler;
   He could call the birds from the trees,
Charm the black snake out of the ledges,   75
   And bring back the swarming bees.

All the virtues of herbs and metals,
　All the lore of the woods, he knew,
And the arts of the Old World mingled
　With the marvels of the New.   80

Well he knew the tricks of magic,
　And the lapstone on his knee
Had the gift of the Mormon's goggles
　Or the stone of Doctor Dee.°

For the mighty master Agrippa°   85
　Wrought it with spell and rhyme
From a fragment of mystic moonstone
　In the tower of Nettesheim.

To a cobbler Minnesinger°
　The marvellous stone gave he, —   90
And he gave it, in turn, to Keezar,
　Who brought it over the sea.

He held up that mystic lapstone,
　He held it up like a lens,
And he counted the long years coming   95
　By twenties and by tens.

"One hundred years," quoth Keezar.
　"And fifty have I told:
Now open the new before me,
　And shut me out the old!"   100

Like a cloud of mist, the blackness
　Rolled from the magic stone,

And a marvellous picture mingled
   The unknown and the known.

Still ran the stream to the river,   105
   And river and ocean joined;
And there were the bluffs and the blue sea-line,
   And cold north hills behind.

But the mighty forest was broken
   By many a steepled town,   110
By many a white-walled farm-house,
   And many a garner brown.

Turning a score of mill-wheels,
   The stream no more ran free;
White sails on the winding river,   115
   White sails on the far-off sea.

Below in the noisy village
   The flags were floating gay,
And shone on a thousand faces
   The light of a holiday.   120

Swiftly the rival ploughmen
   Turned the brown earth from their shares;
Here were the farmer's treasures,
   There were the craftsman's wares.

Golden the good-wife's butter,   125
   Ruby her currant-wine;
Grand were the strutting turkeys,
   Fat were the beeves and swine.

P

Yellow and red were the apples,
   And the ripe pears russet-brown,   130
And the peaches had stolen blushes
   From the girls who shook them down.

And with blooms of hill and wildwood,
   That shame the toil of art,
Mingled the gorgeous blossoms   135
   Of the garden's tropic heart.

"What is it I see?" said Keezar:
   "Am I here or am I there?
Is it a fête at Bingen?°
   Do I look on Frankfort° fair?   140

"But where are the clowns and puppets,
   And imps with horns and tail?
And where are the Rhenish flagons?
   And where is the foaming ale?

"Strange things, I know, will happen, —   145
   Strange things the Lord permits;
But that droughty° folk should be jolly
   Puzzles my poor old wits.

"Here are smiling manly faces,
   And the maiden's step is gay;   150
Nor sad by thinking, nor mad by drinking,
   Nor mopes, nor fools, are they.

"Here's pleasure without regretting,
   And good without abuse,

The holiday and the bridal 155
    Of beauty and of use.

"Here's a priest and there is a Quaker, —
    Do the cat and the dog agree?
Have they burned the stocks for oven-wood?
    Have they cut down the gallows-tree? 160

"Would the old folk know their children?
    Would they own the graceless town,
With never a ranter to worry
    And never a witch to drown?"

Loud laughed the cobbler Keezar, 165
    Laughed like a school-boy gay;
Tossing his arms above him,
    The lapstone rolled away.

It rolled down the rugged hillside,
    It spun like a wheel bewitched, 170
It plunged through the leaning willows,
    And into the river pitched.

There, in the deep, dark water,
    The magic stone lies still,
Under the leaning willows 175
    In the shadow of the hill.

But oft the idle fisher
    Sits on the shadowy bank,
And his dreams make marvellous pictures
    Where the wizard's lapstone sank. 180

And still, in the summer twilights,
    When the river seems to run
Out from the inner glory,
    Warm with the melted sun,

The weary mill-girl lingers   185
    Beside the charmèd stream,
And the sky and the golden water
    Shape and color her dream.

Fair wave the sunset gardens,
    The rosy signals fly;   190
Her homestead beckons from the cloud,
    And love goes sailing by!

THE MAYFLOWERS

SAD Mayflower°! watched by winter stars,
    And nursed by winter gales,
With petals of the sleeted spars,
    And leaves of frozen sails!

What had she in those dreary hours,   5
    Within her ice-rimmed bay,
In common with the wild-wood flowers,
    The first sweet smiles of May?

Yet, "God be praised!" the Pilgrim said,
    Who saw the blossoms peer   10
Above the brown leaves, dry and dead,
    "Behold our Mayflower here!"

"God wills it : here our rest shall be,
   Our years of wandering° o'er ;
For us the Mayflower of the sea,   15
   Shall spread her sails no more."

O sacred flowers of faith and hope,
   As sweetly now as then
Ye bloom on many a birchen slope,
   In many a pine-dark glen.   20

Behind the sea-wall's rugged length,
   Unchanged, your leaves unfold,
Like love behind the manly strength
   Of the brave hearts of old.

So live the fathers in their sons,   25
   Their sturdy faith be ours,
And ours the love that overruns
   Its rocky strength with flowers.

The Pilgrim's wild and wintry day
   Its shadow round us draws ;   30
The Mayflower of his stormy bay,
   Our Freedom's struggling cause.

But warmer suns erelong shall bring
   To life the frozen sod ;
And, through dead leaves of hope, shall spring 35
   Afresh the flowers of God !

RALPH WALDO EMERSON

GOOD–BYE°

GOOD-BYE, proud world! I'm going home:
Thou art not my friend, and I'm not thine.
Long through thy weary crowds I roam;
A river-ark on the ocean brine,
Long I've been tossed like the driven foam;   5
But now, proud world! I'm going home.

Good-bye to Flattery's fawning face;
To Grandeur with his wise grimace;
To upstart Wealth's averted eye;
To supple Office, low and high;   10
To crowded halls, to court and street;
To frozen hearts and hasting feet;
To those who go, and those who come;
Good-bye, proud world! I'm going home.

I am going to my own hearth-stone,   15
Bosomed in yon green hills alone, —
A secret nook in a pleasant land,
Whose groves the frolic fairies planned;
Where arches green, the livelong day,
Echo the blackbird's roundelay,   20
And vulgar feet have never trod
A spot that is sacred to thought and God.

O, when I am safe in my sylvan home,
I tread on the pride of Greece and Rome;
And when I am stretched beneath the pines,   25
Where the evening star so holy shines,
I laugh at the lore° and the pride of man,
At the sophist° schools and the learned clan;
For what are they all, in their high conceit,
Where man in the bush with God may meet?   30

EACH AND ALL

LITTLE thinks, in the field, yon red-cloaked clown
Of thee from the hill-top looking down;
The heifer that lows in the upland farm,
Far-heard, lows not thine ear to charm;
The sexton, tolling his bell at noon,   5
Deems not that great Napoleon
Stops his horse, and lists with delight,
Whilst his files sweep round yon Alpine height;
Nor knowest thou what argument
Thy life to thy neighbor's creed has lent.   10
All are needed by each one;
Nothing is fair or good alone.
I thought the sparrow's note from heaven,
Singing at dawn on the alder bough;
I brought him home, in his nest, at even;   15
He sings the song, but it cheers not now,
For I did not bring home the river and sky; —
He sang to my ear, — they sang to my eye.
The delicate shells lay on the shore;

The bubbles of the latest wave   20
Fresh pearls to their enamel gave,
And the bellowing of the savage sea
Greeted their safe escape to me.
I wiped away the weeds and foam,
I fetched my sea-born treasures home;   25
But the poor, unsightly, noisome° things
Had left their beauty on the shore
With the sun and the sand and the wild uproar.
The lover watched his graceful maid,
As 'mid the virgin train she strayed,   30
Nor knew her beauty's best attire
Was woven still by the snow-white choir.
At last she came to his hermitage,
Like the bird from the woodlands to the cage; —
The gay enchantment was undone,   35
A gentle wife, but fairy none.
Then I said, "I covet truth;
Beauty is unripe childhood's cheat;
I leave it behind with the games of youth:" —
As I spoke, beneath my feet   40
The ground-pine curled its pretty wreath,
Running over the club-moss burrs;
I inhaled the violet's breath;
Around me stood the oaks and firs;
Pine-cones and acorns lay on the ground;   45
Over me soared the eternal sky,
Full of light and of deity;
Again I saw, again I heard,
The rolling river, the morning bird; —
Beauty through my senses stole;   50
I yielded myself to the perfect whole.

THE PROBLEM °

I LIKE a church; I like a cowl;
I love a prophet of the soul;
And on my heart monastic aisles
Fall like sweet strains, or pensive smiles;
Yet not for all his faith can see   5
Would I that cowlèd churchman be.

Why should the vest on him allure,
Which I could not on me endure?

Not from a vain or shallow thought
His awful Jove young Phidias brought;   10
Never from lips of cunning fell
The thrilling Delphic oracle;
Out from the heart of nature rolled
The burdens of the Bible old;
The litanies of nations came,   15
Like the volcano's tongue of flame,
Up from the burning core below, —
The canticles° of love and woe:
The hand that rounded Peter's dome°
And groined° the aisles of Christian Rome; 20
Wrought in a sad sincerity;
Himself from God he could not free;
He builded better than he knew; —
The conscious stone to beauty grew.

Know'st thou what wove yon woodbird's nest 25
Of leaves, and feathers from her breast?

Or how the fish outbuilt her shell,
Painting with morn° each annual cell?
Or how the sacred pine-tree adds
To her old leaves new myriads?   30
Such and so grew these holy piles,
Whilst love and terror laid the tiles.
Earth proudly wears the Parthenon,
As the best gem upon her zone,
And Morning opes with haste her lids   35
To gaze upon the Pyramids;
O'er England's abbeys bends the sky,
As on its friends, with kindred eye;
For out of Thought's interior sphere
These wonders rose to upper air°;   40
And Nature gladly gave them place,
Adopted them into her race,
And granted them an equal date
With Andes and with Ararat.°

These temples grew as grows the grass;   45
Art might obey, but not surpass.
The passive Master lent his hand
To the vast soul that o'er him planned;
And the same power that reared the shrine
Bestrode the tribes that knelt within.   50
Ever the fiery Pentecost°
Girds with one flame the countless host,
Trances the heart through chanting choirs,
And through the priest the mind inspires.
The word unto the prophet spoken   55
Was writ on tables yet unbroken;

The word by seers or sibyls told,
In groves of oak, or fanes of gold,
Still floats upon the morning wind,
Still whispers to the willing mind.   60
One accent of the Holy Ghost
The heedless world hath never lost.
I know what say the fathers wise,—
The book itself before me lies,
Old *Chrysostom,*° best Augustine,°   65
And he who blent both in his line,
The younger *Golden Lips* or mines,
Taylor, the Shakspeare of divines.°
His words are music in my ear,
I see his cowlèd portrait dear;   70
And yet, for all his faith could see,
I would not the good bishop be.

THE RHODORA

On Being Asked, Whence is the Flower?

In May, when sea-winds pierced our solitudes,
I found the fresh Rhodora in the woods,
Spreading its leafless blooms in a damp nook,
To please the desert and the sluggish brook,
The purple petals, fallen in the pool,   5
Made the black water with their beauty gay;
Here might the red-bird come his plumes to cool,
And court the flower that cheapens his array.
Rhodora! if the sages ask thee why
This charm is wasted on the earth and sky,   10

Tell them, dear, that if eyes were made for seeing,
Then Beauty is its own excuse for being:
Why thou wert there, O rival of the rose!
I never thought to ask, I never knew:
But, in my simple ignorance, suppose
The self-same Power that brought me there brought you. 15

THE HUMBLE-BEE

Burly, dozing humble-bee,
Where thou art is clime for me.
Let them sail for Porto Rique,
Far-off heats through seas to seek;
I will follow thee alone, 5
Thou animated torrid-zone!°
Zigzag steerer, desert cheerer,
Let me chase thy waving lines;
Keep me nearer, me thy hearer,
Singing over shrubs and vines. 10

Insect lover of the sun,
Joy of thy dominion!
Sailor of the atmosphere;
Swimmer through the waves of air;
Voyager of light and noon; 15
Epicurean° of June;
Wait, I prithee, till I come
Within earshot of thy hum,—
All without is martyrdom.

When the south wind, in May days, 20
With a net of shining haze

Silvers the horizon wall,
And with softness touching all,
Tints the human countenance
With a color of romance,
And infusing subtle heats,
Turns the sod to violets,
Thou, in sunny solitudes,
Rover of the underwoods,
The green silence dost displace
With thy mellow, breezy bass.

Hot midsummer's petted crone,
Sweet to me thy drowsy tone
Tells of countless sunny hours,
Long days, and solid banks of flowers;
Of gulfs of sweetness without bound
In Indian wildernesses found;
Of Syrian peace, immortal leisure,
Firmest cheer, and bird-like pleasure.

Aught unsavory or unclean
Hath my insect never seen;
But violets and bilberry bells,
Maple-sap and daffodels,
Grass with green flag half-mast high,
Succory to match the sky,
Columbine with horn of honey,
Scented fern, and agrimony,
Clover, catchfly, adder's-tongue
And brier-roses, dwelt among;
All beside was unknown waste,
All was picture as he passed.

25

30

35

40

45

50

Wiser far than human seer,
Yellow-breeched philosopher!
Seeing only what is fair,
Sipping only what is sweet,   55
Thou dost mock at fate and care,
Leave the chaff, and take the wheat.
When the fierce northwestern blast,
Cools sea and land so far and fast,
Thou already slumberest deep;   60
Woe and want thou canst outsleep;
Want and woe, which torture us,
Thy sleep makes ridiculous.

THE SNOW-STORM°

ANNOUNCED by all the trumpets of the sky,
Arrives the snow, and, driving o'er the fields,
Seems nowhere to alight: the whited air
Hides hills and woods, the river, and the heaven,
And veils the farm-house at the garden's end.   5
The sled and traveller stopped, the courier's feet
Delayed, all friends shut out, the housemates sit
Around the radiant fireplace, enclosed
In a tumultuous privacy of storm.°

      Come and see the north wind's masonry.   10
Out of an unseen quarry evermore
Furnished with tile, the fierce artificer
Curves his white bastions° with projected roof
Round every windward stake, or tree, or door.
Speeding, the myriad-handed, his wild work   15

So fanciful, so savage, nought cares he
For number or proportion.   Mockingly,
On coop or kennel he hangs Parian wreaths°;
A swan-like form invests the hidden thorn;
Fills up the farmer's lane from wall to wall,   20
Maugre° the farmer's sighs; and at the gate
A tapering turret overtops the work.
And when his hours are numbered, and the world
Is all his own, retiring, as he were not,
Leaves, when the sun appears, astonished Art   25
To mimic in slow structures, stone by stone,
Built in an age, the mad wind's night-work,
The frolic architecture of the snow.

FABLE°

    THE mountain and the squirrel
    Had a quarrel,
And the former called the latter "Little Prig";
    Bun replied,
"You are doubtless very big;   5
But all sorts of things and weather
Must be taken in together,
    To make up a year
    And a sphere.
And I think it no disgrace   10
    To occupy my place.
If I'm not so large as you,
You are not so small as I,
    And not half so spry.
I'll not deny you make   15

A very pretty squirrel track;
Talents differ; all is well and wisely put;
If I cannot carry forests on my back,
Neither can you crack a nut."

FORBEARANCE

Hast thou named all the birds without a gun?
Loved the wood-rose, and left it on its stalk?
At rich men's tables eaten bread and pulse?
Unarmed, faced danger with a heart of trust?
And loved so well a high behavior,   5
In man or maid, that thou from speech refrained,
Nobility more nobly to repay?
O, be my friend, and teach me to be thine!

CONCORD HYMN°

Sung at the Completion of the Battle Monument, April 19, 1836

By the rude bridge that arched the flood,
   Their flag to April's breeze unfurled,
Here once the embattled farmers stood
   And fired the shot heard round the world.

The foe long since in silence slept;   5
   Alike the conqueror silent sleeps;
And Time the ruined bridge has swept
   Down the dark stream which seaward creeps.

On this green bank, by this soft stream,
   We set to-day a votive stone;   10
That memory may. their deed redeem,
   When, like our sires, our sons are gone.

Spirit, that made those heroes dare
   To die, and leave their children free,
Bid Time and Nature gently spare   15
   The shaft we raise to them and thee.

BOSTON HYMN

The word of the Lord by night
To the watching Pilgrims came,
As they sat beside the seaside,
And filled their hearts with flame.

God said, I am tired of kings,   5
I suffer them no more;
Up to my ear the morning brings
The outrage of the poor.

Think ye I made this ball
A field of havoc and war,   10
Where tyrants great and tyrants small
Might harry the weak and poor?

My angel,—his name is Freedom,—
Choose him to be your king;
He shall cut pathways east and west   15
And fend° you with his wing.

Q

Lo! I uncover the land
Which I hid of old time in the West,
As the sculptor uncovers the statue
When he has wrought his best;   20

I show Columbia, of the rocks
Which dip their foot in the seas
And soar to the air-borne flocks
Of clouds and the boreal° fleece.

I will divide my goods;   25
Call in the wretch and slave:
None shall rule but the humble,
And none but Toil shall have.

I will have never a noble,
No lineage counted great;   30
Fishers and choppers and ploughmen
Shall constitute a state.

Go, cut down trees in the forest
And trim the straightest boughs;
Cut down trees in the forest   35
And build me a wooden house.

Call the people together,
The young men and the sires,
The digger in the harvest-field,
Hireling and him that hires;   40

And here in a pine state-house
They shall choose men to rule

In every needful faculty,
In church and state and school.

Lo, now! if these poor men   45
Can govern the land and the sea
And make just laws below the sun,
As planets faithful be.

And ye shall succor men;
'Tis nobleness to serve;   50
Help them who cannot help again:
Beware from right to swerve.

I break your bonds and masterships,
And I unchain the slave:
Free be his heart and hand henceforth   55
As wind and wandering wave.

I cause from every creature
His proper good to flow:
As much as he is and doeth,
So much he shall bestow.   60

But, laying hands on another
To coin his labor and sweat,
He goes in pawn to his victim
For eternal years in debt.

To-day unbind the captive,   65
So only are ye unbound;
Lift up a people from the dust,
Trump of their rescue, sound!

Pay ransom to the owner
And fill the bag to the brim.   70
Who is the owner?   The slave is owner,
And ever was.   Pay him.

O North! give him beauty for rags,
And honor, O South! for his shame;
Nevada! coin thy golden crags   75
With Freedom's image and name.

Up! and the dusky race
That sat in darkness long,—
Be swift their feet as antelopes,
And as behemoth° strong.   80

Come, East and West and North,
By races, as snow-flakes,
And carry my purpose forth,
Which neither halts nor shakes.

My will fulfilled shall be,   85
For, in daylight or in dark,
My thunderbolt has eyes to see
His way home to the mark.

THE TITMOUSE

You shall not be overbold
When you deal with arctic cold,
As late I found my lukewarm blood
Chilled wading in the snow-choked wood.

How should I fight? my foeman fine   5
Has million arms to one of mine:
East, west, for aid I looked in vain,
East, west, north, south, are his domain.
Miles off, three dangerous miles, is home;
Must borrow his winds who there would come. 10
Up and away for life! be fleet!—
The frost-king ties my fumbling feet,
Sings in my ears, my hands are stones,
Curdles the blood to the marble bones,
Tugs at the heart-strings, numbs the sense,   15
And hems in life with narrowing fence.
Well, in this broad bed lie and sleep,—
The punctual stars will vigil keep,—
Embalmed by purifying cold;
The winds shall sing their dead-march old,   20
The snow is no ignoble shroud,
The moon thy mourner, and the cloud.

     Softly—but this way fate was pointing,
'Twas coming fast to such anointing,
When piped a tiny voice hard by,   25
Gay and polite, a cheerful cry,
Chic-chic-a-dee-dee! saucy note
Out of sound heart and merry throat,
As if it said, "Good day, good sir!
Fine afternoon, old passenger!   30
Happy to meet you in these places,
Where January brings few faces."

     This poet, though he lived apart,
Moved by his hospitable heart,

Sped, when I passed his sylvan fort,   35
To do the honors of his court,
As fits a feathered lord of land;
Flew near, with soft wing grazed my hand,
Hopped on the bough, then, darting low,
Prints his small impress on the snow,   40
Shows feats of his gymnastic play,
Head downward, clinging to the spray.

    Here was this atom in full breath,
Hurling defiance at vast death;
This scrap of valor just for play   45
Fronts the north-wind in waistcoat gray,
As if to shame my weak behavior;
I greeted loud my little savior,
"You pet! what dost here? and what for?
In these woods, thy small Labrador,   50
At this pinch, wee San Salvador!
What fire burns in that little chest
So frolic, stout and self-possest?
Henceforth I wear no stripe but thine;
Ashes and jet all hues outshine.   55
Why are not diamonds black and gray,
To ape thy dare-devil array?
And I affirm, the spacious North
Exists to draw thy virtue forth.
I think no virtue goes with size;   60
The reason of all cowardice
Is, that men are overgrown,
And, to be valiant, must come down
To the titmouse dimension."

'Tis good will makes intelligence,   65
And I began to catch the sense
Of my bird's song : "Live out of doors
In the great woods, on prairie floors.
I dine in the sun; when he sinks in the sea,
I too have a hole in a hollow tree;   70
And I like less when Summer beats
With stifling beams on these retreats,
Than noontide twilights which snow makes
With tempest of the blinding flakes.
For well the soul, if stout within,   75
Can arm impregnably° the skin;
And polar frost my frame defied,
Made of the air that blows outside."

With glad remembrance of my debt,
I homeward turn; farewell, my pet!   80
When here again thy pilgrim comes,
He shall bring store of seeds and crumbs.
Doubt not, so long as earth has bread,
Thou first and foremost shalt be fed;
The Providence that is most large   85
Takes hearts like thine in special charge,
Helps who for their own need are strong,
And the sky dotes on cheerful song.
Henceforth I prize thy wiry chant
O'er all that mass and minster vaunt;   90
For men mis-hear thy call in Spring,
As 'twould accost some frivolous wing,
Crying out of the hazel copse, *Phe-be!*
And, in winter, *Chic-a-dee-dee!*
I think old Caesar must have heard   95

In northern Gaul my dauntless bird,
And, echoed in some frosty wold,°
Borrowed thy battle-numbers bold.
And I will write our annals new,
And thank thee for a better clew,
I, who dreamed not when I came here
To find the antidote of fear,
Now hear thee say in Roman key,
Pœan!   Veni, vidi, vici.

100

JAMES RUSSELL LOWELL

HAKON'S LAY°

Then Thorstein looked at Hakon, where he sate,
Mute as a cloud amid the stormy hall,
And said: "O Skald,° sing now an olden song,
Such as our fathers heard who led great lives;
And, as the bravest on a shield is borne   5
Along the waving host that shouts him king,
So rode their thrones upon the thronging seas!"

Then the old man arose; white-haired he stood,
White-bearded, and with eyes that looked afar
From their still region of perpetual snow,°   10
Over the little smokes and stirs of men:
His head was bowed with gathered flakes of years,
As winter bends the sea-foreboding pine,
But something triumphed in his brow and eye,
Which whoso saw it, could not see and crouch: 15
Loud rang the emptied beakers as he mused,
Brooding his eyried° thoughts; then, as an eagle
Circles smooth-winged above the wind-vexed woods,
So wheeled his soul into the air of song
High o'er the stormy hall; and thus he sang°:   20

"The fletcher° for his arrow-shaft picks out
Wood closest-grained, long-seasoned, straight as light;

233

And, from a quiver full of such as these,
The wary bow-man, matched against his peers,.
Long doubting, singles yet once more the best.   25
Who is it that can make such shafts as Fate?
What archer of his arrows is so choice,
Or hits the white so surely?   They are men,
The chosen of her quiver; nor for her
Will every reed suffice, or cross-grained stick   30
At random from life's vulgar fagot plucked°:
Such answer household ends; but she will have
Souls straight and clear, of toughest fibre, sound
Down to the heart of heart; from these she strips
All needless stuff, all sapwood°; hardens them;   35
From circumstance untoward feathers plucks
Crumpled and cheap°; and barbs with iron will:
The hour that passes is her quiver-boy;
When she draws bow, 'tis not across the wind,
Nor 'gainst the sun,° her haste-snatched arrow sings,   40
For sun and wind have plighted faith to her:
Ere men have heard the sinew twang, behold,
In the butt's° heart her trembling messenger!

"The song is old and simple that I sing;
Good were the days of yore, when men were tried   45
By ring of shields, as now by ring of gold;
But, while the gods are left, and hearts of men,
And the free ocean, still the days are good;
Through the broad Earth roams Opportunity
And knocks at every door of hut or hall,   50
Until she finds the brave soul that she wants."

He ceased, and instantly the frothy° tide
Of interrupted wassail roared along;
But Leif, the son of Eric,° sat apart
Musing, and, with his eyes upon the fire,   55
Saw shapes of arrows, lost as soon as seen;
But then with that resolve his heart was bent,
Which, like a humming shaft, through many a stripe
Of day and night across the unventured seas,
Shot the brave prow to cut on Vinland sands   60
The first rune in the Saga of the West.°

FLOWERS°

(Selection)

O POET! above all men blest,
Take heed that thus thou store them;
Love, Hope, and Faith shall ever rest,
Sweet birds (upon how sweet a nest!)
Watchfully brooding o'er them.   5
And from those flowers of Paradise
Scatter thou many a blessèd seed,
Wherefrom an offspring may arise
To cheer the hearts and light the eyes
Of after-voyagers in their need.   10
They shall not fall on stony ground,
But, yielding all their hundred-fold,°
Shall shed a peacefulness around,
Whose strengthening joy may not be told!
So shall thy name be blest of all,   15
And thy remembrance never die;

For of that seed shall surely fall
In the fair garden of Eternity.°
Exult then in the nobleness
Of this thy work so holy,   20
Yet be not thou one jot the less
Humble and meek and lowly,
But let thine exultation be
The reverence of a bended knee;
And by thy life a poem write,   25
Built strongly day by day —
And on the rock of Truth and Right
Its deep foundations lay.

IMPARTIALITY

I

I CANNOT say a scene is fair
Because it is beloved of thee,
But I shall love to linger there,
For sake of thy dear memory;
I would not be so coldly just   5
As to love only what I must.

II

I cannot say a thought is good
Because thou foundest joy in it;
Each soul must choose its proper food
Which Nature hath decreed most fit;   10
But I shall ever deem it so
Because it made thy heart o'erflow.

III

I love thee for that thou art fair;
And that thy spirit joys in aught
Createth a new beauty there,   15
With thine own dearest image fraught;
And love, for others' sake that springs,
Gives half their charm to lovely things.

MY LOVE

I

Not as all other women are
Is she that to my soul is dear;
Her glorious fancies come from far,
Beneath the silver evening-star,
And yet her heart is ever near.   5

II

Great feelings has she of her own,
Which lesser souls may never know;
God giveth them to her alone,
And sweet they are as any tone
Wherewith the wind may choose to blow.   10

III

Yet in herself she dwelleth not,
Although no home were half so fair;
No simplest duty is forgot,
Life hath no dim and lowly spot
That doth not in her sunshine share.   15

IV

She doeth little kindnesses,
Which most leave undone, or despise;
For naught that sets one heart at ease,
And giveth happiness or peace,
Is low-esteemèd in her eyes.   20

V

She hath no scorn of common things,
And, though she seem of other birth,
Round us her heart entwines and clings,
And patiently she folds her wings
To tread the humble paths of earth.   25

VI

Blessing she is: God made her so,
And deeds of week-day holiness
Fall from her noiseless as the snow,
Nor hath she ever chanced to know
That aught were easier than to bless.   30

VII

She is most fair, and thereunto
Her life doth rightly harmonize;
Feeling or thought that was not true
Ne'er made less beautiful the blue
Unclouded heaven of her eyes.   35

VIII

She is a woman: one in whom
The spring-time of her childish years

Hath never lost its fresh perfume,
Though knowing well that life hath room
For many blights and many tears.   40

IX

I love her with a love as still
As a broad river's peaceful might,
Which, by high tower and lowly mill,
Goes wandering at its own will,
And yet doth ever flow aright.   45

X

And, on its full, deep breast serene,
Like quiet isles my duties lie;
It flows around them and between,
And makes them fresh and fair and green,
Sweet homes wherein to live and die.   50

THE FOUNTAIN

INTO the sunshine,
   Full of the light,
Leaping and flashing
   From morn till night!

Into the moonlight,   5
   Whiter than snow,
Waving so flower-like
   When the winds blow!

Into the starlight,
   Rushing in spray,   10
Happy at midnight,
   Happy by day!

Ever in motion,
   Blithesome and cheery.
Still climbing heavenward,   15
   Never aweary —

Glad of all weathers,
   Still seeming best,
Upward or downward,
   Motion thy rest; —   20

Full of a nature
   Nothing can tame,
Changed every moment,
   Ever the same; —

Ceaseless aspiring,   25
   Ceaseless content,
Darkness or sunshine
   Thy element; —

Glorious fountain!
   Let my heart be   30
Fresh, changeful, constant,
   Upward, like thee!

THE SHEPHERD OF KING ADMETUS

THERE came a youth upon the earth,
   Some thousand years ago,
Whose slender hands were nothing worth,
Whether to plow, to reap, or sow.

Upon an empty tortoise-shell   5
   He stretched some chords, and drew
Music that made men's bosoms swell
Fearless, or brimmed their eyes with dew.

Then King Admetus, one who had
   Pure taste by right divine,   10
Decreed his singing not too bad
To hear between the cups of wine:

And so, well-pleased with being soothed
   Into a sweet half-sleep,
Three times his kingly beard he smoothed,   15
And made him viceroy° o'er his sheep.

His words were simple words enough,
   And yet he used them so,
That what in other mouths was rough
In his seemed musical and low.   20

Men called him but a shiftless youth,
   In whom no good they saw;
And yet, unwittingly, in truth,
They made his careless words their law.

R

They knew not how he learned at all,   25
    For idly, hour by hour,
He sat and watched the dead leaves fall,
Or mused upon a common flower.

It seemed the loveliness of things
    Did teach him all their use,   30
For, in mere weeds, and stones, and springs,
He found a healing power profuse.

Men granted that his speech was wise,
    But, when a glance they caught
Of his slim grace and woman's eyes,   35
They laughed, and called him good-for-naught.

Yet after he was dead and gone,
    And e'en his memory dim,
Earth seemed more sweet to live upon,
More full of love, because of him.   40

And day by day more holy grew
    Each spot where he had trod,
Till after-poets only knew
Their first-born brother as a god.°

ODE RECITED AT THE HARVARD COMMEMORATION
July 21, 1865

(Selection)

I

WEAK-WINGED is song,
Nor aims at that clear-ethered height
Whither the brave deed climbs for light:
    We seem to do them wrong,
Bringing our robin's-leaf to deck their hearse   5
Who in warm life-blood wrote their nobler verse,
Our trivial song to honor those who come
With ears attuned to strenuous trump and drum,
And shaped in squadron-strophes their desire,°
Live battle-odes whose lines were steel and fire: 10
    Yet sometimes feathered words are strong,
A gracious memory to buoy up and save
From Lethe's dreamless ooze, the common grave
    Of the unventurous throng.

*   *   *   *   *   *   *

III

Many loved Truth, and lavished Life's best oil   15
    Amid the dust of books to find her,
Content at last, for guerdon° of their toil,
    With the cast mantle she hath left behind her.
      Many in sad faith sought for her,
      Many with crossed hands sighed for her;   20
      But these, our brothers, fought for her;

At life's dear peril wrought for her,
So loved her that they died for her,
Tasting the raptured fleetness
Of her divine completeness :   25
Their higher instinct knew
Those love her best who to themselves are true,
And what they dare to dream of, dare to do ;
They followed her and found her
Where all may hope to find,   30
Not in the ashes of the burnt-out mind,
But beautiful, with danger's sweetness round her.
Where faith made whole with deed
Breathes its awakening breath
Into the lifeless creed,°   35
They saw her plumed and mailed,
With sweet, stern face unveiled,
And all-repaying eyes, look proud on them in death.

IV

Our slender life runs rippling by, and glides
Into the silent hollow of the past ;
What is there that abides   40
To make the next age better for the last?
Is earth too poor to give us
Something to live for here that shall outlive us?
Some more substantial boon   45
Than such as flows and ebbs with Fortune's fickle moon?
The little that we see
From doubt is never free ;
The little that we do
Is but half-nobly true ;   50
With our laborious hiving

What men call treasure, and the gods call dross,
   Life seems a jest of Fate's contriving,
   Only secure in every one's conniving,
A long account of nothings paid with loss,   55
Where we poor puppets, jerked by unseen wires,
   After our little hour of strut and rave,
With all our pasteboard passions and desires,
Loves, hates, ambitions, and immortal fires,
   Are tossed pell-mell together in the grave.°   60
But stay! no age was e'er degenerate,
   Unless men held it at too cheap a rate,
   For in our likeness still we shape our fate.

   *   *   *   *   *   *   *

V

   Whither leads the path
   To ampler fates that leads?   65
   Not down through flowery meads,
   To reap an aftermath°
Of youth's vainglorious weeds,
   But up the steep, amid the wrath
   And shock of deadly-hostile creeds,   70
   Where the world's best hope and stay
By battle's flashes gropes a desperate way,
And every turf the fierce foot clings to bleeds.
   Peace hath her not ignoble wreath,
   Ere yet the sharp, decisive word   75
Light the black lips of cannon, and the sword
   Dreams in its easeful sheath;
But some day the live coal behind the thought,
   Whether from Baal's° stone obscene,

Or from the shrine serene   30
Of God's pure altar brought,
Bursts up in flame; the war of tongue and pen
Learns with what deadly purpose it was fraught,
And, helpless in the fiery passion caught,
Shakes all the pillared state with shock of men :   85
Some day the soft Ideal that we wooed
Confronts us fiercely, foe-beset, pursued,
And cries reproachful : "Was it, then, my praise,
And not myself was loved?   Prove now thy truth;
I claim of thee the promise of thy youth;   90
Give me thy life, or cower in empty phrase,
The victim of thy genius, not its mate!"
    Life may be given in many ways,
    And loyalty to Truth be sealed
As bravely in the closet as the field,   95
        So bountiful is Fate;
        But then to stand beside her,
        When craven churls deride her,
To front a lie in arms and not to yield,
        This shows, methinks, God's plan   100
        And measure of a stalwart man,
        Limbed like the old heroic breeds,
        Who stands self-poised on manhood's solid earth,
    Not forced to frame excuses for his birth,
Fed from within with all the strength he needs.°   105

VI

Such was he, our Martyr-Chief,
    Whom late the Nation he had led,
    With ashes on her head,
Wept with the passion of an angry grief:

Forgive me, if from present things I turn   110
To speak what in my heart will beat and burn,
And hang my wreath on his world-honored urn.
    Nature, they say, doth dote,°
  And cannot make a man
    Save on some worn-out plan,   115
      Repeating us by rote:
For him her Old-World moulds aside she threw,
  And, choosing sweet clay from the breast
    Of the unexhausted West,
With stuff untainted shaped a hero new,   120
Wise, steadfast in the strength of God, and true.
    How beautiful to see
  Once more a shepherd of mankind indeed,
  Who loved his charge, but never loved to lead;
One whose meek flock the people joyed to be,   125
    Not lured by any cheat of birth,
    But by his clear-grained human worth,
And brave old wisdom of sincerity!
    They knew that outward grace is dust;
    They could not choose but trust   130
In that sure-footed mind's unfaltering skill,
    And supple-tempered will
That bent like perfect steel to spring again and thrust.
    His was no lonely mountain-peak of mind,
    Thrusting to thin air o'er our cloudy bars,   135
    A sea-mark now, now lost in vapors blind;
  Broad prairie rather, genial, level-lined,
  Fruitful and friendly for all human kind,
Yet also nigh to heaven and loved of loftiest stars.
    Nothing of Europe here,   140
Or, then, of Europe fronting mornward still,

Ere any names of Serf and Peer
Could Nature's equal scheme deface
And thwart her genial will;
Here was a type of the true elder race,   145
And one of Plutarch's men° talked with us face to face.
I praise him not; it were too late;
And some innative° weakness there must be
In him who condescends to victory
Such as the Present gives, and cannot wait,   150
Safe in himself as in a fate.
So always firmly he:
He knew to bide his time,
And can his fame abide,
Still patient in his simple faith sublime,   155
Till the wise years decide.
Great captains, with their guns and drums,
Disturb our judgment for the hour,
But at last silence comes;
These all are gone, and, standing like a tower,   160
Our children shall behold his fame,
The kindly-earnest, brave, foreseeing man,
Sagacious, patient, dreading praise, not blame,
New birth of our new soil, the first American.

*   *   *   *   *   *   *

THE VISION OF SIR LAUNFAL

Prelude to Part First

Over his keys the musing organist,
    Beginning doubtfully and far away,
First lets his fingers wander as they list,
    And builds a bridge from Dreamland for his lay:
Then, as the touch of his loved instrument   5
    Gives hope and fervor, nearer draws his theme,
First guessed by faint auroral° flushes sent
    Along the wavering vista of his dream.

Not only around our infancy
    Doth heaven with all its splendors lie;   10
Daily, with souls that cringe and plot,
    We Sinais° climb and know it not.

Over our manhood bend the skies;
    Against our fallen and traitor lives
The great winds utter prophecies;   15
    With our faint hearts the mountain strives;
Its arms outstretched, the druid wood
    Waits with its benedicite;
And to our age's drowsy blood
    Still shouts the inspiring sea.°   20

Earth gets its price for what Earth gives us;
    The beggar is taxed for a corner to die in,
The priest hath his fee who comes and shrives us,
    We bargain for the graves we lie in;

At the devil's booth are all things sold,   25
Each ounce of dross costs its ounce of gold;
  For a cap and bells our lives we pay,
  Bubbles° we buy with a whole soul's tasking:
    'Tis heaven alone that is given away,
    'Tis only God may be had for the asking;   30
No price is set on the lavish summer;
June may be had by the poorest comer.°

And what is so rare as a day in June?
  Then, if ever, come perfect days;
Then Heaven tries the earth if it be in tune,   35
  And over it softly her warm ear lays:
Whether we look, or whether we listen,
We hear life murmur, or see it glisten;
Every clod feels a stir of might,
  An instinct within it that reaches and towers,   40
And, groping blindly above it for light,
  Climbs to a soul in grass and flowers;
The flush of life may well be seen
  Thrilling back over hills and valleys;
The cowslip startles in meadows green,   45
  The buttercup catches the sun in its chalice,
And there's never a leaf nor a blade too mean
  To be some happy creature's palace;
The little bird sits at his door in the sun,
  Atilt like a blossom among the leaves,   50
And lets his illumined being o'errun
  With the deluge of summer it receives;
His mate feels the eggs beneath her wings,
And the heart in her dumb breast flutters and sings;

He sings to the wide world, and she to her nest, — 55
In the nice ear of Nature which song is the best?

Now is the high-tide of the year,
   And whatever of life hath ebbed away
Comes flooding back with a ripply cheer,
   Into every bare inlet and creek and bay; 60
Now the heart is so full that a drop overfills it,
We are happy now because God wills it;
No matter how barren the past may have been,
'Tis enough for us now that the leaves are green;
We sit in the warm shade and feel right well 65
How the sap creeps up and the blossoms swell;
We may shut our eyes but we cannot help knowing
That skies are clear and grass is growing;
The breeze comes whispering in our ear,
That dandelions are blossoming near, 70
   That maize has sprouted, that streams are flowing,
That the river is bluer than the sky,
That the robin is plastering his house hard by;
And if the breeze kept the good news back,
For other couriers we should not lack; 75
   We could guess it all by yon heifer's lowing, —
And hark! how clear bold chanticleer,
Warmed with the new wine of the year,
   Tells all in his lusty crowing!°

Joy comes, grief goes, we know not how; 80
Everything is happy now,
   Everything is upward striving;
'Tis as easy now for the heart to be true

As for grass to be green or skies to be blue, —
  'Tis the natural way of living: 85
Who knows whither the clouds have fled?
  In the unscarred heaven they leave no wake;
And the eyes forget the tears they have shed,
  The heart forgets its sorrow and ache;
The soul partakes the season's youth,   90
  And the sulphurous° rifts of passion and woe
Lie deep 'neath a silence pure and smooth,
  Like burnt-out craters healed with snow.
What wonder if Sir Launfal now
Remembered the keeping of his vow?"   95

BIGLOW PAPERS

I. What Mr. Robinson Thinks

Guvener B.° is a sensible man;
  He stays to his home an' looks arter his folks;
He draws his furrer ez straight ez he can,
  An' into nobody's tater-patch pokes; —
      But John P.   5
      Robinson° he
  Sez he wunt vote fer Guvener B.

My! aint it terrible? Wut shall we du?
  We can't never choose him o' course, — thet's flat;
Guess we shall hev to come round, (don't you?)   10
  An' go in fer thunder an' guns, an' all that;
      Fer John P.
      Robinson he
  Sez he wunt vote fer Guvener B.

Gineral C.° is a dreffle smart man: 15
  He's ben on all sides thet give places or pelf°;
But consistency still wuz a part of his plan, —
  He's been true to *one* party — an' thet is himself; —
      So John P.
      Robinson he 20
  Sez he shall vote fer Gineral C.

Gineral C. he goes in fer the war;
  He don't vally° principle more 'n an old cud;
Wut did God make us raytional creeturs fer,
  But glory an' gunpowder, plunder an' blood? 25
      So John P.
      Robinson he
  Sez he shall vote fer Gineral C.

We were gittin' on nicely up here to our village,
  With good old idees o' wut's right an' wut aint, 30
We kind o' thought Christ went agin war an' pillage,
  An' thet eppyletts° worn't the best mark of a saint,
      But John P.
      Robinson he
  Sez this kind o' thing's an exploded idee. 35

The side of our country must ollers be took,
  An' Presidunt Polk, you know, *he* is our country.
An' the angel thet writes all our sins in a book
  Puts the *debit* to him, an' to us the *per contry*°;
      An' John P. 40
      Robinson he
  Sez this is his view o' the thing to a T.

Parson Wilbur he calls all these argimunts lies;
  Sez they're nothin' on airth but jest *fee, faw, fum:*
An' thet all this big talk of our destinies
  Is half on it ign'ance, an' t' other half rum,   45
      But John P.
      Robinson he
Sez it aint no sech thing; an', of course, so must we.

Parson Wilbur sez *he* never heerd in his life   50
  Thet th' Apostles rigged out in their swaller-tail coats,
An' marched round in front of a drum an' a fife,
  To git some on 'em office, an' some on 'em votes,
      But John P.
      Robinson he
Sez they didn't know everthin' down in Judee.   55

Wal, it's a marcy we've gut folks to tell us
  The rights an' the wrongs o' these matters, I vow, —
God sends country lawyers, an' other wise fellers,
  To start the world's team wen it gits in a slough;   60
      Fer John P.
      Robinson he
Sez the world 'll go right, ef he hollers out Gee!

II. THE COURTIN'

GOD makes sech nights, all white an' still
  Fur 'z you can look or listen,
Moonshine an' snow on field an' hill,
  All silence an' all glisten.

Zekle crep' up quite unbeknown   5
  An' peeked in thru' the winder,
An' there sot Huldy all alone,
  'Ith no one nigh to hender.

A fireplace filled the room's one side
  With half a cord o' wood in —   10
There warn't no stoves (tell comfort died)
  To bake ye to a puddin'.

The wa'nut logs shot sparkles out
  Towards the pootiest, bless her,
An' leetle flames danced all about   15
  The chiny on the dresser.

Agin the chimbley crook-necks° hung,
  An' in amongst 'em rusted
The ole queen's arm° thet gran'ther Young
  Fetched back from Concord busted.   20

The very room, coz she was in,
  Seemed warm from floor to ceilin',
An' she looked full ez rosy agin
  Ez the apples she was peelin'.

'Twas kin' o' kingdom-come to look   25
  On sech a blessed cretur,
A dogrose blushin' to a brook
  Ain't modester nor sweeter.

He was six foot o' man, A 1,
  Clean grit an' human natur';   30

None couldn't quicker pitch a ton
    Nor dror a furrer straighter.

He'd sparked it with full twenty gals,
    He'd squired 'em, danced 'em, druv 'em,°
Fust this one, an' then thet, by spells —   35
    All is, he couldn't love 'em.

But long o' her his veins 'ould run
    All crinkly like curled maple,
The side she breshed felt full o' sun
    Ez a south slope in Ap'il.   40

She thought no v'ice hed sech a swing
    Ez hisn in the choir;
My! when he made Ole Hunderd ring,
    She *knowed* the Lord was nigher.

An' she'd blush scarlit, right in prayer,   45
    When her new meetin'-bunnet
Felt somehow thru' its crown a pair
    O' blue eyes sot upun it.

Thet night, I tell ye, she looked *some!*
    She seemed to 've gut a new soul,   50
For she felt sartin-sure he'd come,
    Down to her very shoe-sole.

She heered a foot, an' knowed it tu,
    A-raspin' on the scraper, —
All ways to once her feelin's flew   55
    Like sparks in burnt-up paper.

He kin' o' l'itered on the mat,
  Some doubtfle o' the sekle,°
His heart kep' goin' pity-pat,
  But hern went pity Zekle.   60

An' yit she gin her cheer a jerk
  Ez though she wished him furder,
An' on her apples kep' to work,
  Parin' away like murder.

"You want to see my Pa, I s'pose?"   65
  "Wal . . . no . . . I come dasignin'" —
"To see my Ma? She's sprinklin' clo'es
  Agin to-morrer's i'nin'."

To say why gals acts so or so,
  Or don't, 'ould be presumin';   70
Mebby to mean *yes* an' say *no*
  Comes nateral to women.

He stood a spell on one foot fust,
  Then stood a spell on t'other,
An' on which one he felt the wust   75
  He couldn't ha' told ye nuther.

Says he, "I'd better call agin;"
  Says she, "Think likely, Mister;"
Thet last word pricked him like a pin,
  An' . . . Wal, he up an' kist her.   80

When Ma bimeby upon 'em slips,
  Huldy sot pale ez ashes,

S

All kin' o' smily roun' the lips
   An' teary roun' the lashes.

For she was jes' the quiet kind   85
   Whose naturs never vary,
Like streams that keep a summer mind
   Snowhid in Jenooary.

The blood clost roun' her heart felt glued
   Too tight for all expressin',   90
Tell mother see how metters stood,
   And gin 'em both her blessin'.

Then her red come back like the tide
   Down to the Bay o' Fundy,°
An' all I know is they was cried   95
   In meetin' come nex' Sunday.

III. SUNTHIN' IN THE PASTORAL LINE

ONCE git a smell o' musk into a draw,
An' it clings hold like precerdents° in law:
Your gra'ma'am put it there, — when, goodness knows, —
To jes' this-worldify° her Sunday-clo'es;
But the old chist wun't sarve her gran'son's wife,   5
(For, 'thout new funnitoor, wut good in life?)
An' so ole clawfoot,° from the precinks dread
O' the spare chamber, slinks into the shed,
Where, dim with dust, it fust or last subsides
To holdin' seeds an' fifty things besides;   10
But better days stick fast in heart an' husk,
An' all you keep in't gits a scent o' musk.

Jes' so with poets: wut they've airly read
Gits kind o' worked into their heart an' head,
So 's 't they can't seem to write but jest on sheers   15
With furrin countries or played-out ideers,
Nor hev a feelin', ef it doosn't smack
O' wut some critter chose to feel 'way back:
This makes 'em talk o' daisies, larks, an' things,
Ez though we'd nothin' here that blows an' sings, —   20
(Why, I'd give more for one live bobolink
Than a square mile o' larks in printer's ink,) —
This makes 'em think our fust o' May is May,
Which 't ain't, for all the almanicks can say.
O little city-gals, don't never go it   25
Blind on the word o' noospaper or poet!
They're apt to puff, an' May-day seldom looks
Up in the country ez it doos in books;
They're no more like than hornets'-nests an' hives,
Or printed sarmons be to holy lives.   30
I, with my trouses perched on cow-hide boots,
Tuggin' my foundered feet out by the roots,
Hev seen ye come to fling on April's hearse
Your muslin nosegays from the milliner's,
Puzzlin' to find dry ground your queen to choose,   35
An' dance your throats sore in morocker shoes:
I've seen ye an' felt proud, thet, come wut would,
Our Pilgrim stock wuz pithed with hardihood.°
Pleasure doos make us Yankees kind o' winch,
Ez though 'twuz sunthin' paid for by the inch;   40
But yit we du contrive to worry thru,
Ef Dooty tells us thet the thing's to du,
An' kerry a hollerday, ef we set out,
Ez stiddily ez though 'twuz a redoubt.

I, country-born an' bred, know where to find   45
Some blooms thet make the season suit the mind,
An' seem to metch the doubtin' bluebird's notes, —
Half-vent'rin' liverworts in furry coats,
Bloodroots, whose rolled-up leaves ef you oncurl,
Each on 'em 's cradle to a baby-pearl,° —   50
But these are jes' Spring's pickets; sure ez sin,
The rebble frosts'll try to drive 'em in;
For half our May's so awfully like Mayn't,
'Twould rile a Shaker or an evrige saint;
Though I own up I like our back'ard springs   55
Thet kind o' haggle° with their greens an' things,
An' when you 'most give up, 'ithout more words
Toss the fields full o' blossoms, leaves, an' birds:
Thet's Northun natur', slow an' apt to doubt,
But when it *doos* git stirred, ther' 's no gin-out!   60

Fust come the blackbirds clatt'rin' in tall trees,
An' settlin' things in windy Congresses, —
Queer politicians, though, for I'll be skinned
Ef all on 'em don't head against the wind.
'Fore long the trees begin to show belief, —   65
The maple crimsons to a coral-reef,
Then saffern swarms swing off from all the willers
So plump they look like yaller caterpillars,
Then gray hossches'nuts leetle hands unfold
Softer'n a baby's be at three days old: 70
Thet's robin-redbreast's almanick; he knows
Thet arter this ther' 's only blossom-snows;
So, choosin' out a handy crotch an' spouse,
He goes to plast'rin' his adobe house.

Then seems to come a hitch, — things lag behind,   75
Till some fine mornin' Spring makes up her mind,
An' ez, when snow-swelled rivers cresh their dams
Heaped-up with ice thet dovetails in an' jams,
A leak comes spirtin' thru some pin-hole cleft,
Grows stronger, fercer, tears out right an' left,   80
Then all the waters bow themselves an' come,
Suddin, in one gret slope o' shedderin' foam,
Jes' so our Spring gits everythin' in tune
An' gives one leap from April into June :
Then all comes crowdin' in ; afore you think,   85
Young oak-leaves mist the side-hill woods with pink ;
The catbird in the laylock-bush is loud ;
The orchards turn to heaps o' rosy cloud ;
Red-cedars blossom tu, though few folks know it,
An' look all dipt in sunshine like a poet ;   90
The lime-trees pile their solid stacks o' shade
An' drows'ly simmer with the bees' sweet trade ;
In ellum-shrouds the flashin' hangbird clings
An' for the summer vy'ge his hammock slings ;
All down the loose-walled lanes in archin' bowers   95
The barb'ry droops its strings o' golden flowers,
Whose shrinkin' hearts the school-gals love to try
With pins, — they'll worry yourn so, boys, bimeby !
But I don't love your cat'logue style, — do you ? —
Ez ef to sell off Natur' by vendoo° ;   100
One word with blood in 't 's twice ez good ez two :
'Nuff sed, June's bridesman, poet o' the year,
Gladness on wings, the bobolink, is here ;
Half-hid in tip-top apple-blooms he swings,
Or climbs aginst the breeze with quiverin' wings,   105
Or, givin' way to't in a mock despair,

Runs down, a brook o' laughter, thru the air.
I ollus feels the sap start in my veins
In Spring, with curus heats an' prickly pains,
Thet drive me, when I git a chance, to walk   116
Off by myself to hev a privit talk
With a queer critter thet can't seem to 'gree
Along o' me like most folks, — Mister Me.
Ther' 's times when I'm unsoshle ez a stone,
An' sort o' suffocate to be alone, —   115
I'm crowded jes' to think thet folks are nigh,
An' can't bear nothin' closer than the sky°;
Now the wind's full ez shifty in the mind
Ez wut it is ou'-doors, ef I ain't blind,
An' sometimes, in the fairest sou'west weather,   120
My innard vane pints east for weeks together,
My natur' gits all goose-flesh, an' my sins
Come drizzlin' on my conscience sharp ez pins:
Wal, et sech times I jes' slip out o' sight
An' take it out in a fair stan'-up fight   125
With the one cuss I can't lay on the shelf,
The crook'dest stick in all the heap, — Myself.

'Twuz so las' Sabbath arter meetin'-time:
Findin' my feelin's wouldn't noways rhyme
With nobody's, but off the hendle flew   130
An' took things from an east-wind pint o' view,
I started off to lose me in the hills
Where the pines be, up back o' Siah's Mills:
Pines, ef you're blue, are the best friends I know,
They mope an' sigh an' sheer your feelin's so, —   135
They hesh the ground beneath so, tu, I swan,
You half-forgit you've gut a body on.

Ther' 's a small school'us' there where four roads meet,
The door-steps hollered out by little feet,
An' side-posts carved with names whose owners grew 140
To gret men, some on 'em, an' deacons, tu;
'Tain't used no longer, coz the town hez gut
A high-school, where they teach the Lord knows wut:
Three-story larnin' 's pop'lar now°; I guess
We thriv' ez wal on jes' two stories less,   145
For it strikes me ther' 's sech a thing ez sinnin'
By overloadin' children's underpinnin':
Wal, here it wuz I larned my A B C,
An' it's a kind o' favorite spot with me.
We're curus critters: Now ain't jes' the minute   150
Thet ever fits us easy while we're in it;
Long ez 'twuz futur', 'twould be perfect bliss, —
Soon ez it's past, *thet* time's wuth ten o' this;
An' yit there ain't a man thet need be told
Thet Now's the only bird lays eggs o' gold.°   155
A knee-high lad, I used to plot an' plan
An' think 'twuz life's cap-sheaf° to be a man;
Now, gittin' gray, there's nothin' I enjoy
Like dreamin' back along into a boy:
So the ole school'us' is a place I choose   160
Afore all others, ef I want to muse;
I set down where I used to set, an' git
My boyhood back, an' better things with it, —
Faith, Hope, an' sunthin', ef it isn't Cherrity,
It's want o' guile, an' thet's ez gret a rerrity.°   165
Now, 'fore I knowed, thet Sabbath arternoon
Thet I sot out to tramp myself in tune,
I found me in the school'us' on my seat,
Drummin' the march to No-wheres with my feet.

Thinkin' o' nothin', I've heerd ole folks say,   170
Is a hard kind o' dooty in its way:
It's thinkin' everythin' you ever knew,
Or ever hearn, to make your feelin's blue.

*   *   *   *   *   *   *

From this to thet I let my worryin' creep
Till finally I must ha' fell asleep.   175

Our lives in sleep are some like streams thet glide
'Twixt flesh an' sperrit boundin' on each side,
Where both shores' shadders kind o' mix an' mingle
In sunthin' thet ain't jes' like either single;
An' when you cast off moorin's from To-day,   180
An' down towards To-morrer drift away,
The imiges thet tengle on the stream
Make a new upside-down'ard world o' dream:
Sometimes they seem like sunrise-streaks an' warnin's
O' wut'll be in Heaven on Sabbath-mornin's,   185
An', mixed right in ez ef jest out o' spite,
Sunthin' thet says your supper ain't gone right.
I'm gret on dreams, an' often, when I wake,
I've lived so much it makes my mem'ry ache,
An' can't skurce take a cat-nap in my cheer   190
'Thout hevin' 'em, some good, some bad, all queer.

Now I wuz settin' where I'd ben, it seemed,
An' ain't sure yit whether I r'ally dreamed,
Nor, ef I did, how long I might ha' slep',
When I hearn some un stompin' up the step,   195
An' lookin' round, ef two an' two make four,
I see a Pilgrim Father in the door.

He wore a steeple-hat, tall boots, an' spurs
With rowels to 'em big ez ches'nut-burrs,
An' his gret sword behind him sloped away   200
Long'z a man's speech thet dunno wut to say. —
"Ef your name's Biglow, an' your given-name
Hosee," sez he, "it's arter you I came;
I'm your gret-gran'ther multiplied by three." —
"My *wut?*" sez I. — "Your gret-gret-gret," sez he: 205
"You wouldn't ha' never ben here but for me.
Two hundred an' three year ago this May
The ship I come in sailed up Boston Bay;
I'd been a cunnle in our Civil War,° —
But wut on airth hev *you* gut up one for?   210
Coz we du things in England, 'tain't for you
To git a notion you can du 'em tu:
I'm told you write in public prints: ef true,
It's nateral you should know a thing or two." —
"Thet air's an argymunt I can't endorse, —   215
'Twould prove, coz you wear spurs, you kep' a horse:

*   *   *   *   *   *   *

But du pray tell me, 'fore we furder go,
How in all Natur' did you come to know
'Bout our affairs," sez I, "in Kingdom-Come?" —
"Wal, I worked round at sperrit-rappin' some,   220
An' danced the tables till their legs wuz gone,
In hopes o' larnin' wut wuz goin' on,"
Sez he, "but mejums lie so like all-split
Thet I concluded it wuz best to quit.
But, come now, ef you wun't confess to knowin',   225
You've some conjectures how the thing's a-goin'." —
"Gran'ther," sez I, "a vane warn't never known

Nor asked to hev a jedgment of its own ;
An' yit, ef 'tain't gut rusty in the jints,
It's safe to trust its say on certin pints :   230
It knows the wind's opinions to a T,
An' the wind settles wut the weather'll be."
"I never thought a scion of our stock
Could grow the wood to make a weathercock ;
When I wuz younger'n you, skurce more'n a shaver,   235
No airthly wind," sez he, "could make me waver!"
(Ez he said this, he clinched his jaw an' forehead,
Hitchin' his belt to bring his sword-hilt forrard.) —
"Jes' so it wuz with me," sez I, "I swow,
When *I* wuz younger'n wut you see me now, —   240
Nothin' from Adam's fall° to Huldy's bonnet,
Thet I warn't full-cocked with my jedgment on it ;
But now I'm gittin' on in life, I find
It's a sight harder to make up my mind, —
Nor I don't often try tu, when events   245
Will du it for me free of all expense.
The moral question's ollus plain enough, —
It's jes' the human-natur' side thet's tough ;
Wut's best to think mayn't puzzle me nor you, —
The pinch comes in decidin' wut to *du ;*   250
Ef you *read* History, all runs smooth ez grease,
Coz there the men ain't nothin' more'n idees, —
But come to *make* it, ez we must to-day,
Th' idees hev arms an' legs an' stop the way :
It's easy fixin' things in facts an' figgers, —   255
They can't resist, nor warn't brought up with niggers ;
But come to try your the'ry on, — why, then
Your facts an' figgers change to ign'ant men
Actin' ez ugly —" — "Smite 'em hip an' thigh!"

Sez gran'ther, "and let every man-child die!   260
Oh for three weeks o' Crommle° an' the Lord!
Up, Isr'el, to your tents an' grind the sword!" —
"Thet kind o' thing worked wal in ole Judee,
But you forgit how long it's ben A. D.;
You think thet's ellerkence, — I call it shoddy,   265
A thing," sez I, "wun't cover soul nor body;
I like the plain all-wool o' common-sense,
Thet warms ye now, an' will a twelvemonth hence.
You took to follerin' where the Prophets beckoned,
An', fust you knowed on, back come Charles the Second°; 270
Now wut I want's to hev all *we* gain stick,
An' not to start Millennium° too quick;
We hain't to punish only, but to keep,
An' the cure's gut to go a cent'ry deep."
"Wal, milk-an'-water ain't the best o' glue,"   275
Sez he, "an' so you'll find before you're thru;

*   *   *   *   *   *   *

"Strike soon," sez he, "or you'll be deadly ailin', —
Folks thet's afeared to fail are sure o' failin';
God hates your sneakin' creturs thet believe
He'll settle things they run away an' leave!"   280
He brought his foot down fercely, ez he spoke,
An' give me sech a startle thet I woke.

AN INDIAN-SUMMER REVERIE

WHAT visionary tints the year puts on,
When falling leaves falter through motionless air
  Or numbly cling and shiver to be gone!
How shimmer the low flats and pastures bare,
  As with her nectar Hebe Autumn° fills   5
  The bowl between me and those distant hills,
And smiles and shakes abroad her misty, tremulous hair!

No more the landscape holds its wealth apart.
Making me poorer in my poverty,
  But mingles with my senses and my heart;   10
My own projected spirit° seems to me
  In her own reverie the world to steep;
  'Tis she that waves to sympathetic sleep,
Moving, as she is moved, each field and hill, and tree.

How fuse and mix, with what unfelt degrees,   15
Clasped by the faint horizon's languid arms,
  Each into each, the hazy distances!
The softened season all the landscape charms;
  Those hills, my native village that embay,
  In waves of dreamier purple roll away,   20
And floating in mirage seem all the glimmering farms.

Far distant sounds the hidden chickadee
Close at my side; far distant sound the leaves;
  The fields seem fields of dream, where Memory
Wanders like gleaning Ruth; and as the sheaves   25
  Of wheat and barley wavered in the eye
  Of Boaz as the maiden's glow went by,
So tremble and seem remote all things the sense receives.°

The cock's shrill trump that tells of scattered corn,
Passed breezily on by all his flapping mates,   30
  Faint and more faint, from barn to barn is borne,
Southward, perhaps to far Magellan's Straits°;
   Dimly I catch the throb of distant flails;
   Silently overhead the henhawk sails,
With watchful, measuring eye, and for his quarry waits.   35

  The sobered robin, hunger-silent now,
Seeks cedar-berries blue, his autumn cheer;
  The squirrel on the shingly shagbark's bough,
Now saws, now lists with downward eye and ear,
   Then drops his nut, and, with a chipping bound,   40
   Whisks to his winding fastness underground;
The clouds like swans drift down the streaming atmosphere.

  O'er yon bare knoll the pointed cedar shadows
Drowse on the crisp, gray moss; the ploughman's call
  Creeps faint as smoke from black, fresh-furrowed
    meadows;   45
The single crow a single caw lets fall;
   And all around me every bush and tree
   Says Autumn's here, and Winter soon will be
Who snows his soft, white sleep and silence over all.

  The birch, most shy and lady-like of trees,   50
Her poverty, as best she may, retrieves,°
  And hints at her foregone gentilities
With some saved relics of her wealth of leaves;
   The swamp-oak, with his royal purple on,
   Glares red as blood across the sinking sun,   55
As one who proudlier to a falling fortune cleaves

He looks a sachem, in red blanket wrapt,
Who, mid some council of the sad-garbed whites,
  Erect and stern, in his own memories lapt,°
With distant eye broods over other sights,   60
  Sees the hushed wood the city's flare replace,
  The wounded turf heal o'er the railway's trace,
And roams the savage Past of his undwindled rights.

  The red-oak, softer-grained, yields all for lost,
And, with his crumpled foliage stiff and dry,   65
  After the first betrayal of the frost,
Rebuffs the kiss of the relenting sky;
  The chestnuts, lavish of their long-hid gold,
  To the faint Summer, beggared now and old,
Pour back the sunshine hoarded 'neath her favoring eye.   70

  The ash her purple drops forgivingly
And sadly, breaking not the general hush;
  The maple-swamps glow like a sunset sea,
Each leaf a ripple with its separate flush;
  All round the wood's edge creeps the skirting blaze   75
  Of bushes low, as when, on cloudy days,
Ere the rain falls, the cautious farmer burns his brush.°

  O'er yon low wall, which guards one unkempt zone,
Where vines, and weeds, and scrub-oaks intertwine
  Safe from the plough, whose rough, discordant stone   80
Is massed to one soft gray by lichens fine,
  The tangled blackberry, crossed and recrossed, weaves
  A prickly network of ensanguined° leaves;
Hard by, with coral beads, the prim black-alders shine.

Pillaring with flame this crumbling boundary,   85
Whose loose blocks topple 'neath the ploughboy's foot,
Who, with each sense shut fast except the eye,
Creeps close and scares the jay he hoped to shoot,
The woodbine up the elm's straight stem aspires.
Coiling it, harmless, with autumnal fires;   90
In the ivy's paler blaze the martyr oak stands mute.

Below, the Charles — a stripe of nether sky,°
Now hid by rounded apple-trees between,
Whose gaps the misplaced sail sweeps bellying by,
Now flickering golden through a woodland screen,   95
Then spreading out at his next turn beyond,
A silver circle like an inland pond —
Slips seaward silently through marshes purple and green.

Dear marshes!° vain to him the gift of sight
Who cannot in their various incomes share,   100
From every season drawn, of shade and light,
Who sees in them but levels brown and bare;
Each change of storm or sunshine scatters free
On them its largesse of variety,
For nature with cheap means still works her wonders rare. 105

In Spring they lie one broad expanse of green,
O'er which the light winds run with glimmering feet;
Here, yellower stripes track out the creek unseen,
There, darker growths o'er hidden ditches meet;
And purpler stains show where the blossoms crowd,   110
As if the silent shadow of a cloud
Hung there becalmed, with the next breath to fleet.

All round, upon the river's slippery edge,
Witching to deeper calm the drowsy tide,
    Whispers and leans the breeze-entangling sedge;   115
Through emerald glooms the lingering waters slide,
    Or, sometimes wavering, throw back the sun,
    And the stiff banks in eddies melt and run
Of dimpling light, and with the current seem to glide.

    In Summer 'tis a blithesome sight to see,   120
As, step by step, with measured swing, they pass,
    The wide-ranked mowers wading to the knee,
Their sharp scythes panting through the thick-set grass;
    Then, stretched beneath a rick's shade in a ring,
    Their nooning take, while one begins to sing   125
A stave that droops and dies 'neath the close sky of brass.

    Meanwhile the devil-may-care, the bobolink,
Remembering duty, in mid-quaver stops
    Just ere he sweeps o'er rapture's tremulous brink,
And 'twixt the winrows most demurely drops,   130
    A decorous bird of business, who provides
    For his brown mate and fledglings six besides,
And looks from right to left, a farmer mid his crops.°

    Another change subdues them in the Fall,
But saddens not; they still show merrier tints,   135
    Though sober russet seems to cover all;
When the first sunshine through their dew-drops glints,
    Look how the yellow clearness, streamed across,
    Redeems with rarer hues the season's loss,   139
As Dawn's feet there had touched and left their rosy prints.°

Or come when sunset gives its freshened zest,
Lean o'er the bridge and let the ruddy thrill,
  While the shorn sun swells down the hazy west,
Glow opposite; — the marshes drink their fill
  And swoon with purple veins, then slowly fade   145
  Through pink to brown, as eastward moves the shade,
Lengthening with stealthy creep, of Simond's darkening hill.

  Later, and yet ere Winter wholly shuts,
Ere through the first dry snow the runner grates,
  And the loath cart-wheel screams in slippery ruts,   150
While firmer ice the eager boy awaits,
  Trying each buckle and strap beside the fire,
  And until bed-time plays with his desire,
Twenty times putting on and off his new-bought skates; —

Then, every morn, the river's banks shine bright   155
With smooth plate-armor, treacherous and frail,
  By the frost's clinking hammers forged at night,°
'Gainst which the lances of the sun prevail,
  Giving a pretty emblem of the day
  When guiltier arms in light shall melt away,   160
And states shall move free-limbed, loosed from war's cramp-
    ing mail.

  And now those waterfalls the ebbing river
Twice every day creates on either side°
  Tinkle, as through their fresh-sparred grots they shiver
In grass-arched channels to the sun denied;   165
  High flaps in sparkling blue the far-heard crow,
  The silvered flats gleam frostily below,
Suddenly drops the gull and breaks the glassy tide.

    T

But, crowned in turn by vying seasons three,
Their winter halo hath a fuller ring;   170
   This glory seems to rest immovably, —
The others were too fleet and vanishing;
    When the hid tide is at its highest flow,
    O'er marsh and stream one breathless trance of snow
With brooding fulness awes and hushes everything.   175

The sunshine seems blown off by the bleak wind,
As pale as formal candles lit by day;
   Gropes to the sea the river dumb and blind°;
The brown ricks, snow-thatched by the storm in play,
    Show pearly breakers combing o'er their lee,   180
    White crests as of some just enchanted sea,
Checked in their maddest leap and hanging poised midway.°

But when the eastern blow, with rain aslant,
From mid-sea's prairies green and rolling plains
   Drives in his wallowing herds of billows gaunt,   185
And the roused Charles remembers in his veins
    Old Ocean's blood and snaps his gyves° of frost,
    That tyrannous silence on the shores is tost
In dreary wreck, and crumbling desolation reigns.

Edgewise or flat, in Druid-like device,°   190
With leaden pools between or gullies bare,
   The blocks lie strewn, a bleak Stonehenge of ice;
No life, no sound, to break the grim despair,
    Save sullen plunge, as through the sedges stiff
    Down crackles riverward some thaw-sapped cliff,   195
Or when the close-wedged fields of ice crunch here and there.

But let me turn from fancy-pictured scenes
To that whose pastoral calm before me lies:
  Here nothing harsh or rugged intervenes;
The early evening with her misty dyes   200
    Smooths off the ravelled edges of the nigh,°
    Relieves the distant with her cooler sky,
And tones the landscape down, and soothes the wearied eyes.

  There gleams my native village, dear to me,
Though higher change's waves each day are seen,   205
    Whelming fields famed in boyhood's history,
Sanding with houses the diminished green;
    There, in red brick, which softening time defies,
    Stand square and stiff the Muses' factories°; —
How with my life knit up is every well-known scene!   210

  Flow on, dear river! not alone you flow
To outward sight, and through your marshes wind;
    Fed from the mystic springs of long-ago,
Your twin flows silent through my world of mind:
    Grow dim, dear marshes, in the evening's gray!   215
    Before my inner sight ye stretch away,
And will forever, though these fleshly eyes grow blind.°

*   *   *   *   *   *   *

A FABLE FOR CRITICS

(Selections)

I. *Emerson.*

"THERE comes Emerson first, whose rich words, every one,
Are like gold nails in temples to hang trophies on,
Whose prose is grand verse, while his verse, the Lord knows,
Is some of it pr —— No, 'tis not even prose;
I'm speaking of metres; some poems have welled   5
From those rare depths of soul that have ne'er been excelled;
They're not epics, but that doesn't matter a pin,
In creating, the only hard thing's to begin;
A grass-blade's no easier to make than an oak,
If you've once found the way you've achieved the grand
        stroke;   10
In the worst of his poems are mines of rich matter,
But thrown in a heap with a crash and a clatter·
Now it is not one thing nor another alone
Makes a poem, but rather the general tone,
The something pervading, uniting the whole,   15
The before unconceived, unconceivable soul,
So that just in removing this trifle or that, you
Take away, as it were, a chief limb of the statue;
Roots, wood, bark, and leaves, singly perfect may be,
But, clapt hodge-podge together, they don't make a tree.   20

"But, to come back to Emerson, (whom by the way,
I believe we left waiting,) — his is, we may say,
A Greek head on right Yankee shoulders, whose range
Has Olympus for one pole, for t' other the Exchange;

*   *   *   *   *   *   *

Life, nature, love, God, and affairs of that sort,   25
He looks at as merely ideas; in short,
As if they were fossils stuck round in a cabinet,
Of such vast extent that our earth's a mere dab in it;
Composed just as he is inclined to conjecture her,
Namely, one part pure earth, ninety-nine parts pure lecturer; 30
You are filled with delight at his clear demonstration,
Each figure, word, gesture, just fits the occasion,
With the quiet precision of science he'll sort 'em,
But you can't help suspecting the whole a *post mortem*.

II. *Bryant.*

"There is Bryant, as quiet, as cool, and as dignified,   35
As a smooth, silent iceberg, that never is ignified,°
Save when by reflection 'tis kindled o' nights
With a semblance of flame by the chill Northern Lights.
He may rank (Griswold says so) first bard of your nation,
(There's no doubt that he stands in supreme iceolation,)°   40
Your topmost Parnassus° he may set his heel on,
But no warm applauses come, peal following peal on, —
He's too smooth and too polished to hang any zeal on:
Unqualified merits, I'll grant, if you choose, he has 'em,
But he lacks the one merit of kindling enthusiasm;   45
If he stir you at all, it is just, on my soul,
Like being stirred up with the very North Pole.

"He is very nice reading in summer, but *inter
Nos,*° we don't want *extra* freezing in winter;
Take him up in the depth of July, my advice is,   50
When you feel an Egyptian devotion to ices.°
But, deduct all you can, there's enough that's right good in
    him,

He has a true soul for field, river, and wood in him ;
And his heart, in the midst of brick walls, or where'er it is,
Glows, softens, and thrills with the tenderest charities,   55
To you mortals that delve in this trade-ridden planet?
No, to old Berkshire's hills, with their lime stone and granite.

III. *Whittier.*

"There is Whittier, whose swelling and vehement heart
Strains the strait-breasted drab of the Quaker apart,
And reveals the live Man, still supreme and erect,   60
Underneath the bemummying° wrappers of sect ;
There was ne'er a man born who had more of the swing
Of the true lyric bard and all that kind of thing ;
And his failures arise, (though perhaps he don't know it,)
From the very same cause that has made him a poet, —   65
A fervor of mind which knows no separation
'Twixt simple excitement and pure inspiration,
As my Pythoness° erst sometimes erred from not knowing
If 'twere I or mere wind through her tripod° was blowing ;
Let his mind once get head in its favorite direction   70
And the torrent of verse bursts the dams of reflection,
While, borne with the rush of the metre along,
The poet may chance to go right or go wrong,
Content with the whirl and delirium of song ;
Then his grammar's not always correct, nor his rhymes,   75
And he's prone to repeat his own lyrics sometimes,
Not his best, though, for those are struck off at white-heats
When the heart in his breast like a trip-hammer beats,
And can ne'er be repeated again any more
Than they could have been carefully plotted before :   80

     *   *   *   *   *   *   *

"All honor and praise to the right-hearted bard
Who was true to The Voice when such service was hard,
Who himself was so free he dared sing for the slave;
When to look but a protest in silence was brave;

IV. *Hawthorne.*

"There is Hawthorne, with genius so shrinking and rare   85
That you hardly at first see the strength that is there;
A frame so robust, with a nature so sweet,
So earnest, so graceful, so solid, so fleet,
Is worth a descent from Olympus to meet;
'Tis as if a rough oak that for ages had stood,   90
With his gnarled bony branches like ribs of the wood,
Should bloom, after cycles of struggle and scathe,°
With a single anemone trembly and rathe°;
His strength is so tender; his wildness so meek,
That a suitable parallel sets one to seek, —   95
He's a John Bunyan Fouqué,° a Puritan Tieck°;
When nature was shaping him, clay was not granted
For making so full-sized a man as she wanted,
So, to fill out her model, a little she spared
From some finer-grained stuff for a woman prepared,   100
And she could not have hit a more excellent plan
For making him fully and perfectly man.
The success of her scheme gave her so much delight,
That she tried it again, shortly after, in Dwight;
Only, while she was kneading and shaping the clay,   105
She sang to her work in her sweet childish way,
And found, when she'd put the last touch to his soul,
That the music had somehow got mixed with the whole.

V. *Cooper.*

"Here's Cooper, who's written six volumes to show
He's as good as a lord°: well, let's grant that he's so;   110
If a person prefer that description of praise,
Why, a coronet's certainly cheaper than bays°;
But he need take no pains to convince us he's not
(As his enemies say) the American Scott.
Choose any twelve men, and let C. read aloud   115
That one of his novels of which he's most proud,
And I'd lay any bet that, without ever quitting
Their box, they'd be all, to a man, for acquitting.
He has drawn you one character, though, that is new,
One wildflower he's plucked that is wet with the dew   120
Of this fresh Western world, and, the thing not to mince,
He has done naught but copy it ill ever since;
His Indians, with proper respect be it said,
Are just Natty Bumpo° daubed over with red,
And his very Long Toms° are the same useful Nat,   125
Rigged up in duck pants and a sou'-wester hat,
(Though once in a Coffin, a good chance was found
To have slipt the old fellow away underground.)
All his other men-figures are clothes upon sticks,
The *dernière chemise*° of a man in a fix,   130
(As a captain besieged, when his garrison's small,
Sets up caps upon poles to be seen o'er the wall;)
And the women he draws from one model don't vary,
All sappy as maples and flat as a prairie.
When a character's wanted, he goes to the task   135
As a cooper would do in composing a cask;
He picks out the staves, of their qualities heedful,
Just hoops them together as tight as is needful,

And, if the best fortune should crown the attempt, he
Has made at the most something wooden and empty.   140

"Don't suppose I would underrate Cooper's abilities
If I thought you'd do that, I should feel very ill at ease;
The men who have given to *one* character life
And objective existence, are not very rife,
You may number them all, both prose-writers and singers, 145
Without overrunning the bounds of your fingers,
And Natty won't go to oblivion quicker
Than Adams the parson° or Primrose the vicar.°

"There is one thing in Cooper I like, too, and that is
That on manners he lectures his countrymen gratis,   150
Not precisely so either, because, for a rarity,
He is paid for his tickets in unpopularity.
Now he may overcharge his American pictures,
But you'll grant there's a good deal of truth in his strictures;
And I honor the man who is willing to sink   155
Half his present repute for the freedom to think,
And, when he has thought, be his cause strong or weak,
Will risk t'other half for the freedom to speak,
Caring naught for what vengeance the mob has in store,
Let that mob be the upper ten thousand or lower.   160

VI. *Poe and Longfellow.*

"There comes Poe, with his raven, like Barnaby Rudge,°
Three-fifths of him genius and two-fifths sheer fudge,°
Who talks like a book of iambs and pentameters,
In a way to make people of common-sense damn metres,
Who has written some things quite the best of their kind, 165
But the heart somehow seems all squeezed out by the mind,

Who — but hey-day! What's this? Messieurs Mathews
    and Poe,
You mustn't fling mud-balls at Longfellow so,
Does it make a man worse that his character's such
As to make his friends love him (as you think) too much? 170
Why, there is not a bard at this moment alive
More willing than he that his fellows should thrive,
While you are abusing him thus, even now
He would help either one of you out of a slough;
You may say that he's smooth and all that till you're hoarse
But remember that elegance also is force;   176
After polishing granite as much as you will,
The heart keeps its tough old persistency still;
Deduct all you can that still keeps you at bay, —
Why, he'll live till men weary of Collins and Gray.°   180

*   *   *   *   *   *   *

          'Tis truth that I speak
Had Theocritus° written in English, not Greek,
I believe that his exquisite sense would scarce change a line
In that rare, tender, virgin-like pastoral Evangeline.
That's not ancient nor modern, its place is apart   185
Where time has no sway, in the realm of pure Art,
'Tis a shrine of retreat from Earth's hubbub and strife
As quiet and chaste as the author's own life.

VII. *Irving.*

  "What! Irving? thrice welcome, warm heart and fine brain,
You bring back the happiest spirit from Spain,°   190
And the gravest sweet humor, that ever were there
Since Cervantes met death in his gentle despair;

Nay, don't be embarrassed, nor look so beseeching, —
I shan't run directly against my own preaching,
And, having just laughed at their Raphaels and Dantes,   195
Go to setting you up beside matchless Cervantes° ;
But allow me to speak what I honestly feel, —
To a true poet-heart add the fun of Dick Steele,
Throw in all of Addison, *minus* the chill,
With the whole of that partnership's stock and good will,° 200
Mix well, and while stirring, hum o'er, as a spell,
The fine *old* English Gentleman, simmer it well,
Sweeten just to your own private liking, then strain
That only the finest and clearest remain,
Let it stand out of doors till a soul it receives   205
From the warm lazy sun loitering down through green leaves,
And you'll find a choice nature, not wholly deserving
A name either English or Yankee, — just Irving.

VIII.   *Holmes.*

    "There's Holmes, who is matchless among you for wit ;
A Leyden-jar always full-charged, from which flit   210
The electrical tingles of hit after hit ;
In long poems 'tis painful sometimes, and invites
A thought of the way the new Telegraph writes,
Which pricks down its little sharp sentences spitefully
As if you got more than you'd title to rightfully,   215
And you find yourself hoping its wild father Lightning
Would flame in for a second and give you a fright'ning.
He has perfect sway of what *I* call a sham metre,
But many admire it, the English pentameter,
And Campbell, I think, wrote most commonly worse,   220
With less nerve, swing, and fire in the same kind of verse,

Nor e'er achieved aught in 't so worthy of praise
As the tribute of Holmes to the grand *Marseillaise*.
You went crazy last year over Bulwer's New Timon°;
Why, if B., to the day of his dying, should rhyme on,   225
Heaping verses on verses and tomes upon tomes,
He could ne'er reach the best point and vigor of Holmes.
His are just the fine hands, too, to weave you a lyric
Full of fancy, fun, feeling, or spiced with satyric
In a measure so kindly, you doubt if the toes   230
That are trodden upon are your own or your foes'.

IX.   *Lowell.*

"There is Lowell, who's striving Parnassus to climb
With a whole bale of *isms* tied together with rhyme,
He might get on alone, spite of brambles and boulders,
But he can't with that bundle he has on his shoulders,   235
The top of the hill he will ne'er come nigh reaching
Till he learns the distinction 'twixt singing and preaching°;
His lyre has some chords that would ring pretty well,
But he'd rather by half make a drum of the shell,
And rattle away till he's old as Methusalem,   240
At the head of a march to the last new Jerusalem.

X.   *Spirit of Ancient Poetry.*

"My friends, in the happier days of the muse,
We were luckily free from such things as reviews,
Then naught came between with its fog to make clearer
The heart of the poet to that of his hearer;   245
Then the poet brought heaven to the people, and they
Felt that they, too, were poets in hearing his lay;

Then the poet was prophet, the past in his soul
Pre-created the future, both parts of one whole;
Then for him there was nothing too great or too small,   250
For one natural deity sanctified all;
Then the bard owned no clipper and meter° of moods
Save the spirit of silence that hovers and broods
O'er the seas and the mountains, the rivers and woods;
He asked not earth's verdict, forgetting the clods,   255
His soul soared and sang to an 'audience of gods.
'Twas for them that he measured the thought and the line,
And shaped for their vision the perfect design,
With as glorious a foresight, a balance as true,
As swung out the worlds in the infinite blue;   260
Then a glory and greatness invested man's heart,
The universal, which now stands estranged and apart,
In the free individual moulded, was Art;
Then the forms of the Artist seemed thrilled with desire
For something as yet unattained, fuller, higher,   265
As once with her lips, lifted hands, and eyes listening,
And her whole upward soul in her countenance glistening,
Eurydice stood — like a beacon unfired,
Which, once touched with flame, will leap heav'nward in-
    spired —
And waited with answering kindle to mark   270
The first gleam of Orpheus that pained the red Dark.°
Then painting, song, sculpture, did more than relieve
The need that men feel to create and believe,
And as, in all beauty, who listens with love,
Hears these words oft repeated — 'beyond and above,'   275
So these seemed to be but the visible sign
Of the grasp of the soul after things more divine;
They were ladders the Artist erected to climb

O'er the narrow horizon of space and of time,
And we see there the footsteps by which men had gained
To the one rapturous glimpse of the never-attained,   281
As shepherds could erst sometimes trace in the sod
The last spurning print of a sky-cleaving god.

OLIVER WENDELL HOLMES

OLD IRONSIDES°

Ay, tear her tattered ensign down!
  Long has it waved on high,
And many an eye has danced to see
  That banner in the sky;
Beneath it rung the battle shout,   5
  And burst the cannon's roar; —
The meteor of the ocean air
  Shall sweep the clouds no more!

Her deck, once red with heroes' blood,
  Where knelt the vanquished foe,   10
When winds were hurrying o'er the flood,
  And waves were white below,
No more shall feel the victor's tread,
  Or know the conquered knee; —
The harpies of the shore shall pluck   15
  The eagle of the sea!

O better that her shattered hulk
  Should sink beneath the wave;
Her thunders shook the mighty deep,
  And there should be her grave;   20
Nail to the mast her holy flag,
  Set every threadbare sail,
And give her to the god of storms,
  The lightning and the gale!

287

THE LAST LEAF°

I saw him once before,
As he passed by the door,
   And again
The pavement stones resound,
As he totters o'er the ground   5
   With his cane.

They say that in his prime,
Ere the pruning-knife of Time
   Cut him down,
Not a better man was found   10
By the Crier on his round
   Through the town.

But now he walks the streets,
And he looks at all he meets
   Sad and wan,
And he shakes his feeble head,   15
That it seems as if he said,
   "They are gone."

The mossy marbles rest
On the lips that he has prest   20
   In their bloom,
And the names he loved to hear
Have been carved for many a year
   On the tomb.

My grandmamma has said —   25
Poor old lady, she is dead
   Long ago —

That he had a Roman nose,
And his cheek was like a rose
   In the snow.   30

But now his nose is thin,
And it rests upon his chin
   Like a staff,
And a crook is in his back,
And a melancholy crack   35
   In his laugh.

I know it is a sin
For me to sit and grin
   At him here;
But the old three-cornered hat,   40
And the breeches, and all that,
   Are so queer!

And if I should live to be
The last leaf upon the tree
   In the spring,   45
Let them smile, as I do now,
At the old forsaken bough
   Where I cling.

MY AUNT

My aunt! my dear unmarried aunt!
   Long years have o'er her flown;
Yet still she strains the aching clasp
   That binds her virgin zone;

U

I know it hurts her, — though she looks   5
    As cheerful as she can;
Her waist is ampler than her life,
    For life is but a span.

My aunt! my poor deluded aunt!
    Her hair is almost gray;   10
Why will she train that winter curl
    In such a spring-like way?
How can she lay her glasses down,
    And say she reads as well,
When through a double convex lens,   15
    She just makes out to spell?

Her father — grandpapa! forgive
    This erring lip its smiles —
Vowed she should make the finest girl
    Within a hundred miles;   20
He sent her to a stylish school;
    'Twas in her thirteenth June;
And with her, as the rules required,
    "Two towels and a spoon."

They braced my aunt against a board,   25
    To make her straight and tall;
They laced her up, they starved her down,
    To make her light and small;
They pinched her feet, they singed her hair,
    They screwed it up with pins; —   30
O never mortal suffered more
    In penance for her sins.

So, when my precious aunt was done,
  My grandsire brought her back;
(By daylight, lest some rabid youth   35
  Might follow on the track;)
"Ah!" said my grandsire, as he shook
  Some powder in his pan,
"What could this lovely creature do
  Against a desperate man!"   40

Alas! nor chariot, nor barouche,
  Nor bandit cavalcade,
Tore from the trembling father's arms
  His all-accomplished maid.
For her how happy had it been!   45
  And Heaven had spared to me
To see one sad, ungathered rose
  On my ancestral tree.

THE CHAMBERED NAUTILUS

THIS is the ship of pearl, which, poets feign,
  Sails the unshadowed main, —
    The venturous bark that flings
On the sweet summer wind its purpled wings
In gulfs enchanted, where the Siren sings,   5
  And coral reefs lie bare,
Where the cold sea-maids rise to sun their streaming hair.

Its webs of living gauze no more unfurl;
  Wrecked is the ship of pearl!
    And every chambered cell,   10
Where its dim dreaming life was wont to dwell,

As the frail tenant shaped his growing shell,
    Before thee lies revealed, —
Its irised° ceiling rent, its sunless crypt° unsealed!

Year after year beheld the silent toil   15
    That spread his lustrous coil;
    Still, as the spiral grew,
He left the past year's dwelling for the new,
Stole with soft step its shining archway through,
    Built up its idle door,   20
Stretched in his last-found home, and knew the old no more.°

Thanks for the heavenly message brought by thee,
    Child of the wandering sea,
    Cast from her lap, forlorn!
From thy dead lips a clearer note is born   25
Than ever Triton blew from wreathèd horn!
    While on mine ear it rings,
Through the deep caves of thought I hear a voice that
    sings: —

Build thee more stately mansions, O my soul,
    As the swift seasons roll!   30
    Leave thy low-vaulted past!
Let each new temple, nobler than the last,
Shut thee from heaven with a dome more vast,
    Till thou at length art free,
Leaving thine outgrown shell by life's unresting sea!   35

CONTENTMENT

"Man wants but little here below."

LITTLE I ask; my wants are few;
  I only wish a hut of stone,
(A *very plain* brown stone° will do,)
  That I may call my own; —
And close at hand is such a one,   5
In yonder street that fronts the sun.

Plain food is quite enough for me;
  Three courses are as good as ten; —
If Nature can subsist on three,
  Thank Heaven for three. Amen!   10
I always thought cold victual nice; —
My *choice* would be vanilla-ice.

I care not much for gold or land; —
  Give me a mortgage here and there, —
Some good bank-stock, some note of hand, 15
  Or trifling railroad share, —
I only ask that Fortune send
A *little* more than I shall spend.

Honors are silly toys, I know,
  And titles are but empty names;   20
I would, *perhaps*, be Plenipo, —
  But only near St. James°;
I'm very sure I should not care
To fill our Gubernator's chair.

Jewels are bawbles; 'tis a sin   25
  To care for such unfruitful things; —
One good-sized diamond in a pin, —
  Some, *not so large*, in rings, —
A ruby, and a pearl, or so,
Will do for me; — I laugh at show.   30

My dame should dress in cheap attire;
  (Good, heavy silks are never dear;)
I own perhaps I *might* desire
  Some shawls of true Cashmere, —
Some marrowy° crapes of China silk,   35
Like wrinkled skins on scalded milk.

I would not have the horse I drive
  So fast that folks must stop and stare;
An easy gait — two, forty-five —
  Suits me; I do not care; —   40
Perhaps, for just a *single spurt*,
Some seconds less would do no hurt.

Of pictures, I should like to own
  Titians and Raphaels three or four,
I love so much their style and tone, —   45
  One Turner, and no more,°
(A landscape, — foreground golden dirt, —
The sunshine painted with a squirt.)

Of books but few, — some fifty score
  For daily use, and bound for wear;   50
The rest upon an upper floor; —
  Some *little* luxury *there*

Of red morocco's gilded gleam,
And vellum° rich as country cream.

Busts, cameos, gems, — such things as these, 55
 Which others often show for pride,
I value for their power to please,
 And selfish churls deride ; —
One Stradivarius,° I confess,
Two Meerschaums, I would fain possess. 60

Wealth's wasteful tricks I will not learn
 Nor ape the glittering upstart fool ; —
Shall not carved tables serve my turn,
 But *all* must be of buhl?°
Give grasping pomp its double share, — 65
I ask but *one* recumbent chair.

Thus humble let me live and die,
 Nor long for Midas' golden touch ;
If Heaven more generous gifts deny,
 I shall not miss them *much*, — 70
Too grateful for the blessing lent
Of simple tastes and mind content!

THE DEACON'S MASTERPIECE; OR, THE WONDERFUL "ONE–HOSS SHAY"

A Logical Story

HAVE you heard of the wonderful one-hoss shay,
That was built in such a logical way
It ran a hundred years to a day,
And then, of a sudden, it — ah, but stay,
I'll tell you what happened without delay,   5
Scaring the parson into fits,
Frightening people out of their wits, —
Have you ever heard of that, I say?

Seventeen hundred and fifty-five,
Georgius Secundus° was then alive, —   10
Snuffy old drone from the German hive.
That was the year when Lisbon-town
Saw the earth open and gulp her down,
And Braddock's army was done so brown,
Left without a scalp to its crown.   15
It was on the terrible Earthquake-day
That the Deacon finished the one-hoss shay.

Now in building of chaises, I tell you what,
There is always *somewhere* a weakest spot, —
In hub, tire, felloe,° in spring or thill,   20
In panel, or crossbar, or floor, or sill,
In screw, bolt, thoroughbrace, — lurking still,
Find it somewhere you must and will, —
Above or below, or within or without, —

And that's the reason, beyond a doubt,   25
That a chaise *breaks down*, but doesn't *wear out*.

But the Deacon swore (as Deacons do,
With an "I dew vum," or an "I tell *yeou*,")
He would build one shay to beat the taown
'n' the keounty 'n' all the kentry raoun';   30
It should be so built that it *couldn'* break daown:
"Fur," said the Deacon, "'t's mighty plain
Thut the weakes' place mus' stan' the strain;
'n' the way t' fix it, uz I maintain,
                 Is only jest   35
T' make that place uz strong uz the rest."

So the Deacon inquired of the village folk
Where he could find the strongest oak,
That couldn't be split nor bent nor broke, —
That was for spokes and floor and sills;   40
He sent for lancewood to make the thills;
The crossbars were ash, from the straightest trees,
The panels of white-wood, that cuts like cheese,
But lasts like iron for things like these;
The hubs of logs from the "Settler's ellum," —   45
Last of its timber, — they couldn't sell 'em,
Never an axe had seen their chips,
And the wedges flew from between their lips,
Their blunt ends frizzled like celery-tips;
Step and prop-iron, bolt and screw,   50
Spring, tire, axle, and linchpin too,
Steel of the finest, bright and blue;
Thoroughbrace bison-skin, thick and wide;

Boot, top, dasher, from tough old hide
Found in the pit when the tanner died.   55
That was the way he "put her through." —
"There!" said the Deacon, "naow she'll dew!"

Do! I tell you, I rather guess
She was a wonder, and nothing less!
Colts grew horses, beards turned gray,   60
Deacon and deaconess dropped away,
Children and grandchildren — where were they?
But there stood the stout old one-hoss shay
As fresh as on Lisbon-earthquake-day!

Eighteen Hundred; — it came and found   65
The Deacon's masterpiece strong and sound.
Eighteen hundred increased by ten; —
"Hahnsum kerridge" they called it then.
Eighteen hundred and twenty came; —
Running as usual; much the same.   70
Thirty and forty at last arrive,
And then come fifty, and Fifty-five.

Little of all we value here
Wakes on the morn of its hundredth year
Without both feeling and looking queer.   75
In fact, there's nothing that keeps its youth,
So far as I know but a tree and truth.
(This is a moral that runs at large;
Take it. — You're welcome. — No extra charge.)

First of November, — the Earthquake-day —   80
There are traces of age in the one-hoss shay,

A general flavor of mild decay,
But nothing local, as one may say.
There couldn't be, — for the Deacon's art
Had made it so like in every part   85
That there wasn't a chance for one to start.
For the wheels were just as strong as the thills,
And the floor was just as strong as the sills,
And the panels just as strong as the floor,
And the whipple-tree neither less nor more,   90
And the back-crossbar as strong as the fore,
And spring and axle and hub *encore.*°
And yet, *as a whole*, it is past a doubt
In another hour it will be *worn out!*

First of November, 'Fifty-five!   95
This morning the parson takes a drive.
Now, small boys, get out of the way!
Here comes the wonderful one-hoss shay,
Drawn by a rat-tailed, ewe-necked bay.
"Huddup!" said the parson. — Off went they.   100
The parson was working his Sunday's text, —
Had got to *fifthly*, and stopped perplexed
At what the — Moses — was coming next.

All at once the horse stood still,
Close by the meet'n'-house on the hill.   105
—First a shiver, and then a thrill,
Then something decidedly like a spill, —
And the parson was sitting upon a rock,
At half past nine by the meet'n'-house clock —
Just the hour of the Earthquake shock!   110

— What do you think the parson found,
When he got up and stared around?
The poor old chaise in a heap or mound,
As if it had been to the mill and ground!
You see, of course, if you're not a dunce,   115
How it went to pieces all at once, —
All at once, and nothing first, —
Just as bubbles do when they burst.

End of the wonderful one-hoss shay.
Logic is logic.   That's all I say.   120

THOMAS BUCHANAN READ

STORM ON ST. BERNARD

Oh, Heaven, it is a fearful thing
Beneath the tempest's beating wing
To struggle, like a stricken hare
When swoops the monarch bird of air;
To breast the loud winds' fitful spasms,   5
To brave the cloud and shun the chasms,
Tossed like a fretted shallop-sail
Between the ocean and the gale.

Along the valley, loud and fleet,
The rising tempest leapt and roared,   10
And scaled the Alp, till from his seat
 The throned Eternity of Snow
His frequent avalanches poured
 In thunder to the storm below.
   * * * *

And now, to crown their fears, a roar   15
Like ocean battling with the shore,
Or like that sound which night and day
Breaks through Niagara's veil of spray,
From some great height within the cloud,
 To some immeasured valley driven,   20
Swept down, and with a voice so loud
 It seemed·as it would shatter heaven!
The bravest quailed; it swept so near,
 It made the ruddiest cheek to blanch,
While look replied to look in fear,   25
 "The avalanche!   The avalanche!"

It forced the foremost to recoil,
    Before its sideward billows thrown, —
Who cried, "O God! Here ends our toil!
    The path is overswept and gone!"   30

The night came down. The ghostly dark,
    Made ghostlier by its sheet of snow,
    Wailed round them its tempestuous wo,
Like Death's announcing courier! "Hark!
There, heard you not the alp-hound's bark?   35
And there again! and there! Ah, no,
'Tis but the blast that mocks us so!"

Then through the thick and blackening mist
Death glared on them, and breathed so near,
    Some felt his breath grow almost warm,   40
The while he whispered in their ear
    Of sleep that should out-dream the storm.
Then lower drooped their lids, — when, "List!
Now, heard you not the storm-bell ring?
    And there again, and twice and thrice!   45
Ah, no, 'tis but the thundering
    Of tempests on a crag of ice!"

Death smiled on them, and it seemed good
    On such a mellow bed to lie:
    The storm was like a lullaby,   50
And drowsy pleasure soothed their blood.
But still the sturdy, practised guide
His unremitting labour plied;
Now this one shook until he woke,
And closer wrapt the other's cloak, —   55
Still shouting with his utmost breath,

To startle back the hand of Death,
Brave words of cheer! "But, hark again, —
Between the blasts the sound is plain;
The storm, inhaling, lulls, — and hark!   60
It is — it is! the alp-dog's bark!
And on the tempest's passing swell —
    The voice of cheer so long debarred —
There swings the Convent's guiding-bell,
    The sacred bell of Saint Bernard!"   65

DRIFTING

        My soul to-day
        Is far away,
    Sailing the Vesuvian Bay;
        My wingéd boat
        A bird afloat,   5
    Swings round the purple peaks remote: —

        Round purple peaks
        It sails, and seeks
    Blue inlets and their crystal creeks,
        Where high rocks throw,   10
        Through deeps below,
    A duplicated golden glow.

        Far, vague, and dim,
        The mountains swim;
    While on Vesuvius' misty brim,   15

With outstretched hands,
The gray smoke stands
O'erlooking the volcanic lands.

Here Ischia° smiles
O'er liquid miles;   20
And yonder, bluest of the isles,
Calm Capri° waits,
Her sapphire gates
Beguiling to her bright estates.

I heed not, if   25
My rippling skiff
Float swift or slow from cliff to cliff;
With dreamful eyes
My spirit lies
Under the walls of Paradise.   30

Under the walls
Where swells and falls
The Bay's deep breast at intervals
At peace I lie,
Blown softly by,   35
A cloud upon this liquid sky.

The day, so mild,
Is Heaven's own child,
With Earth and Ocean reconciled;
The airs I feel   40
Around me steal
Are murmuring to the murmuring keel.

Over the rail
My hand I trail
Within the shadow of the sail,⠀⠀⠀⠀⠀⠀45
A joy intense,
The cooling sense
Glides down my drowsy indolence.

With dreamful eyes
My spirit lies⠀⠀⠀⠀⠀⠀50
Where Summer sings and never dies, —
O'erveiled with vines
She glows and shines
Among her future oil and wines.

Her children, hid⠀⠀⠀⠀⠀⠀55
The cliffs amid,
Are gambolling with the gambolling kid;
Or down the walls,
With tipsy calls,
Laugh on the rocks like waterfalls.⠀⠀⠀⠀⠀⠀60

The fisher's child,
With tresses wild,
Unto the smooth, bright sand beguiled,
With glowing lips
Sings as she skips,⠀⠀⠀⠀⠀⠀65
Or gazes at the far-off ships.

Yon deep bark goes
Where traffic blows,
From lands of sun to lands of snows;

x

This happier one, —   70
    Its course is run
From lands of snow to lands of sun.

    O happy ship,
    To rise and dip
With the blue crystal at your lip!   75
    O happy crew,
    My heart with you
Sails, and sails, and sings anew!

    No more, no more
    The worldly shore   80
Upbraids me with its loud uproar:
    With dreamful eyes
    My spirit lies
Under the walls of Paradise!

WALT WHITMAN

PIONEERS! O PIONEERS

(Selection)

Come, my tan-faced children,
Follow well in order, get your weapons ready;
Have you your pistols? have you your sharp-edged axes?
    Pioneers! O pioneers!

For we cannot tarry here; 5
We must march, my darlings, we must bear the brunt of
    danger,
We the youthful sinewy races, all the rest on us depend,
    Pioneers! O pioneers!

O you youths, Western youths,
So impatient, full of action, full of manly pride and friend-
    ship, 10
Plain I see you, Western youths, see you tramping with the
    foremost,
    Pioneers! O pioneers!

Have the elder races halted?
Do they droop and end their lesson, wearied over there be-
    yond the seas?
We take up the task eternal, and the burden and the lesson, 15
    Pioneers! O pioneers!

307

All the past we leave behind,
We debouch° upon a newer mightier world, varied world;
Fresh and strong the world we seize, world of labor and the
     march,
    Pioneers! O pioneers!   20

We detachments steady throwing,
Down the edges, through the passes, up the mountains
     steep,
Conquering, holding, daring, venturing as we go the unknown
     ways,
    Pioneers! O pioneers!

We primeval forests felling,   25
We the rivers stemming, vexing we and piercing deep the
     mines within,
We the surface broad surveying, we the virgin soil upheav-
     ing,
    Pioneers! O pioneers!

Colorado men are we;
From the peaks gigantic, from the great sierras and the high
     plateaus,   30
From the mine and from the gully, from the hunting trail,
     we come,
    Pioneers! O pioneers!

From Nebraska, from Arkansas,
Central inland race are we, from Missouri, with the conti-
     nental blood intervein'd;
All the hands of comrades clasping, all the Southern, all the
     Northern,   35
    Pioneers! O pioneers!

O resistless restless race!
O beloved race in all! O my breast aches with tender love
    for all!
O I mourn and yet exult, I am rapt with love for all,
    Pioneers! O pioneers!   40

    Raise the mighty mother mistress,
Waving high the delicate mistress, over all the starry mis-
    tress (bend your heads all),
Raise the fang'd and warlike mistress, stern, impassive,
    weapon'd mistress,
    Pioneers! O pioneers!

    See, my children, resolute children,   45
By those swarms upon our rear we must never yield or falter,
Ages back in ghostly millions frowning there behind us urg-
    ing,
    Pioneers! O pioneers!

    On and on the compact ranks,
With accessions ever waiting, with the places of the dead
    quickly fill'd,   50
Through the battle, through defeat, moving yet and never
    stopping,
    Pioneers! O pioneers!

    Minstrels latent on the prairies
(Shrouded bards of other lands, you may rest, you have done
    your work),
Soon I hear you coming warbling, soon you rise and tramp
    amid us,   55
    Pioneers! O pioneers!

Not for delectations sweet,
Not the cushion and the slipper, not the peaceful and the
    studious,
Not the riches safe and palling, not for us the tame enjoy-
    ment,
    Pioneers! O pioneers!
                                                                    60

Do the feasters gluttonous feast?
Do the corpulent sleepers sleep? have they lock'd and bolted
    doors?
Still be ours the diet hard, and the blanket on the ground,
    Pioneers! O pioneers!

Has the night descended?
                                                                    65
Was the road of late so toilsome? did we stop discouraged
    nodding on our way?
Yet a passing hour I yield you in your tracks to pause
    oblivious,
    Pioneers! O pioneers!

Till with sound of trumpet,
Far, far off the daybreak call — hark! how loud and clear I
    hear it wind!
Swift! to the head of the army! — swift! spring to your
    places,   70
    Pioneers! O pioneers!

O CAPTAIN! MY CAPTAIN!°

O CAPTAIN! my Captain! our fearful trip is done;
The ship has weather'd every rack, the prize we sought is
    won;
The port is near, the bells I hear, the people all exulting,
While follow eyes the steady keel, the vessel grim and daring.
    But O heart! heart! heart!   5
        O the bleeding drops of red,
            Where on the deck my Captain lies,
                Fallen cold and dead.

O Captain! my Captain! rise up and hear the bells;
Rise up — for you the flag is flung — for you the bugle
    trills —   10
For you bouquets and ribbon'd wreaths — for you the shores
    a-crowding —
For you they call, the swaying mass, their eager faces turning.
    Here, Captain! dear father!
        This arm beneath your head!
            It is some dream that on the deck   15
                You've fallen cold and dead.

My Captain does not answer, his lips are pale and still;
My father does not feel my arm, he has no pulse nor will.
The ship is anchor'd safe and sound, its voyage closed and
    done;
From fearful trip the victor ship comes in with object won. 20
    Exult, O shores! and ring, O bells!
        But I with mournful tread
            Walk the deck my Captain lies,
                Fallen cold and dead.

O CAPTAIN! MY CAPTAIN!

O Captain! my Captain! our fearful trip is done,
The ship has weather'd every rack, the prize we sought is
    won,
The port is near, the bells I hear, the people all exulting,
While follow eyes the steady keel, the vessel grim and daring;
          But O heart! heart! heart!
            O the bleeding drops of red,
              Where on the deck my Captain lies,
                Fallen cold and dead.

O Captain! my Captain! rise up and hear the bells;
Rise up—for you the flag is flung—for you the bugle
    trills,
For you bouquets and ribbon'd wreaths—for you the shores
    a-crowding,
For you they call, the swaying mass, their eager faces turning;
            Here Captain! dear father!
              This arm beneath your head!
                It is some dream that on the deck,
                  You've fallen cold and dead.

My Captain does not answer, his lips are pale and still,
My father does not feel my arm, he has no pulse nor will,
The ship is anchor'd safe and sound, its voyage closed and
    done,
From fearful trip the victor ship comes in with object won;
          Exult O shores, and ring O bells!
            But I with mournful tread,
              Walk the deck my Captain lies,
                Fallen cold and dead.

NOTES

ANNE DUDLEY BRADSTREET (1612–1672)

" One wishes she were more winning : yet there is no gainsaying that she was clever ; wonderfully well instructed for those days ; a keen and close observer ; often dexterous in her verse — catching betimes upon epithets that are very picturesque : But — the Tenth Muse is too rash."

— DONALD G. MITCHELL.

Born in England, she married at sixteen and came to Boston, where she always considered herself an exile. In 1644 her husband moved deeper into the wilderness and there " the first professional poet of New England " wrote her poems and brought up a family of eight children. Her English publisher called her the " Tenth Muse, lately sprung up in America."

CONTEMPLATION (page 1)

2. Phœbus : Apollo, the Greek sun god, hence in poetry the sun.

7. delectable : giving pleasure.

13. dight : adorned.

MICHAEL WIGGLESWORTH (1631–1705)

" He was, himself, in nearly all respects, the embodiment of what was great, earnest, and sad, in Colonial New England. . . . In spite, however, of all offences, of all defects, there are in his poetry an irresistible sincerity, a reality, a vividness, reminding one of similar qualities in the prose of John Bunyan."
— M. C. TYLER.

Born in England, he was brought to America at the age of seven. He graduated from Harvard College and then became a preacher. He later added the profession of medicine and practiced both professions.

THE DAY OF DOOM (page 3)

There seems to be no doubt that this poem was the most popular piece of literature, aside from the Bible, in the New England Puritan colonies. Children memorized it, and its considerable length made it sufficient for many Sunday afternoons. Notice the double attempt at rhyme ; the first, third, fifth, and seventh lines rhyme within themselves ; the second line rhymes with the fourth, the sixth with the eighth. The pronunciation in such lines as 35, 77, 79, 93, 99, 105, and 107 requires adaptation to rhyme, as does the grammar in line 81, for example.

3. carnal : belonging merely to this world as opposed to spiritual.

11–15. See *Matthew* 25 : 1–13.

40. wonted steads : customary places.

PHILIP FRENEAU (1752–1832)

" The greatest poet born in America before the Revolutionary War. . . . His best poems are a few short lyrics, remarkable for their simplicity, sincerity, and love of nature."

— REUBEN P. HALLECK.

Born in New York, he graduated from Princeton at the age of nineteen and became school teacher, sea captain, interpreter, editor, and poet. He lost his way in a severe storm and was found dead the next day.

TO A HONEY BEE (page 9)

29–30. Pharaoh : King of Egypt in the time of Joseph, who perished in the Red Sea. See *Exodus*, Chapter xiv.

34. epitaph : an inscription in memory of the dead.

35. Charon : the Greek mythical boatman on the River Styx.

EUTAW SPRINGS (page 12)

Eutaw Springs. Sept. 8th, 1781, the Americans under General Greene fought a battle which was successful for the Americans, since Georgia and the Carolinas were freed from English invasion.

21. Greene : Nathanael Greene of Rhode Island was one of the men who became a leader early in the war and who in spite of opposition and failure stood by the American cause through all the hard days of the war.

25. Parthian : the soldiers of Parthia were celebrated as horse-archers. Their mail-clad horsemen spread like a cloud round the hostile army and poured in a shower of darts. Then they evaded any closer conflict by a rapid flight, during which they still shot their arrows backwards upon the enemy. See Smith, *Classical Dictionary.*

FRANCIS HOPKINSON (1737–1791)

He was " a mathematician, a chemist, a physicist, a mechanician, an inventor, a musician and a composer of music, a man of literary knowledge and practice, a writer of airy and dainty songs, a clever artist with pencil and brush, and a humorist of unmistakable power."

— MOSES COIT TYLER.

Born in Philadelphia, he graduated from the College of Philadelphia and began the practice of law. He signed the Declaration of Independence and held various offices under the federal government. " The Battle of the Kegs " is his best-known production.

THE BATTLE OF THE KEGS (page 14)

59. Stomach : courage.

JOSEPH HOPKINSON (1770–1842)

" His legal essays and decisions were long accepted as authoritative ; but he will be longest remembered for his national song, 'Hail Columbia,' written in 1798, which attained immediate popularity and did much to fortify wavering patriotism." — NEW INTERNATIONAL ENCYCLOPÆDIA.

The Ballad of Nathan Hale (page 21)

For the story of Nathan Hale see any good history of the American Revolution. He is honored by the students of Yale as one of its noblest graduates, and the building in which he lived has been remodeled and marked with a memorial tablet, while a bronze statue stands before it. This is the last of Yale's old buildings and will now remain for many years.

31. minions : servile favorites.

48. presage : foretell.

TIMOTHY DWIGHT (1752–1817)

" He was in many ways the first of the great modern college presidents; if his was the day of small things, he nevertheless did so many of them and did them so well that he deserves admiration." — William P. Trent.

Born in Northampton, Mass., he graduated from Yale and was then made a tutor there. He became an army chaplain in 1777, but his father's death made his return home necessary. He became a preacher later and finally president of Yale. His hymn, " Love to the Church," is the one thing we most want to keep of all his several volumes.

SAMUEL WOODWORTH (1785–1842)

" Our best patriotic ballads and popular lyrics are, of course, based upon sentiment, aptly expressed by the poet and instinctively felt by the reader. Hence just is the fame and true is the love bestowed upon the choicest songs of our 'single-

poem poets': upon Samuel Woodworth's 'Old Oaken
Bucket,' etc."   — CHARLES F. RICHARDSON.

Born at Scituate, Mass., he had very little education. His
father apprenticed him to a Boston printer while he was a
young boy. He remained in the newspaper business all his
life, and wrote numerous poems, and several operas which
were produced.

WILLIAM CULLEN BRYANT (1794–1878)

"A moralist, dealing chiefly with death and the more sombre
phases of life, a lover and interpreter of nature, a champion
of democracy and human freedom, in each of these capacities
he was destined to do effective service for his countrymen,
and this work was, as it were, cut out for him in his youth,
when he was laboring in the fields, attending corn-huskings
and cabin-raisings, or musing beside forest streams."
        — W. P. TRENT.

Born in a mill-town village in western Massachusetts, he
passed his boyhood on the farm. Unable to complete his college course, he practiced law until 1824, when he became editor
of the *New York Review*. He continued all his life to be a
man of letters.

The poems by Bryant are used by permission of D. Appleton and Company, authorized publishers of his works.

THANATOPSIS (page 30)

34. patriarchs of the infant world : the leaders of the
Hebrews before the days of history.

51. Barcan wilderness : waste of North Africa.

54. Why does Bryant suggest " the wings of the morning " to begin such a survey of the world ? Would he choose the Oregon now ?

THE YELLOW VIOLET (page 33)

28. ape : mimic.

TO A WATERFOWL (page 34)

This poem is very simple in its form and is typical of Bryant's nature poems. First, is his observation of the waterfowl's flight and his question about it. Secondly, the answer is given. Thirdly, the application is made to human nature. Do you find such a comparison of nature and human nature in any other poems by Bryant ?

9. plashy : swampy.
15. illimitable : boundless.

GREEN RIVER (page 35)

Green River, flows near Great Barrington where Bryant practised law.

33. simpler : a collector of herbs for medicinal use.

58. This reference to Bryant's profession is noteworthy. His ambition for a thorough literary training was abandoned on account of poverty. He then took up the study of law and practiced it in Great Barrington, Mass., for nine years. His dislike of this profession is here very plainly shown. He abandoned it entirely in 1824 and gave himself to literature. " I Broke the Spell That Held Me Long " also throws light on his choice of a life work.

THE WEST WIND (page 38)

With this may be compared with profit Shelley's " Ode to
the West Wind " and Kingsley's " Ode to the Northeast
Wind." State the contrast between the ideas of the west
wind held by Shelley and by Bryant.

A FOREST HYMN (page 40)

2. architrave : the beam resting on the top of the column
and supporting the frieze.

5. From these details can you form a picture of this temple
in its exterior and interior ? Is it like a modern church ?

darkling : dimly seen ; a poetic word. Do you find any
other adjectives in this poem which are poetic words ?

23. Why is the poem divided here ? Is the thought divided ? Connected ? Can you account in the same way for
the divisions at lines 68 and 89 ?

34. vaults : arched ceilings.

44. instinct : alive, animated by.

66. emanation : that which proceeds from a source, as
fragrance is an emanation from flowers.

89. This idea that death is the source of other life everywhere in nature is a favorite one with Bryant. It is the fun-
damental thought in his first poem, " Thanatopsis " (A View
of Death), which may be read in connection with " The Forest
Hymn."

96. Emerson discusses this question in " The Problem."
See selections from Emerson.

THE DEATH OF THE FLOWERS (page 44)

26. Bryant's favorite sister, Mrs. Sarah Bryant Shaw, died shortly after her marriage, of tuberculosis. This poem alludes to her and is in its early lines the saddest poem Bryant ever wrote. Notice the change of tone near the end.

29. unmeet : unsuitable.

THE GLADNESS OF NATURE (page 45)

5. hang-bird : the American oriole, which hangs its nest from a branch.

8. wilding : the wild bee which belongs to no hive.

TO THE FRINGED GENTIAN (page 46)

No description of this flower can give an adequate idea of its beauty. The following account, from Reed's " Flower Guide, East of the Rockies," expresses the charm of the flower well : " Fringed Gentian because of its exquisite beauty and comparative rarity is one of the most highly prized of our wild flowers." " During September and October we may find these blossoms fully expanded, delicate, vase-shaped creations with four spreading deeply fringed lobes bearing no resemblance in shape or form to any other American species. The color is a violet-blue, the color that is most attractive to bumblebees, and it is to these insects that the flower is indebted for the setting of its seed. . . . The flowers are wide open only during sunshine, furling in their peculiar twisted manner on cloudy days and at night. In moist woods from Maine to Minnesota and southwards."

Y

This guide gives a good colored picture of the flower as do Matthews' "Field Guide to American Wildflowers" and many other flower books.

8. ground-bird : the vesper sparrow, so called because of its habit of singing in the late evening. Its nest is made of grass and placed in a depression on the ground.

11. portend : indicate by a sign that some event, usually evil, is about to happen.

16. cerulean : deep, clear blue.

SONG OF MARION'S MEN (page 47)

4. Marion, Francis (1732–1795), in 1780 took command of the militia of South Carolina and carried on a vigorous partisan warfare against the English. Colonel Tarleton failed to find "the old swamp fox," as he named him, because the swamp paths of South Carolina were well known to him. See McCrady, "South Carolina in the Revolution," for full particulars of his life.

21. deem : expect.

30. up : over, as in the current expression, "the time is up."

41. barb : a horse of the breed introduced by the Moors from Barbary into Spain and noted for speed and endurance.

49. Santee : a river in South Carolina.

THE CROWDED STREET (page 49)

32. throes : agony.

44. Compare this final thought with the solution in "To a Waterfowl."

The Snow-Shower (page 51)

All the New England poets felt the charm of falling snow, and several have written on the theme. In connection with this poem read Emerson's "Snow-Storm" and Whittier's "The Frost Spirit." The best known of all is Whittier's "Snow-Bound"; the first hundred and fifty lines may well be read here.

9. living swarm: like a swarm of bees from the hidden chambers of the hive.

12. prone: straight down.

17. snow-stars: what are the shapes of snowflakes?

20. Milky way: the white path which seems to lead across the sky at night and which is composed of millions of stars.

21. burlier: larger and stronger.

35. myriads: vast, indefinite number.

37. middle: as the cloud seems to be between us and the blue sky, so the snowflakes before they fell occupied a middle position.

Robert of Lincoln (page 53)

"Robert of Lincoln" is the happiest, merriest poem written by Bryant. It is characteristic of the man that it should deal with a nature topic. In what ways does he secure the merriment?

Analyze each stanza as to structure. Does the punctuation help to indicate the speaker?

Look up the Bobolink in the *Bird Guide* or some similar book. How much actual information did Bryant have about the bird ? Compare the amount of bird-lore given here with that of Shelley's or Wordsworth's " To a Skylark." Which is more poetic ? Which interests you more ?

THE POET (page 56)

5. **deem** : consider. Compare with the use in the " Song of Marion's Men," 1. 21.

8. **wreak** : carry them out in your verse. The word usually has an angry idea associated with it. The suggestion may be here of the frenzy of a poet.

26. **unaptly** : not suitable to the occasion.

30. Only in a moment of great emotion (rapture) should the poet revise a poem which was penned when his heart was on fire with the idea of the poem.

38. **limn** : describe vividly.

54. By this test where would you place Bryant himself ? Did he do what he here advises ? In what poems do you see evidences of such a method ? Compare your idea of him with Lowell's estimate in " A Fable for Critics," ll. 35–56.

ABRAHAM LINCOLN (page 58)

In connection with this poem the following stanza from " The Battle-Field " seems very appropriate :

> "Truth, crushed to Earth, shall rise again ;
>   The eternal years of God are hers ;
> But Error, wounded, writhes with pain,
>   And dies among his worshippers."

The American people certainly felt that Truth was crushed to Earth with Lincoln's death, but believed that it would triumph.

FRANCIS SCOTT KEY (1780–1843)

Born in Maryland, he graduated from St. John's College, Md., and practiced law in Frederick City, Md. He was district attorney for the District of Columbia during the War of 1812 and while imprisoned by the British on board the ship *Minden*, Sept. 13, 1814, he witnessed the British attack on Fort McHenry and wrote this national anthem.

THE STAR-SPANGLED BANNER (page 59)

30. Why is this mentioned as our motto?

JOSEPH RODMAN DRAKE (1795–1820)

The "Culprit Fay" "is so much better than American poetry had previously been that one is at first disposed to speak of it enthusiastically. An obvious comparison puts it in true perspective. Drake's life happened nearly to coincide with that of Keats. . . . Amid the full fervor of European experience Keats produced immortal work ; Drake, whose whole life was passed amid the national inexperience of New York, produced only pretty fancies."
— BARRETT WENDELL.

Born in New York, he practiced medicine there. He died of tuberculosis at the age of twenty-five, and left behind him manuscript verses which were later published by his daughter. "The Culprit Fay," from which selections are here given, is generally considered one of the best productions of early American literature.

The American Flag (page 61)

6. milky baldric : the white band supposed by the ancients to circle the earth and called the zodiac. He may here mean the Milky Way as part of this band.

46. careering : rushing swiftly.

47. bellied : rounded, filled out by the gale.

56. welkin : sky.

The Culprit Fay (page 63)

25. ising-stars : particles of mica.

30. minim : smallest. What objection may be made to this word ?

37. Ouphe : elf or goblin.

45. behest : command.

78. shardy : resembling a shell or a scale.

94. oozy : muddy.

107. colen-bell : coined by Drake, probably [the columbine.

114. nightshade : a flower also called henbane or belladonna.   **dern** : drear.

119. thrids : threads, makes his way through.

160. prong : probably a prawn ; used in this sense only in this one passage.

165. quarl : jelly fish.

178. wake-line : showing by a line of foam the course over which he has passed.

193. amain : at full speed.

210. banned : cursed as by a supernatural power.

216. henbane: see note on line 114.

223. fatal : destined to determine his fate.

245. sculler's notch : depression in which the oar rested.

255. wimpled : undulated.

257. athwart : across.

306. glossed : having gloss, or brightness.

329. This is only the first of the exploits of the Culprit Fay. The second quest is described by the monarch as follows :

> "If the spray-bead gem be won,
>   The stain of thy wing is washed away,
> But another errand must be done
>   Ere thy crime be lost for aye ;
> Thy flame-wood lamp is quenched and dark,
> Thou must re-illume its spark.
> Mount thy steed and spur him high
> To the heaven's blue canopy ;
> And when thou seest a shooting star,
> Follow it fast, and follow it far —
> The last faint spark of its burning train
> Shall light the elfin lamp again."

FITZ–GREENE HALLECK (1790–1867)

" The poems of Halleck are written with great care and finish, and manifest the possession of a fine sense of harmony and of genial and elevated sentiments."

— ENCYCLOPÆDIA BRITANNICA.

Born in Guilford, Conn., he was the closest friend of Drake, at whose death he wrote his best poem, which is given in this collection. " Marco Bozzaris " aroused great enthusiasm, which has now waned in favor of his simple lines, " On the Death of Joseph Rodman Drake."

The poems by Halleck are used by permission of D. Appleton and Company, authorized publishers of his works.

MARCO BOZZARIS (page 75)

Marco Bozzaris (c. 1790–1823) was a prominent leader in the struggle for Greek liberty and won many victories from the Turks. During the night of August 20, 1823, the Greeks won a complete victory which was saddened by the loss of Bozzaris, who fell while leading his men to the final attack.

13. Suliote: a tribe of Turkish subjects of mixed Greek and Albanian blood, who steadily opposed Turkish rule and won for themselves a reputation for bravery. They fought for Grecian independence under Marco Bozzaris.

16–22. These lines refer to the military history of Greece. See Encyclopædia Britannica — article on Greece (Persian Wars subtitle) for account of the Persian invasion and battle of Platæa.

79. What land did Columbus see first ? Where did he come from ? Why then is he called a Genoese ?

107. pilgrim-circled : visited by pilgrims as are shrines.

JOHN HOWARD PAYNE (1791–1852)

Born in New York, he graduated from Union College and later went on the stage. He was appointed U. S. Consul to

Tunis, where he died. He is now best remembered by " Home, Sweet Home " from one of his operas.

EDGAR ALLAN POE (1809–1849)

" Small as the quantity of his true verse is, it more sustains his peculiar genius in American eyes than does his prose; and this is because it is so unique. He stands absolutely alone as a poet, with none like him." — GEORGE E. WOODBERRY.

Born in Boston, he spent most of his literary years in New York. His parents, both actors, died when he was still a little child, and he was adopted by Mr. Allan, who educated him in Europe. He served as literary editor and hack writer for several journals and finally died in poverty.

To HELEN (page 81)

"To Helen" is said to have been written in 1823, when Poe was only fourteen years old. It refers to Mrs. Jane Stith Stanard, the mother of one of his school friends, whose death was a terrible blow to the sensitive, lonely lad. This loss was the cause of numerous poems of sorrow for death and permanently influenced his work.

2. **Nicéan** : Nicæa, the modern Iznik in Turkey, was anciently a Greek province.

2. **Nicéan barks** : the Greek ships that bore the **wanderer**, Ulysses, from Phæacia to his home. Read " The Wanderings of Ulysses " in Gayley's *Classic Myths*, Chapter XXVII.

7. **hyacinth** : like Hyacinthus, the fabled favorite of Apollo ; hence lovely, beautiful.

8. Naiad : a nymph presiding over fountains, lakes, brooks, and wells.

14. Psyche, a beautiful maiden beloved of Cupid, whose adventure with the lamp is told in all classical mythologies.

ISRAFEL (page 82)

Israfel, according to the Koran, is the angel with the sweetest voice among God's creatures. He will blow the trump on the day of resurrection.

2. The idea that Israfel's lute was more than human is taken from Moore's " Lalla Rookh," although these very words do not occur there. The reference will be found in the last hundred lines of the poem.

12. levin : lightning.

26. Houri : one of the beautiful girls who, according to the Moslem faith, are to be companions of the faithful in paradise.

LENORE (page 84)

13. Peccavimus : we have sinned.

20. Avaunt : Begone ! Away !

26. Pæan : song of joy or triumph.

THE COLISEUM (page 85)

10. Eld : antiquity.

14. See *Matthew* 26 : 36–56.

16. The Chaldæans were the world's greatest astrologers.

26–29. Poe here uses technical architectural terms with success.

plinth : the block upon which a column or a statue rests.

shafts : the main part of a column between the base and the capital.

entablatures : the part of a building borne by the columns.

frieze : an ornamented horizontal band in the entablature.

cornices : the horizontal molded top of the entablatures.

32. corrosive : worn away by degrees ; used figuratively of time.

36. At Thebes there is a statue which is supposed to be Memnon, the mythical king of Ethiopia, and which at daybreak was said to emit the music of the lyre.

EULALIE. — A SONG (page 89)

19. Astarté : the Phœnician goddess of love.

THE RAVEN (page 90)

41. Pallas : Greek goddess of wisdom.

46–47. Night's Plutonian shore : Pluto ruled over the powers of the lower world and over the dead. Darkness and gloom are constantly associated with him ; the cypress tree was sacred to him and black victims were sacrificed to him. Why does the coming of the raven suggest this realm to the poet ?

50. relevancy : appropriateness.

80. Seraphim : one of the highest orders of angels.

82. respite and nepenthe : period of peace and forgetting.

89. balm in Gilead. See *Jeremiah* 8 : 22 ; 46 : 11 and *Genesis* 37 : 25.

93. Aideen, fanciful spelling of Eden.

106. This line has been often criticized on the ground

that a lamp could not cause any shadow on the floor if the bird sat above the door. Poe answered this charge by saying : "My conception was that of the bracket candelabrum affixed against the wall, high up above the door and bust, as is often seen in English palaces, and even in some of the better houses of New York."

What effect does this poem have upon you ? Work out the rhyme scheme in the first and second stanzas. Are they alike ? Does this rhyme scheme help to produce the effect of the poem ? Have you noticed a similar use of "more" in any other poem ? Point out striking examples of repetition, of alliteration. Are there many figures of speech here ?

To Helen (page 96)

This Helen is Mrs. Whitman.

15. parterre : a flower garden whose beds are arranged in a pattern and separated by walks.

48. Dian : Roman goddess representing the moon.

60. elysian : supremely happy.

65. scintillant : sending forth flashes of light.

66. Venuses : morning stars.

The Bells (page 100)

"The Bells" originally consisted of eighteen lines, and was gradually enlarged to its present form.

10. Runic : secret, mysterious.

11. Why does Poe use this peculiar word ? Compare its use with that of "euphony," l. 26, "jangling," l. 62, "monotone," l. 83.

26. euphony : the quality of having a pleasant sound.

72. monody : a musical composition in which some one voice-part predominates.

88. Ghouls : imaginary evil beings of the East who rob graves.

ELDORADO (page 104)

6. Eldorado : any region where wealth may be obtained in abundance ; hence, figuratively, the source of any abundance, as here.

21. Valley of the Shadow suggests death and is a fitting close to Poe's poetic work.

HENRY WADSWORTH LONGFELLOW (1807–1882)

"His verse blooms like a flower, night and day ;
  Bees cluster round his rhymes ; and twitterings
Of lark and swallow, in an endless May,
  Are mingling with the tender songs he sings.
Nor shall he cease to sing — in every lay
Of Nature's voice he sings — and will alway."
— JAMES WHITCOMB RILEY.

Born in Portland, Maine, he graduated from Bowdoin College in 1825 and went abroad to prepare himself to teach the modern languages. He taught until 1854, when he became a professional author. During the remaining years of his life he lived quietly at Craigie House in Cambridge and there he died.

The poems by Longfellow are used by permission of, and by special arrangement with, Houghton Mifflin Company, authorized publishers of his works.

Hymn to the Night (page 106)

'Ασπασίη, τρίλλιστος : "Night, thrice welcome."
"Night, undesired by Troy, but to the Greeks
Thrice welcome for its interposing gloom."
— Cowper, trans. of Iliad VIII, 488.

21. Orestes-like. Orestes, the son of Agamemnon and Clytemnestra, avenged the death of his father by killing his mother. The Furies chased him for many years through the world until at last he found pardon and peace. The story is told in several Greek plays, but perhaps best in Æschylus' "Libation Pourers" and "Furies."

A Psalm of Life (page 107)

"I kept it," he said, "some time in manuscript, unwilling to show it to any one, it being a voice from my inmost heart."

7. "Dust thou art" : quoted from *Genesis* 3 : 19, "Dust thou art, and unto dust shalt thou return."
10. Pope in Epistle IV of his "Essay on Man" says : "O happiness ! our being's end and aim." How does Longfellow differ with him ?

The Skeleton in Armor (page 108)

The Skeleton in Armor. "The following Ballad was suggested to me while riding on the seashore at Newport. A year or two previous a skeleton had been dug up at Fall River,

clad in broken and corroded armor ; and the idea occurred to
me of connecting it with the Round Tower at Newport, generally known hitherto as the Old Windmill, though now
claimed by the Danes as a work of their early ancestors."

19. Skald : a Scandinavian minstrel who composed and
sang or recited verses in celebration of famous deeds, heroes,
and events.

> "And there, in many a stormy vale,
> The Scald had told his wondrous tale."
> — SCOTT, *Lay of the Last Minstrel*, can. 6, st. 22.

20. Saga : myth or heroic story.

28. ger-falcon : large falcon, much used in northern
Europe in falconry.

38. were-wolf : a person who had taken the form of a wolf
and had become a cannibal.   The superstition was that those
who had voluntarily become wolves could become men again
at will.

42. corsair : pirate.   Originally " corsair " was applied
to privateers off the Barbary Coast who preyed upon Christian
shipping under the authority of their governments.

49. " wassail-bout " : festivity at which healths are drunk.

53. Berserk. Berserker was a legendary Scandinavian
hero who never wore a shirt of mail.   In general, a warrior
who could assume the form and ferocity of wild beasts, and
whom fire and iron could not harm.

94. Sea-mew : a kind of European gull.

110. Skaw : a cape on the coast of Denmark.

159. Skoal ! : Hail ! a toast or friendly greeting used by the
Norse especially in poetry.

THE WRECK OF THE HESPERUS (page 114)

On Dec. 17, 1839, Longfellow wrote in his journal : "News of shipwrecks, horrible, on the coast. Forty bodies washed ashore near Gloucester, one lashed to a piece of the wreck. There is a reef called Norman's Woe, where many of these took place ; among others the schooner *Hesperus*."

On Dec. 30 he added: "Sat till one o'clock by the fire, smoking, when suddenly it came into my head to write the Ballad of the schooner *Hesperus*, which I accordingly did. Then went to bed, but could not sleep. New thoughts were running in my mind, and I got up to add them to the ballad. It was three by the clock." . . . "I feel pleased with the ballad. It hardly cost me an effort. It did not come into my mind by lines but by stanzas."

In a letter to Mr. Charles Lanman on Nov. 24, 1871, Mr. Longfellow said : "I had quite forgotten about its first publication ; but I find a letter from Park Benjamin, dated Jan. 7, 1840, beginning . . . as follows : —

"'Your ballad, The Wreck of the *Hesperus*, is grand. Enclosed are twenty-five dollars (the sum you mentioned) for it, paid by the proprietors of *The New World*, in which glorious paper it will resplendently coruscate on Saturday next.'"

11. flaw : a sudden puff of wind.

14. Spanish Main : a term applied to that portion of the Caribbean Sea near the northeast coast of South America, including the route followed by Spanish merchant ships in traveling between Europe and America.

37–48. This little dialogue reminds us of the "Erlkönig," a ballad by Goethe.

56. See *Luke* 8 : 22–25.

60. Norman's Woe : a reef in W. Gloucester harbor, Mass.

70. carded wool. The process of carding wool, cotton, flax, etc. removes by a wire-toothed brush foreign matter and dirt, and leaves it combed out and cleansed.

THE VILLAGE BLACKSMITH (page 118)

7. Crisp, and black, and long. Mr. Longfellow says that before this poem was published, he read it to his barber. The man objected that crisp black hair was never long, and as a result the author delayed publication until he was convinced in his own mind that no other adjectives would give a truer picture of the blacksmith as he saw him.

39–42. Mr. Longfellow's friends agree that these lines depict his own industry and temperament better than any others can.

IT IS NOT ALWAYS MAY (page 120)

No hay pájaros en los nidos de antaño. Translated in lines 12 and 24.

8. freighted : heavily laden.

EXCELSIOR (page 121)

Mr. Longfellow explained fully the allegory of this poem in a letter to Mr. Henry T. Tuckerman. He said : " This (his intention) was no more than to display, in a series of pictures, the life of a man of genius, resisting all temptations, laying aside all fears, heedless of all warnings, and pressing right on to accomplish his purpose. His motto is Excelsior, — ' higher.' He passes through the Alpine village, — through

z

the rough, cold paths of the world — where the peasants cannot understand him, and where his watchword is ' an unknown tongue.' He disregards the happiness of domestic peace, and sees the glaciers — his fate — before him. He disregards the warnings of the old man's wisdom. . . . He answers to all, ' Higher yet ' ! The monks of St. Bernard are the representatives of religious forms and ceremonies, and with their oft-repeated prayer mingles the sound of his voice, telling them there is something higher than forms and ceremonies. Filled with these aspirations he perishes without having reached the perfection he longed for ; and the voice heard in the air is the promise of immortality and progress ever upward."

Compare with this Tennyson's " Merlin and The Gleam," in which he tells his own experience.

7. falchion : a sword with a broad and slightly curved blade, used in the Middle Ages ; hence, poetically, any type of sword.

The Day is Done (page 124)

25. In this stanza and the two following Longfellow describes what his poems have come to mean to us and the place they hold in American life. Compare with Whittier's " Dedication " to " Songs of Labor," ll. 26–36.

Walter von der Vogelweide (page 126)

Walter von der Vogelweide : the most celebrated of medieval German lyric poets; who lived about the year 1200. He belonged to the lower order of " nobility of service." He lived in Tyrol, then the home of famous minnesingers from whom he learned his art.

4. Walter von der Vogelweide is buried in the cloisters adjoining the Neumünster church in Würtzburg, which dates from the eleventh century.

10. The debt of the poet to the birds has been dwelt upon in many poems, the best known of which are Shelley's " Skylark " and Wordsworth's " To the Cuckoo."

27. War of Wartburg. In 1207 there occurred in this German castle, the Wartburg, a contest of the minstrels of the time. Wagner has immortalized this contest in " Tannhäuser," in which he describes the victory of Walter von der Vogelweide over all the other singers.

42. Gothic spire. See note on " The Builders " ll. 17–19.

The Builders (page 128)

17–19. The perfection of detail in the structure and sculpture of Gothic cathedrals may be seen in the cathedrals of Chartres and Amiens. Numerous beautiful illustrations may be found in Marriage, " The Sculptures of Chartres Cathedral," and in Ruskin, " The Bible of Amiens."

Santa Filomena (page 129)

Santa Filomena stands for Miss Florence Nightingale, who did remarkable work among the soldiers wounded in the Crimean War (1854–56). This poem was published in 1857 while the story of her aid was fresh in the minds of the world.

42. The palm, the lily, and the spear : St. Filomena is

represented in many Catholic churches and usually with these three emblems to signify her victory, purity, and martyrdom. Sometimes an anchor replaces the palm.

The Discoverer of the North Cape (page 131)

King Alfred's Orosius. Orosius, a Spaniard of the fifth century A.D., wrote at the request of the church a history of the world down to 414 A.D. King Alfred (849–901) translated this work and added at least one important story, that of the voyages of Ohthere and Wulfstan. The part of the story used by Longfellow may be found in Cook and Tinkers's *Translations from Old English Prose*, in Bosworth's, and in Sweet's editions.

2. Helgoland: an island in the North Sea, belonging to Prussia.

42. Hebrides: islands west of Scotland.

90. a nameless sea. They sailed along the coast of Lapland and into the White Sea.

96–100. Alfred reports simply, " He says he was one of a party of six who killed sixty of these in two days."

115. The original says : " He made this voyage, in addition to his purpose of seeing the country, chiefly for walruses, for they have very good bone in their teeth — they brought some of these teeth to the king — and their hides are very good for ship-ropes."

Sandalphon (page 135)

Sandalphon: one of the oldest angel figures in the Jewish system. In the second century a Jewish writing described him as follows : " He is an angel who stands on the earth . . . ; he is taller than his fellows by the length of a journey of 500 years ; he binds crowns for his Creator." These crowns are symbols of praise, and with them he brings before the Deity the prayers of men. See the *Jewish Encyclopaedia* for further particulars.

1. Talmud: the work which embodies the Jewish law of church and state. It consists of texts and many commentaries and illustrations.

12. Refers to *Genesis* 28 : 10–22.

39. Rabbinical: pertaining to the Jewish rabbis or teachers of law.

44. welkin: poetical term for the sky.

48. nebulous: indistinct.

THE LANDLORD'S TALE (page 138)

The " Tales of a Wayside Inn " were series of stories told on three separate days by the travelers at the Inn at Sudbury, Mass. It is the same device used by writers since the days of Chaucer, but cleverly handled furnishes an interesting setting for a variety of tales. Some of Longfellow's best-known narratives are in these series, among them the following selections.

The story is self-explanatory. It is probably the best example of the simple poetic narrative of an historic event.

107–110. The reference is to one of the seven men who were killed at Lexington — possibly to Jonathan Harrington, Jr., who dragged himself to his own door-step before he died. Many books tell the story, but the following are the most interesting ; Gettemy, Chas. F., *True Story of Paul Revere*; Colburn, F., *The Battle of April 19, 1775*.

The Sicilian's Tale (page 142)

This story of King Robert of Sicily is very old, as it is found among the short stories of the Gesta Romanorum written in the thirteenth and fourteenth centuries.

17. seditious : tending towards disorder and treason.

52. besprent : poetic for besprinkled.

56. seneschal : the official in the household of a prince or high noble who had the supervision of feasts and ceremonies.

106. Saturnian : the fabled reign of the god Saturn was the golden age of the world, characterized by simplicity, virtue, and happiness.

110. Enceladus, the giant. Longfellow's poem "Enceladus" emphasizes this reference. For the story of the giants and the punishment of Enceladus see any good Greek mythology.

The Theologian's Tale (page 150)

9. dial : the sun-dial was the clock of the time.

41. iteration : repetition.

49. dole : portion.

51. almoner : official dispenser of alms.

100. See *Matthew* 25 : 40.

JOHN GREENLEAF WHITTIER (1807–1892)

"Best loved and saintliest of our singing train,
    Earth's noblest tributes to thy name belong.
A lifelong record closed without a stain,
    A blameless memory shrined in deathless song."
        — Oliver Wendell Holmes.

Born at East Haverhill, Mass., in surroundings which he faithfully describes in " Snow-Bound," he had little education. At the age of twenty-two he secured an editorial position in Boston and continued to write all his life. For some years he devoted all his literary ability to the cause of abolition, and not until the success of " Snow-Bound " in 1866 was he free from poverty.

The poems by Whittier are used by permission of, and by special arrangement with, Houghton Mifflin Company, authorized publishers of his works.

PROEM (page 155)

Proem : preface or introduction.

3. Spenser, Edmund (1552–1599). His best-known work is the " Faerie Queen."

4. Arcadian Sidney: Sir Philip Sidney (1554–1586) ; an English courtier, soldier, and author. He stands as a model of chivalry. He was mortally wounded at the battle of Zutphen. " Arcadia " was his greatest work ; hence the epithet here.

23. plummet-line : a weight suspended by a line used to test the verticality of walls, etc. Here used as if in a sounding process.

30. Compare this opinion of his own work with Lowell's comments in " A Fable for Critics." How do they agree ?

32. For Whittier's opinion of Milton see also " Raphael," l. 70, and " Burns," l. 104.

33. Marvell, Andrew (1621–1678) : an English statesman, poet, and satirist, friend of Milton.

THE FROST SPIRIT (page 156)

Whittier has an intense love and appreciation of winter. With this poem may be read " Snow Bound," the last stanzas of " Flowers in Winter," and " Lumbermen." Many others may be added to this list. Do you find this same idea in other poets?

11. Hecla : a volcano in Iceland which has had 28 known eruptions — one as late as 1878. It rises 5100 feet above the sea and has a bare, irregular-shaped cone. Its appearance is extremely wild and desolate.

SONGS OF LABOR. DEDICATION (page 158)

8. The o'er-sunned bloom. . . . In this collection of poems are a few written in his youth, the more mature works of the " summer " of his life, and the later works of his old age. The figure here is carefully carried through and gives a clear, simplified picture of his literary life.

22. Whittier himself noted that he was indebted for this line to Emerson's " Rhodora."

26–35. Compare Longfellow's " The Day is Done " for another idea of the influence of poetry.

36. Compare *Genesis* 3 : 17–19.

43–45. Compare *Luke* 2 : 51–52.

THE LUMBERMEN (page 160)

33. Ambijejis : lake in central Maine.

35. Millnoket : a lake in central Maine.

39. Penobscot : one of the most beautiful of Maine rivers.

It is about 300 miles along and flows through the central part of the state.

42. Katahdin : Mount Katahdin is 5385 feet in height and is usually snow-covered.

BARCLAY OF URY (page 163)

Barclay of Ury : David Barclay (1610–1686). Served under Gustavus Adolphus, was an officer in the Scotch army during Civil War. He bought the estate of Ury, near Aberdeen, in 1648. He was arrested after the Restoration and for a short time was confined to Edinburgh Castle, where he was converted to Quakerism by a fellow prisoner. His son, also a Quaker, heard of the imprisonment mentioned in this poem and attempted to rescue his father. During the years between this trouble in 1676 and his death in 1686, the persecution seems to have been directed largely against his son. (See *Dictionary of National Biography* for details.) Whittier naturally felt keenly on this subject, as he himself was a Quaker.

1. Aberdeen : capital of Aberdeenshire, and chief seaport in north of Scotland ; fourth Scottish town in population, industry, and wealth. The buildings of Aberdeen College, founded in 1494, are the glory of Aberdeen.

7. churl : a rude, low-bred fellow.

10. carlin : a bluff, good-natured man.

35. Lutzen : a town in Saxony where the Swedes under Gustavus Adolphus defeated the Austrians, Nov. 16, 1632.

36. Gustavus Adolphus, " The Great " (1594–1632). He was one of the great Swedish kings, and was very prominent in the Thirty Years' War (1618–1648).

56. Tilly: Johann Tserklaes, Count von Tilly, a German imperial commander in the Thirty Years' War.

57. Walloon: a people akin to the French, inhabiting Belgium and some districts of Prussia. They have greater vivacity than the Flemish, and more endurance than the French.

66. Jewry: Judea.

76. reeve: a bailiff or overseer.

81. snooded. The unmarried women of Scotland formerly wore a band around their heads to distinguish them from married women.

99. Tolbooth: Scotch word for prison.

126. This idea is expanded in the poem "Seed-time and Harvest."

RAPHAEL (page 168)

Raphael Sanzio (1483–1520), the great Italian painter. Trained first by his father, later by the great Perugino. His work was done mainly in Florence and Rome.

6. This picture is the portrait of Raphael when scarcely more than a boy.

17. Gothland's sage: Sweden's wise man, Emanuel Swedenborg.

36. Raphael painted many madonnas, but the word "drooped" limits this description. Several might be included under this: "The Small Holy Family," "The Virgin with the Rose," or, most probable of all to me, "The Madonna of the Chair."

37. the Desert John: John the Baptist.

40. "The Transfiguration" is not as well known as some of the madonnas, but shows in wonderful manner Raphael's ability to handle a large group of people, without detracting from the central figure. It is now in the Vatican Gallery, at Rome.

42. There are few great Old Testament stories which are not depicted by Raphael. Among them are The Passage Through Jordan, The Fall of Jericho, Joshua Staying the Sun, David and Goliath, The Judgment of Solomon, The Building of the Temple, Moses Bringing the Tables of the Law, the Golden Calf, and many others equally well known.

45. Fornarina. This well-known portrait is now in the Palazzo Barberini in Rome.

70. holy song on Milton's tuneful ear. Poetry and painting are here spoken of together as producing permanent effects, and from the figure he uses we may add music to the list. Compare Longfellow's " The Arrow and the Song." In the last stanza the field is still further broadened until his thought is that all we do lives after us.

Seed-Time and Harvest (page 171)

5. Whittier's intense interest in Freedom is here apparent. His earlier poems were largely on the slavery question in America. His best work was not done until he began to devote his poetic ability to a wider range of subjects.

26. See Longfellow, " A Psalm of Life," ll. 9–12 and note.

The Prophecy of Samuel Sewall (page 173)

12. Samuel Sewall is one of the most interesting characters in colonial American history. He was born in England in 1652, but came to America while still a child. He graduated from Harvard College in 1671 and finally became a justice of the peace. He was instrumental in the Salem witchcraft decision, but later bitterly repented. He made in 1697 a public confession of his share in the matter and begged that God would " not visit the sin . . . upon the Land."

28. Hale's Reports. Sir Matthew Hale (1609–1676) was one of the most eminent judges of England. From 1671 to 1676 he occupied the position of Chief Justice of the King's Bench, the highest judicial position in England. Sewall was depending upon an authority of the day.

32. warlock's : a wizard, one who deals in incantations ; synonymous with witch.

46. Theocracy : a state governed directly by the ministers of God.

58. hand-grenade : a hollow shell, filled with explosives, arranged to be thrown by hand among the enemy and to explode on impact.

73. Koordish robber. The Kurds were a nomadic people living in Kurdistan, Persia, and Caucasia. They were very savage and vindictive, specially towards Armenians. The Sheik was the leader of a clan or town and as such had great power.

81. Newbury, Mass. Judge Sewall's father was one of the founders of the town.

130–156. This prophecy is most effective in its use of local color for a spiritual purpose. Beginning with local conditions which might be changed, it broadens to include all nature which shall never grow old.

SKIPPER IRESON'S RIDE (page 178)

Skipper Ireson's Ride. Whittier was told after this poem was published that it was not historically accurate, since the crew and not Skipper Ireson was to blame for the desertion of the wreck. He stated that he had founded his poem on a song sung to him when he was a boy.

3. Apuleius's Golden Ass. Apuleius was a Latin satirical writer whose greatest work was a romance or novel called " The Golden Ass." The hero is by chance changed into an ass, and has all sorts of adventures until he is finally freed from the magic by eating roses in the hands of a priest of Isis.

3. one-eyed Calendar's horse of brass. See the *Arabian Nights' Entertainments* for the story of the one-eyed beggar.

6. Al-Borak: according to the Moslem creed the animal brought by Gabriel to carry Mohammed to the seventh heaven. It had the face of a man, the body of a horse, the wings of an eagle, and spoke with a human voice.

11. Marblehead, in Massachusetts.

30. Mænads: the nymphs who danced and sang in honor of Bacchus, the god of vegetation and the vine.

35. Chaleur Bay, in Newfoundland, a part of the Gulf of St. Lawrence.

THE DOUBLE-HEADED SNAKE OF NEWBURY (page 182)

6. Deucalion flood. The python was a monstrous serpent which arose from the mud left after the flood in which Deucalion survived. The python lived in a cave on Mount Parnassus and there Apollo slew him. Deucalion and his wife

Pyrrha were saved from the flood because Zeus respected their piety.   They obeyed the oracle and threw stones behind them from which sprang men and women to repopulate the earth.

9. See " The Prophecy of Samuel Sewall " for another story of Newbury town.

22. stones of Cheops : an Egyptian king, about 2900 B.C. ; built the great pyramid, which is called by his name.

59. Each town in colonial days set aside certain land for free pasture-land for the inhabitants.

60. double-ganger : a double or apparition of a person ; here, a reptile moving in double form.

76. Cotton Mather (1663–1728). This precocious boy entered Harvard College at eleven and graduated at fifteen. At seventeen he preached his first sermon and all his life was a zealous divine.   He was undoubtedly sincere in his judgments in the cases of witchcraft and was not thoughtlessly cruel. He was a great writer and politician and a public-minded citizen.

85. Wonder-Book of Cotton Mather is his story of early New England life called *Magnalia Christi Americana*.

MAUD MULLER (page 185)

94. astral : a lamp with peculiar construction so that the shadow is not cast directly below it.

BURNS (page 190)

Burns.   In connection with this poem may well be read the following poems by Robert Burns (1759–1796) : " The Twa Dogs," " A Man's a Man for A' That," " Cotter's Saturday

Night" (Selections), "Ye Banks and Braes o' Bonnie Doon," "Highland Mary."

40. allegory : the expression of an idea indirectly by means of a story or narrative. Bunyan's *Pilgrim's Progress* is probably the best-known allegory. What others can you name ?

67. Craigie-burn and **Devon** were favorite Scotch streams.

71. Ayr : a river in Scotland. This whole region is full of associations with Burns. Near it he was born and there is the Auld Brig of Doon of Tam o' Shanter fame. Near the river is a Burns monument. **Doon :** a river of Scotland 30 miles long and running through wild and picturesque country. Burns has made it famous.

91–92. The unpleasant facts of Burns's life, due to weakness of character, should not be allowed to destroy our appreciation of what he accomplished when he was his better self.

99. Magdalen. See *John* 8 : 3–11 and many other instances in the Gospels.

103. The mournful Tuscan : Dante, who wrote " The Divine Comedy."

The Hero (page 195)

1. Bayard, Pierre Terrail (1473–1524) : a French soldier who, on account of his heroism, piety, and magnanimity was called " le chevalier sans peur et sans reproche," the fearless and faultless knight. By his contemporaries he was more often called " le bon chevalier," the good knight.

6. Zutphen : an old town in Holland, which was often besieged, especially during the wars of freedom waged by the

Dutch.   The most celebrated fight under its walls was in September, 1586, when Sir Philip Sidney was mortally wounded.

   12. See *John* 16 : 21.

   28. Sidney.   See note on line 6 and Proem, note on line 4.

   31. Cyllenian ranges : Mount Cyllene, in southern Greece, is the fabled birthplace of Hermes.

   36. Suliote.   See Fitz-Greene Halleck, "Marco Bozzaris," note on line 13.

   42. The reference is to Samuel G. Howe, who fought as a young man for the independence of Greece.

   45. Albanian : pertaining to Albania, a province of western Turkey.

   78. Cadmus: mythological king of Phœnicia ; was regarded as the introducer of the alphabet from Phœnicia into Greece.

   86. Lancelot stands for most of us as the example of a brave knight whose life was ruined by a great weakness. Malory writes of him in " Mort d'Arthur, " and Tennyson has made him well known to us.

THE ETERNAL GOODNESS (page 199)

   24. See *John* 19 : 23 and *Matthew* 9 : 20–22.

   36. After David had suffered, he wrote the greatest of the Psalms which are attributed to him.   The idea of righteous judgment is to be found throughout them all, but seems especially strong in 9 and 147.

   54. Compare Tennyson's *Crossing the Bar.*

THE PIPES AT LUCKNOW (page 202)

9. Lowland : the south and east of Scotland ; distinguished from the Highlands.

13. pibroch : a wild, irregular martial music played on Scotch bagpipes.

18. A small English garrison was in possession of the city of Lucknow at the time of the great Sepoy Mutiny in India. They were besieged, and their rescue is described here.

32. Sir Henry Havelock commanded the relieving army.

36. Sepoy : a native East-Indian soldier, equipped like a European soldier.

51. Goomtee : a river of Hindustan.

77. Gaelic : belonging to Highland Scotch or other Celtic people.

COBBLER KEEZAR'S VISION (page 205)

The element of superstition which enters into many of Whittier's poems is well illustrated here.

19. the Brocken : in the Harz Mountains in Germany.

35. swart : dark-colored.

49. See " Prophecy of Samuel Sewall," note on line 32.

52. Religion among the Pilgrim fathers was a harsh thing. What illustrations of its character did you find in the early part of this book ?

84. Doctor Dee : an English astrologer (1527–1608).

85. Agrippa, Heinrich Cornelius : German physician, theologian, and writer (1486–1535), who tried to turn less precious metals into gold.

2 A

89. Minnesinger. Hans Sachs (1494–1576), the famous cobbler singer, is probably referred to. For another famous minstrel see notes on Longfellow, " Walter von der Vogelweide."

139. Bingen, a city on the Rhine, has been made famous
by the poem written in 1799 by Southey, " God's Judgment
on a Wicked Bishop." Longfellow refers to this legend in
" The Children's Hour."

140. Frankfort (on-the-Main), in Germany.

147. droughty : thirsty, wanting drink.

THE MAYFLOWERS (page 212)

1. Sad Mayflower : the trailing arbutus.

14. Our years of wandering o'er. The Pilgrim fathers
sought refuge in Holland, but found life there unsatisfactory,
as they were not entirely free. They then set out for Virginia
and almost by chance settled in New England.

RALPH WALDO EMERSON (1803–1882)

" He shaped an ideal for the commonest life, he proposed
an object to the humblest seeker after truth. Look for
beauty in the world around you, he said, and you shall see it
everywhere. Look within, with pure eyes and simple trust,
and you shall find the Deity mirrored in your own soul. Trust
yourself because you trust the voice of God in your inmost
consciousness." — OLIVER WENDELL HOLMES.

Born in Boston, Mass., of a family with some literary attain-
ments, he showed little promise of unusual ability during his

years at Harvard. He became pastor of the Second Church in Boston for a time and later settled in Concord. He lectured extensively and wrote much, living a quiet, isolated life.

The poems by Emerson are used by permission of, and by special arrangement with, Houghton Mifflin Company, authorized publishers of his works.

Good-Bye (page 214)

"Good-Bye" was written in 1823 when Emerson, a young boy, was teaching in Boston. It does not refer to his retirement to the country twelve years later, but seems a kind of prophecy.

27. lore : learning.

28. sophist : a professed teacher of wisdom.

Each and All (page 215)

26. noisome offensive.

The Problem (page 217)

18. canticles : hymns belonging to church service.

19. The dome of St. Peter's was the largest in the world at the time of its construction and was a great architectural achievement. Emerson feels that it, like every other work that is worth-while, was the result of a sincere heart.

20. groined : made the roofs inside the churches according to a complicated, intersecting pattern.

28. Notice the figure of speech here. Is it effective ?

39–40. All the mighty buildings of the world were made

first in the mind of the builder or architect, and then took material form.

44. The **Andes** and Mt. **Ararat** are very ancient formations and belong to Nature at her beginning on the earth. These great buildings are so in keeping with Nature that she accepts them and forgets how modern they are.

51. Pentecost : Whitsunday, when the descent of the Holy Spirit is celebrated. Emerson says here that this spirit animates all beautiful music and sincere preaching, as it does all we do at our noblest.

65. Chrysostom, Augustine, and the more modern Taylor are all great religious teachers of the world, and all urged men to enter the service of the church. **Augustine:** Saint Augustine, the great African bishop (354–430). He was influential mainly through his numerous writings, which are still read. His greatest work was his *Confessions*.

68. **Taylor:** Dr. Jeremy Taylor, English bishop and author (1613–1667). One writer assigns to him " the good humour of a gentleman, the eloquence of an orator, the fancy of a poet, the acuteness of a schoolman, the profoundness of a philosopher, the wisdom of a chancellor, the sagacity of a prophet, the reason of an angel, and the piety of a saint." Why should a man so endowed be compared to Shakespeare ?

THE HUMBLE-BEE (page 220)

6. What characteristics of the bumblebee make **animated torrid-zone** applicable ? Why doesn't he need to seek a milder climate in Porto Rico ?

16. **Epicurean:** one addicted to pleasure of senses, specially eating and drinking. How does it apply to the bee ?

The Snow-Storm (page 222)

Emerson called this poem " a lecture on God's architecture, one of his beautiful works, a Day."

9. This picture is strikingly like Whittier's description of a similar day in " Snow-Bound."

13. bastions : sections of fortifications.

18. Parian wreaths were very white because the marble of Paros was pure.

21. Maugre : in spite of.

Fable (page 223)

This fable was written some years before its merits were recognized. Since then it has steadily grown in popularity.

Boston Hymn (page 225)

16. fend : defend.

24. boreal : northern.

80. behemoth : very large beast.

The Titmouse (page 228)

76. impregnably : so that it can resist attack.

97. wold : wood, forest.

JAMES RUSSELL LOWELL (1819–1891)

" As political reformer, as editor, as teacher, above all as an example of the type of scholarly gentleman that the new world was able to produce, he perhaps did more than any of his contemporaries to dignify American literature at home and to win for it respect abroad." — W. B. Cairns.

Born at Cambridge, Mass., he early showed a love of literature and says that while he was a student at Harvard he read
everything except the prescribed textbooks. He opened a
law office in Boston, but spent his time largely in reading and
writing poetry. He became professor of literature at Harvard in 1854 and later edited the *Atlantic Monthly*. Later
he was minister to Spain and to England. In 1885 he returned
to his work at Harvard, where he remained until his death in
the very house in which he was born.

The poems by Lowell are used by permission of, and by special arrangement with, Houghton Mifflin Company, authorized publishers of his works.

HAKON'S LAY (page 233)

This poem is here given in its original form as published by
Lowell in Graham's Magazine in January, 1855. It was after-
wards expanded into the second canto of "The Voyage to
Vinland."

With what other poems in this book may "Hakon's Lay"
be compared?

3. Skald. See Longfellow, "The Skeleton in Armor,"
note on l. 19.

10. Hair and beard were both white, we are told. What
is suggested in this line as white?

17. eyried. An eagle builds its aerie or nest upon a crag
or inaccessible height above ordinary birds. The simile is
here begun before the eagle is mentioned, and the minstrel's
thoughts are spoken of as born in the aerie of his brain, high
above his companions.

20. One of the finest pictures of the singing of a minstrel before his lord is found in Scott's " Waverly."

21. fletcher : arrow-maker.

31. The work of Fate cannot be done by a reed which is proverbially weak or by a stick which is cut cross-grained and hence will split easily. She does not take her arrow at random from all the poor and weak weapons which life offers, but she chooses carefully.

35. sapwood : the new wood next the bark, which is not yet hardened.

37. Much of the value of an arrow lies in its being properly feathered. So when Fate chooses, she removes all valueless feathers which will hinder success.

40. In these ways her aim would be injured.

43. butt's : target's.

52. frothy : trivial.

54. Leif, the son of Eric, near the end of the tenth century went from Greenland to Norway and was converted to Christianity. About 1000 he sailed southward and landed at what is perhaps now Newfoundland, then went on to some part of the New England coast and there spent the winter.

61. The coming of Leif Ericson with his brave ship to Vinland was the first happening in the story of America.

61. rune : a character in the ancient alphabet.

Flowers (page 235)

" Flowers " is another very early poem, but it was included by Lowell in his first volume, " A Year's Life," in 1841. Compare this idea of a poet's duty and opportunity with that of other American writers.

12. Look up *Matthew* 13 : 3–9.

18. Condensed expression ; for some of that seed shall surely fall in such ground that it shall bloom forever.

The Shepherd of King Admetus (page 241)

16. viceroy : ruler in place of the king.

44. Apollo, while he was still young, killed one of the Cyclops of Zeus and Zeus condemned him to serve a mortal man as a shepherd. He served Admetus, as is here described, and secured many special favors for him from the gods.

Commemoration Ode (page 243)

9. The men who fought for the cause they loved expressed their love in the forming of a squadron instead of a poem, and wrote their praise of battle in fighting-lines instead of tetrameters.

17. guerdon : reward.

35. A creed without defenders is lifeless. When to belief in a cause is added action in its behalf, the creed lives.

60. This is as life would be without live creeds and results that will endure. Compare Whittier's " Raphael."

67. aftermath : a second crop.

79. Baal's : belonging to the local deities of the ancient Semitic race.

105. With this stanza may well be compared " The Present Crisis."

113. dote : have the intellect weakened by age.

146. Plutarch's men. Plutarch wrote the lives of the greatest men of Greece and Rome.

NOTES

The Vision of Sir Launfal (Prelude) (page 249)

7. auroral : morning.

12. Sinais. Read *Exodus*, Chapter 19. Why did Moses climb Mount Sinai ? What would be the advantage to us if we knew when we climbed a Mount Sinai ?

9–20. Wordsworth says :

> "Heaven lies about us in our infancy!
> Shades of the prison-house begin to close
> Upon the growing boy," etc.

Lowell does not agree with him, and in these lines he declares that heaven is as near to the aged man as to the child, since the skies, the winds, the wood, and the sea have lessons for us always.

28. bubbles : things as useless and perishable as the child's soap-bubbles.

20–32. The great contrast ! What does Lowell mean by Earth ? Does he define it ? Which does he love better ?

79. Notice how details are accumulated to prove the high-tide. Are his points definite ?

91. sulphurous : so terrible as to suggest the lower world.

Biglow Papers (page 252)

Lowell attempted a large task in the "Biglow Papers," and on the whole he succeeded well. He wished to discuss the current question in America under the guise of humorous Yankee attack. The first series appeared in 1848 and dealt with the problem of the Mexican War ; the second series in 1866 and refers to the Civil War. From the two series are given here only three which are perhaps the best known. Mr. Hosea Biglow purports to be the writer. He is an uneducated Yankee boy who " com home (from Boston) considerabul riled." His father in No. I, a letter, describes the process of composition as follows : " Arter I'd gone to bed I hearn Him a thrashin round like a short-tailed bull in fli-time. The old woman ses she to me ses she, Zekle, ses she, our Hosie's gut the chollery or suthin anuther, ses she, don't you be skeered, ses I, he's oney a-makin poetery, ses I, he's ollers on hand at that ere busyness like Da & martin, and shure enuf, cum mornin, Hosy he cum down stares full chizzle, hare on eend and cote tales flyin, and sot rite of to go reed his varses to Parson Wilbur."

WHAT MR. ROBINSON THINKS (page 252).

1. Guvener B.: George Nixon Briggs of Massachusetts.

6. John P. Robinson was a lawyer (l. 59) of Lowell, Mass. Mr. Lowell had no intention of attacking the individual here ; Mr. Robinson changed his party allegiance and the letter published over his signature called Lowell's attention to him.

15. Gineral C.: General Caleb Cushing, who took a prominent part in the Mexican War, and was at this time the candidate for governor opposed to Governor Briggs.

16. pelf : money.

23. vally : value.

32. eppyletts : epaulets, the mark of an officer in the army or navy.

39. debit, per contry : makes him the debtor and on the other side credits us.

The Courtin' (page 254)

17. crook-necks : gourds.

19. queen's-arm : musket.

33–34. He had taken at least twenty girls to the social events of the town.

58. sekle : sequel, result.

94. The Bay of Fundy has an exceptionally high tide which rises with great rapidity.

Sunthin' in the Pastoral Line (page 258)

2. precerdents : legal decisions previously made which serve as models for later decisions.

4. this-worldify. The women in early New England dressed very simply and sternly, but the odor of musk would make them seem to belong to this world, which has beauty as well as severity.

7. clawfoot : a piece of furniture, here a chest, having claw-feet.

38. pithed with hardihood. New England people had hardihood at the center of their lives.

50. The bloodroot leaf is curled round the tiny white flower bud to protect it.

56. haggle : move slowly and with difficulty.

100. vendoo : vendue, public sale.

117. What American poets express a similar need of nearness to nature ?

144. Lowell's own education was four-story : grammar school, high school, college, law school.

155. A good application of the old story of the man who killed the goose that laid the golden eggs.

157. Cap-sheaf : the top sheaf on a stack and hence the completion of any act.

165. Lowell, himself, seems to be talking in these last lines, and not young Hosea Biglow.

209. English Civil War (1642–1649), which ended in the establishment of the Commonwealth.

241. As Adam's fall " Brought death into the world, and all our woe," it was considered by all Puritans as an event of highest importance ; most men agree that their wives' bonnets stand at the other end of the scale.

261. Cromvle : Oliver Cromwell, under whom the English fought for a Commonwealth.   See note on line 219.

270. After the short period of the Commonwealth, Charles II became ruler of England (1660–1685).

272. Millennium : a period when all government will be free from wickedness.

An Indian-Summer Reverie (page 268)

5. Autumn personified as Hebe, the cupbearer of the Greek gods.

11. projected spirit. The poet's own spirit seems to take on material form in the landscape before him.

28. See the book of *Ruth* in the Old Testament for this exquisite story.

32. Magellan's Strait : passage discovered by Magellan when he sailed around the southern end of South America.

51. retrieves : remedies.

59. lapt : wrapped.

77. Explain this simile. Has color any part in it ?

83. ensanguined : made blood-red by frost.

92. The Charles is so placid and blue that it resembles a line of the sky.

99. In connection with this description of the marshes, Lanier's " The Marshes of Glynn " may well be read, as it is the best description of marshes in American literature.

133. Compare Bryant's " Robert of Lincoln."

140. Compare this figure with Bryant's in " To a Water-fowl," l. 2.

157. Compare with the Prelude to the Second Part of " The Vision of Sir Launfal."

163. The river Charles near its mouth is affected by the ocean tides.

178. Why is the river pictured as dumb and blind ?

182. Compare Whittier's " Snow-Bound."

187. gyves : fetters.

190. Druid-like device. At Stonehenge (l. 192) in England is a confused mass of stones, some of which are in their original positions and which are supposed to have been placed by the Druids. It is possible that the sun was worshiped here, but everything about the Druids is conjecture.

201. A view near at hand is usually too detailed to be attractive. But in the twilight, near-by objects become softened, the distance fades into the horizon, and a soothing picture is formed.

209. The schools and colleges. Probably Harvard College is here included, as Lowell graduated there.

217. Compare this idea with that in the following lines from Wordsworth's " The Daffodils " :

"I gazed — and gazed — but little thought
What wealth the show to me had brought;

For oft, when on my couch I lie
In vacant or in pensive mood,
They flash upon that inward eye
Which is the bliss of solitude;
And then my heart with pleasure fills,
And dances with the daffodils."

The justice of these opinions should be tested by each student from his own experience.

A FABLE FOR CRITICS (page 276)

36. ignified : melted.

40. An example of Lowell's puns, which are generally criticized as belonging to a low order of humor.

41. Parnassus : a mountain in Greece, sacred to Apollo and the Muses, and hence the domain of the arts in general.

49. inter nos : between us.

51. ices. Isis was the Egyptian goddess of the arts and of agriculture.

60. bemummying : a word coined by Lowell to mean causing one to dry up like a mummy.

68. Pythoness : woman with power of prophecy.

69. tripod : a bronze altar over which the Pythoness at Delphi uttered her oracles.

" Most of his judgments are, however, those of posterity

though often, as in the case of Hawthorne, he was characterizing writers who had not done their best work." — CAIRNS.

92. **scathe** : injury.

93. **rathe** : early in the season.

96. **John Bunyan Fouqué** is an extraordinary combination of names as of characteristics. Bunyan is known everywhere for his devotion to truth as he saw it ; the oak in character. Friederich Heinrich Karl, Baron de Lamotte-Fouqué, was a German soldier, but is better known as a romantic writer. His best-known work is " Undine," the anemone in daintiness of fancy and delicacy of expression.

A Puritan Tieck is another anomaly. From the early poems in this anthology the Puritan type is evident ; Tieck was a German writer who revolted against the sternness of life and believed in beauty and romance.

110. In 1821 Scott published *The Pilot*, a novel of the sea, which was very popular. Cooper, however, thought he could improve upon it and so in 1823 he published *The Pilot*, hoping to show his superiority.

112. The bay was used for a garland of honor to a poet.

124. **Nathaniel Bumpo** was " Leatherstocking," who gave his name to the series of Cooper's novels.

125. **Long Tom Coffin** was the hero in *The Pilot*.

130. **dernière chemise.** A pun upon the word " shift," which here means stratagem.

148. **Parson Adams** is one of the most delightful of all fiction characters. Fielding pictures him in his novel *Joseph Andrews* in such a manner that you always sympathize with him even if you must laugh at his simplicity.

Dr. Primrose in Goldsmith's *Vicar of Wakefield* is a direct literary descendant of Parson Adams. He is one of the best-known characters in English fiction. To be classed with these two men is high praise for Natty Bumpo.

161. Barnaby Rudge, the hero of Dickens's novel of that name, kept a tame raven.

162. fudge : nonsense, rubbish.

180. Collins and Gray : English poets. William Collins, an English lyric poet (1721–1759) was a friend of Dr. Johnson. Thomas Gray (1716–1771) is best known by his " Elegy in a Country Churchyard."

182. Theocritus, a Greek poet of the third century B.C., was the founder of pastoral poetry. Since his idea was the original one, his judgment of his followers would be better than that of any one else.

190. Irving had been so long a resident in Europe that America almost despaired of reclaiming him. He did return, however, in 1832, after making himself an authority on Spanish affairs.

196. Cervantes : the author of *Don Quixote*, and the most famous of all Spanish authors. He died on the same day as Shakespeare, April 23, 1616.

200. Addison and Steele together wrote the *Spectator Papers* (1711–1712), which had a great influence on the English reading public. The Sir Roger de Coverley papers are the most widely read of these essays at the present time.

224. New Timon, published in 1846 ; a satire in which Tennyson among others was severely lampooned.

237. The comparison suggests Bunyan's journey with his bundle of sin.

252. no clipper and meter : no person who could cut short or measure the moods of the poet.

271. The story of Orpheus and Eurydice may be found in any Greek mythology.

OLIVER WENDELL HOLMES (1809–1894)

" [In 1830] most of our writers were sentimental ; a few were profound ; and the nation at large began to be deeply agitated over social reforms and political problems. The man who in such a period showed the possibilities of humor, and whose humor was invariably tempered by culture and flavored with kindness, did a service to our literature that can hardly be overestimated." — WILLIAM J. LONG.

Born at Cambridge, Mass., he was brought up under the sternest type of New England theology. He graduated from Harvard College in 1829 after writing much college verse. It was Lowell who stimulated him to his best work. He himself says, " Remembering some crude contributions of mine to an old magazine, it occurred to me that their title might serve for some fresh papers, and so I sat down and wrote off what came into my head under the title, *The Autocrat of the Breakfast Table*." He practiced medicine in Boston and taught Anatomy and Physiology in Harvard until 1882. The latter years of his life were spent happily in Boston, where he died.

2 B

The poems by Holmes are used by permission of, and by special arrangement with, Houghton Mifflin Company, authorized publishers of his works.

OLD IRONSIDES (page 287)

The frigate *Constitution* was popularly known as " Old Ironsides " and this poem was written when the naval authorities proposed to break it up as unfit for service.

THE LAST LEAF (page 288)

Holmes says this poem was suggested by the appearance in Boston of an old man said to be a Revolutionary soldier.

THE CHAMBERED NAUTILUS (page 291)

14. irised : having colors like those in a rainbow.
14. crypt : secret recess.

CONTENTMENT (page 293)

3. In 1857–1858, when this poem was written, the ideal of elegance in eastern cities of America was a " brown stone front " house. The possession of such a mansion indicated large wealth. In the light of this fact the humor of the verse is evident. The same principle is used throughout.
22. The position of Minister Plenipotentiary to the court of St. James — England — was considered the highest diplomatic position in the disposal of the United States. How would such a position compare with filling the governor's chair of any state ?
35. marrowy : rich.

46. The paintings of Raphael and Titian are beyond purchase price now. Most of them belong to the great galleries of Europe. Turner is a modern painter whose work is greatly admired and held almost above price.

54. vellum : fine parchment made of the skin of calves and used for manuscripts. It turns cream-color with age.

59. Stradivarius : a violin made by Antonio Stradivari, who lived (1644–1737) in Cremona, Italy. These instruments created a standard so that they are now the most highly prized violins in existence.

64. buhl : brass, white metal, or tortoise shell inlaid in patterns in the wood of furniture. So named from the French woodworker who perfected it.

THE DEACON'S MASTERPIECE (page 296)

10. Georgius Secundus: King George II of England. He was the son of George I, who was elector of Hanover, as well as king of England.

20. felloe : a part of the rim of a wooden wheel in which the spokes are inserted.

92. encore : we can say the same thing about their strength.

THOMAS BUCHANAN READ (1822–1872)

Born in Pennsylvania, he was early apprenticed to a tailor. He drifted until at last he made his way to Italy, where he studied and painted for several years. Later he made Rome his permanent residence, and died there. He was known as a clever artist and sculptor, but his best work is the two poems here quoted.

The poems by Read are used by special permission of J. B. Lippincott Company, the authorized publishers of the poems.

Storm on St. Bernard (page 301)

Storm on St. Bernard may be compared with *Excelsior* in general subject matter. Do they affect you in the same way? Are they alike in purpose? Which seems most real to you? Why is *Excelsior* the more familiar?

Drifting (page 303)

Read was essentially an artist, and in this poem he expresses his artistic soul more truly than in anything else he ever did.

19. Ischia : an island in the bay of Naples.

22. Capri : an island in the Mediterranean, best known for the Blue Grotto.

WALT WHITMAN (1819–1891)

"Walt Whitman . . . the chanter of adhesiveness, of the love of man for man, may not be attractive to some of us. . . . But Walt Whitman the tender nurse, the cheerer of hospitals, the saver of soldier lives, is much more than attractive — he is inspiring." — W. P. Trent.

Born on Long Island, he entered a printer's office when he was thirteen. By the time he was twenty, he was editing his own paper, but he soon gave it up for work on a New York newspaper. When he was thirty, he traveled through the west ; in " Pioneers " we have a part of the result. During the Civil War he gave himself up to nursing as long as his strength lasted. From 1873 to the time of his death he was a great invalid and poor, but every trial was nobly borne.

The selections from Walt Whitman are included by special permission of Mitchell Kennerley, the publisher of the complete authorized editions of Walt Whitman's Works.

PIONEERS ! O PIONEERS (page 307)

18. debouch : go out into.

O CAPTAIN ! MY CAPTAIN ! (page 311)

Written to express the grief of the nation over the death of Abraham Lincoln at the time when the joy over the saving of the union was most intense.